ANTICOSTI I.

Lawrence River

GASPÉ

Chaleur Bay

GULF OF ST. LAWRENCE

NEWFOUNDLAND

SEAWAY FROM FRANCE
TO THE ST. LAWRENCE CITIES
OF CANADA

MICMAC

ILE ST. JEAN

CAPE BRETON ISLAND

A

Quebec

St. John

Verte Bay

B

ABENAKI

River

NOVA SCOTIA

SEAWAY FROM ENGLAND
TO HER ATLANTIC COLONIES

Kennebec R.

Chaudière

Penobscot R.

C

Minas Basin

MAINE

Port Royal

Halifax

Boston

ATLANTIC

OCEAN

N

⚑ BRITISH FORTS

1. EDWARD
2. Wᵐ HENRY
3. OSWEGO FORTS
4. NECESSITY
5. CUMBERLAND
6. LIGONIER
7. LAWRENCE
8. BULL

⚑ FRENCH FORTS

A. LOUISBOURG
B. BEAUSÉJOUR
C. ST. JEAN
D. ST. FRÉDÉRIC
E. CARILLON (TICONDEROGA)
F. FRONTENAC
G. TORONTO
H. NIAGARA
I. PRESQUE ISLE
J. LE BOEUF

K. VENANGO
L. DUQUESNE
M. MIAMIS
N. VINCENNES
O. ST. JOSEPH
P. LA BAYE
Q. MICHILIMACKINAC
R. STE. MARIE
S. LÉVIS
T. FORT

D1062684

Battle for a Continent

Battle for a Continent

HARRISON BIRD

NEW YORK

OXFORD UNIVERSITY PRESS

1965

To the
Officers, Noncommissioned Officers, and Men
of the
1st Battalion, The Lake Superior Regiment (Motor)
The Canadian Army Overseas
1939–1945
The Living and The Dead

Acknowledgments

One cannot but have a sense of inadequacy in attempting to express, in this brief space, one's deeply felt gratitude to the many persons who have contributed in one way or another to the gathering of the material on which this book is based.

For her patient and untiring efforts in obtaining copies of contemporary diaries, journals, and letters, borrowed with her help from libraries and other institutions all over the United States and Canada, I am particularly grateful to the former Miss E. N. McDowell (now Mrs. Charles Thompson) of the Crandall Free Library in Glens Falls, New York. The Inter-Library Loan Service of the Southern Adirondack Library System, of which the Crandall Library is a member, not only made it possible for Miss McDowell to obtain the loan of the required books for me, but permitted me to study them at my leisure and in my own home. Any author will agree that this is a special boon.

As was the case in previous books, Miss Eleanor Murray of Fort Ticonderoga gave unstintingly of her great fund of knowledge about the campaigns on Lake George and Lake Champlain, and contributed the results of her extensive research regarding the colonial units serving at Fort Ticonderoga. For her help, not only in this instance but throughout our long association at "Ti," I again express my thanks.

The old line of forts extending from Louisbourg, on Cape Breton Island, to the mountains of western Pennsylvania, has to a great degree been preserved, reconstructed, or reproduced. In the course of searching out the material for this book, I visited virtually all of these sites, and I am newly aware of the debt of gratitude that, in company with other Americans, I owe to the public and private organizations whose funds and efforts have recreated for us this aspect of our history. The co-operation and help that I received everywhere from the people engaged in implementing these programs was not only of great practical value, but was activated by a sense of dedication that, to me, was truly an inspiration. Among the sites I visited I must mention, with no slight to others not specifically named, the following: Louisbourg, Beauséjour, Quebec, St. Jean, Chambly, St. Frédéric and Crown Point, William Henry, Fort George, Fort Edward, Rogers Island, Johnson Hall, Stanwix, Niagara, Frontenac, Ligonier, and Necessity. Again, I am particularly indebted to Fort Ticonderoga, the first example (by many years) of the reconstruction of North American historical sites, and to the late Stephen H. P. Pell, who founded the modern Fort Ticonderoga, its museum, and its library; also to his son, John H. P. Pell, President of the Fort Ticonderoga Association, for his kindness and neighborly help.

The numerous historical societies in the United States and in Canada have published letters and journals, as well as other documents, which are invaluable to anyone interested in the seventeenth and eighteenth centuries. I am further indebted to The Company of Military Historians, whose members can always be counted upon for help, and

I must thank particularly the Company's president, Mrs. John Nicholas Brown, from whose great collection have come many of the rare prints used to illustrate my story. Eric Manders kindly made available to me the findings of his painstaking research on British regiments in North America.

I wish to express here my thanks to Professor Howard H. Peckham, Director of the William L. Clements Library at the University of Michigan, for his helpful and constructive comments, so courteously expressed after his careful reading of the manuscript.

Others to whom I am grateful for help of various kinds include Mrs. I. M. B. Dobell and The Honorable William B. Scott, both of Montreal, Colonel John Elting, Mr. Grove McClellan, Mrs. Henry Foster, Mrs. Nils G. Sahlin, Jr., Mr. Byron H. Delavan, Mr. Robert Flack, Mr. Edward Mann, Mr. Earl Stott, and Mr. Malcolm Tweedy.

Contents

Illustrations

Ruins of Notre Dame des Victoires
Louis Joseph, Marquis de Montcalm
Pierre, Marquis de Vaudreuil
A View of Quebec
Chevalier de Levis
Jeffrey Amherst
A View of Montreal

Maps

Battle for a Continent

I

The Beautiful River

The Marquis de Duquesne de Menneville, governor general of New France, sent his canoe brigades up the St. Lawrence very early in the spring of 1754. Ice floes still lay rotting in the backwashes of the river and the launching stages at Lachine were slippery with skim ice as the *voyageurs* and soldiers gingerly carried their big bark canoes down to the water's edge. There was a special urgency in getting the brigades away that spring. As usual, supplies were needed for the western forts and for the Frenchmen and Canadians who had wintered in them. But there was yet another reason for haste. Before the snow had buried the leaves of autumn and stilled their crackling under moccasined feet, Governor Duquesne had heard that the English were reasserting their claim to the Ohio River. From Virginia, the British seaboard colony on the Atlantic coastal plain beyond the barrier ridges of the Allegheny Mountains, had come men who were walking tall and talking big in the lodges of the Indians and among the Frenchmen they met along La Belle Rivière (the Ohio) and at the portage forts linking that river to Le Lac de Conte, as the French called Lake Erie. At his palace in Quebec, the governor had received official notice from Versailles that the Ohio question, amicably settled at the hasty "Peace of Exhaustion" signed in 1748, was now being reinterpreted in London, as well as in Britain's American colonies.

Thus, the canoe brigades which Governor Duquesne sent west so early that spring of 1754 were under orders to make all possible haste. They were big brigades, four of them, carrying men and matériel and supplies to build a new fort at that point where the Monongahela leads down out of the Alleghenies to join the Ohio River at its most strategic point. This fort, to be named Duquesne, would be the governor's conclusive answer to the question of the ownership of the Ohio Valley.

The brigades formed up at Lachine, above Montreal at the fork of the old Ottawa River road to the upper Great Lakes. Hopeful seekers for a northwest passage to the Orient had once thought the stones of the China Rapids to mark the very threshold of Cathay. Time had proven the early explorers to be wrong, and though the old name remained, for long years French traders had been forced by Indian wars to ply the arduous Ottawa River way to the west. But during the latter years of the seventeenth century the diplomacy and strength of the great French governor, Frontenac, had neutralized the unfriendly western Nations of the Iroquois who controlled the lower Great Lakes, thus opening the St. Lawrence River to French trade. Fort Frontenac had been built as a storehouse and staging place where the St. Lawrence begins at the eastern end of Lake Ontario. At the mouth of the Niagara River, the Iroquois had permitted the French to build a great stone house (which was in fact a disguised fort), to protect one end of the long carry around the thundering falls and echoing gorge where Lake Erie spills into Lake Ontario. Other forts and trading posts stepped further to the west and to the north as collecting points and way stations for canoe brigades, both outward and homeward bound. Each year the wealth of the Great Lakes and the vast lands beyond was carried by these brigades down the arterial St. Lawrence, to Canada and the seaway to France.

On the southern shore of Lake Erie, Presque Isle was the first of three forts protecting the best road across country to the launching place on the Allegheny River. Once canoes were launched and their bundles stowed, they were waterborne until they reached the Gulf of Mexico, having safely descended the Ohio and the long reach of the Mississippi to New Orleans in Louisiana.

Of all the routes westward that which followed the Ohio was the most vital to New France, and in 1754 it was the most threatened. It was the quick, easy line of communication between the alternate French terminals at New Orleans and Quebec; it led to all points throughout the vast river system of North America; in itself it was rich, and it must not be broached if New France was to hold all of interior North America. In the spring of 1754 the Ohio route needed a strong French fort to hold it. So it was that Governor Duquesne despatched his conoe brigades westward early that crucial spring.

The canoes bucked a strong south wind all the way up the St. Lawrence, and Chaussegros de Léry, commander of the third brigade, was hard put to keep his place in the parade. He made slow progress up the first rapids at the cedars, and beyond, where the river is wide enough to be Lake St. Francis, his eight big canoes were caught in a storm of wind and rain. Hands that gripped the shank of the paddles grew numb with the cold of the water, and faces stung with the drops of spray. Even at night, when Léry worked his men late patching the frost-brittle bark of the canoes, there was no warmth and little rest in the wet camps. While yet in the upriver settlements the men wandered off to find shelter in the farmhouses, and departure of the brigade was delayed while the sergeant searched out the tired, cold, reluctant soldiers. Léry had ninety men under his command. A third of these were regulars of the Marine. The other sixty were militiamen, called up in the *corvée* and muscled for the plow rather than for the paddle. Because he could find few steersmen in his command, Léry lost his first canoe, split open from stem to stern on the Long Rapids. At that night's bivouac, room had to be made in the remaining canoes for the stranded men and for the forty-five tote-sized bundles from the wreck.

When the third brigade reached the islands above the last rapids, they found shelter from the wind and clear water over which to paddle. But they found confusion, too, in the myriad channels that wound through the islands clogging the Lake Ontario end of the St. Lawrence. Seeking its own way, first one canoe disappeared from sight, then another, and Léry, leading in his own light canoe, found his brigade scattered and himself alone on the river.

For almost a week Léry searched for his lost canoes. He went as far as Fort Frontenac on the north shore and visited for an hour with the fort commander before continuing on his way southward. As the days passed, he picked up the missing canoes one by one, among the islands and in the bays. Even more important, he found news from the Ohio. An express canoe appeared, bound for Montreal, and as the two craft rode for a moment, bow to stern, hands holding the gunwales, the messenger told his tale: how the Sieur de Contrecoeur arrived at the confluence of the Monongahela and the Ohio with his advance party of fort builders to find a British party already in occupancy, their small fort built and named "Prince George." But the British were few in number, and Contrecoeur had overwhelmed them with a show of guns. As the canoes drifted apart, the messenger urged Léry to make all possible haste. As more Frenchmen were coming to the Ohio, so, too, would there be more British.

It was on 19 May that the third brigade came into Famine Bay, where Léry found the other brigade already in bivouac and his captain waiting for him. That night, by the light of his campfire, Léry read the three letters brought down to him by the fourth brigade. The letters were from his wife in Quebec, to whom he expected to be able to return at the end of a year.

Joseph Gaspard Chaussegros de Léry had been born in Canada. Like most young Canadians of his position, he had secured a post in the Marine. Organized into free companies, the men of the Marine were in fact colonial soldiers, authorized, raised, and paid by the navy. In France, this department administered colonial affairs and appointed the governor general, who commanded the troops of the Marine in Canada. There were few troops in the scattered free companies, and many young men in need of Crown patronage and an officer's commission, so those young gentlemen of the Marine who were cadets without a command turned to a variety of governmental duties in the distant forts and with the Indian Nations. Often, they acted as liaison officers between the French military and the Indian war parties. The young Canadians soon grew wily in the ways of savage forest warfare. But Joseph Gaspard de Léry's work as a cadet took a different turn. From his father, he had learned the art of surveying and of military engineering. His training, and later his work, had taken him over the whole expanse of his native Canada. By 1754 Léry had already built and commanded the French fort at Beauséjour, on that narrow neck of land between the Gulf of St. Lawrence and the Bay of Fundy, which since 1714 had been the border between New France and Nova Scotia. While still in his teens, he had mapped the French domain from the fort at

Niagara down the length of the Beautiful River to the fort at the mouth of the Mississippi.

Chaussegros de Léry was now a lieutenant, and the assignment he had drawn (and protested) was to Fort Detroit, guarding the pass from Lake Erie to Lake Huron. He had asked for work on the new Fort Duquesne.

At the camp at Famine Bay, Lieutenant de Léry had expected to find orders reassigning him to the Ohio, but no such orders awaited him.

The combined brigades set out on the morning of 20 May for the lengthy, coasting passage along the south shore of Lake Ontario. Muskets were ready to hand in each canoe, and the men paddled with their heads up, every eye searching the shoreline for sight or sign of the ever unfriendly, possibly hostile, British. The brigades were nearing the fort at Oswego. Built in 1727 on Onondaga land by permission of the Iroquois League of the Six Indian Nations and garrisoned by settlers from Albany, in the New York colony, Oswego was a slim British finger on the jugular of New France. In war, Oswego could become a strangling hand. It bore watching.

At seven o'clock in the morning, the third brigade passed close by the British fort. Flags had been propped up in the French canoes, and the drummer set high on the cargo, his drum between his knees, to give a quick gay beat to the paddlers and a taunt to the listeners ashore. The multi-crossed British Jack hung limp at its staff in the still of the morning. The guns at the embrasures were run back, the tampions securing their muzzles. The French canoes passed by in peace.

Lieutenant de Léry, the engineer, noted with a professional eye that no improvements to Fort Oswego had been made since he had last seen the fort in 1749.

At the end of the fifth day on Lake Ontario, the brigades arrived at Fort Niagara, amid a welcoming display of fireworks and a rush of greetings at the water's edge. The arrival of the spring brigades brought news and letters and a surcease of isolation. To some, the canoes represented a replacement officer and a way of getting home. But in the spring of 1754 there would be few from the western forts who would see Montreal or Quebec that year.

Chaussegros de Léry did not tarry at Fort Niagara. The necessity to hurry forward the supplies was a shoving hand of conscience at his back. Wagons, teams, and porters were quickly organized, and one by one the canoes set off with their heavy loads over the carry road that led around the great falls to Lake Erie.

The night of 27 May Lieutenant de Léry slept beside the portage road. He woke in the morning to a fair day.

In the upper Ohio Valley two hundred miles from Léry's bivouac it had rained all night, and the forty Englishmen from Virginia were soaked to the skin. The trail they had followed had been poor and indistinct—hopeless in the black wet night. Seven men had become lost, but the rest had followed the broad back of their colonel for six miles through the sopping underbrush. It was still dark and still raining when they made their rendezvous with Tanacharison, the Seneca "half-king." Experienced hands recharged muskets from powder kept dry in the hollow horns, while the colonel, George Washington, and the half-king made their reconnaissance forward to where the French war party lay concealed in a rocky hide. Silently, the colonel placed his men around the unsuspecting bivouac. Tanacharison and his seven Indians, of whom one was a young boy, took the far side. At first light, Washington led in the attack. Only a few shots were fired, as the English ran in with bayonets. One of them struck the French commander, Ensign Coulon de Jumonville, standing on his bed-roll, his mouth open and his hand raised in protest at the suddenness of the attack. He fell back, and Tanacharison, rushing in from the other side of the ambush, jumped astride the fallen Frenchman. The Indian had time to recognize and speak to Jumonville before tomahawking him and rending his scalp from his skull.

By then it was all over. Ten Frenchmen and one Englishman lay dead. Twenty-two frightened survivors implored mercy, and red-coated Virginia militiamen looked to their young colonel for orders. He had begun a war.

II

The Wagon Road

George Washington stood a full six feet in his moccasins. The continuing rain had wetted his woods clothes so that they were plastered to the swell of the powerful muscles at his shoulders, over his chest, and along his upper arms. He was three months over twenty-one years of age, a lieutenant colonel in the Virginia Regiment, and on the Ohio side of the Allegheny Mountains, George Washington was the authority and the policy of his native Virginia and of England.

A gray boulder, as big and as high as the governor's state coach, stood alone on the floor of the glade. From what shelter it provided, the young colonel gave his orders for the dead to be buried, the prisoners searched and lined up, and when the battlefield was tidied, for the whole party to return to the army, encamped at the Great Meadows.

The meadows were "great" only in comparison with the Little Meadows, further east. They were a few flat acres of grassland set in a horseshoe of wooded ridges and cut through by a sluggish brook. Above the meadows was a bowl of sky, unscored by the arch of branches, unflecked by the new green leaves of spring. Into the flat wide space of the Great Meadows, George Washington had led his army after almost a month of days and nights among the jutting mountains, stiff-bristled with tangled trees.

Washington's command was an army only in that it was a complete military force of men, cannon, transport, and baggage. A scant 160 soldiers mustered in the meadow to tell and hear of the ambush in the glade. In sapling pens nearby, the poor horses and mean cattle grazed without looking up at the strange sight of French and Canadian prisoners of battle. Ten battered wagons, or what remained of them, were parked in array near the log hut beside the brook which served as a storehouse.

On 2 April the army had left Alexandria, where the Potomac is still a wide arm of Chesapeake Bay, on the march to Winchester. Colonel Washington had drilled and trained the unruly group of men, tempted into service by the prospect of land grants on the Ohio. At Winchester, no inducement or invocation of the law could bring out the seventy-four strong wagons and healthy teams required by the army for its march to the Ohio. After a week's delay, Washington marched on with only ten old wagons (all that he could raise) in his train. The army, virtually undisciplined as yet, crossed the wide stream of the upper Potomac to camp on the high ground along Will's Creek by the Allegheny Ridge, the first of the mountain obstacles that lay ahead.

At the eastern base camp on Will's Creek, soon to expand into Fort Cumberland, George Washington found Captain William Trent. That officer, a veteran of other unaccomplished missions, had been sent ahead with a company of men to build the Virginia fort on the Ohio. Trent himself had found a convenient reason to stay at Will's Creek. His ignorance of his company, which he had sent on to the Ohio under command of Ensign Edward Ward, was only equaled by his indifference. Two days after Washington's arrival, the ensign came down the trail with the forty-one men of Trent's company following behind him. They had

built their Fort Prince George, only to yield it at once to the
compelling argument of the Sieur de Contrecoeur's 500
Frenchmen and eighteen cannon.

With the refugees came two Indians from Washington's
friend Tanacharison, the half-king, urging haste lest the
tribes go over to the side of France. Washington answered
the half-king's appeal by driving forward the road he had
been ordered to build over the mountains for the moving of
wagons and guns.

While the axes rang in time interminable, the men, the
horses, and the wagons crossed over the watershed. They
knew it as such when they bridged the Youghiogeny,
where a soldier who spit into the water could watch his
spittle spin downstream on its way to the Gulf of Mexico.
It was still downhill on the western side as far as the Great
Meadows. From the open land the men could see Chestnut
Ridge on the western horizon, the last they would be called
upon to cross.

The camp on the Great Meadows was an orderly one, for
the slovenly men who had enlisted at Alexandria and at
Winchester had become a part of a united force as they
worked together in building the road. Their wagons were
the first ever to cross over the Alleghenies; their teams had
climbed the steepest hills; their hands had braked the wheel
spokes on the down slopes. As they followed the leadership
of their colonel and the example of their officers, the men
who crossed the mountains had become an army.

The first call to arms came even before the log-and-bark
house for the perishable stores was completed. Tanacharison sent word from the woods for them to be on guard, and
the army stood to during a night. Then Christopher Gist
came in from his place of three houses on Chestnut Hill to
tell Washington that he had seen a French ranger pass by
with a reconnoitering party. Captain Stevens took half the
army in pursuit. That night, 27 May, Tanacharison again

sent word, this time to report that he had found Jumonville's bivouac in the hidden glade. Within an hour forty keen Virginians, armed and accoutered, were at Washington's back, loping through the wet darkness to the attack.

The French prisoners went back over the wagon road to the tidewater settlements of Virginia, their officers protesting that the battle in the glade was an unwarranted massacre. At the Great Meadows the Virginians prepared for a French attack. Colonel Washington and his men, infected with the elation of victory, built their small palisade around the storehouse, mounted their swivel cannon, and viewed with satisfaction their work and its prospect. But the French did not come to try the field of fire around the log walls of Fort Necessity. The days of May ran out and warm June came, bringing the summer foliage and ringing the Great Meadows with a thick wall of leaves.

Like a silent drum, the frontier is a seemingly empty place until the tap of war beats on its taut surface. Then it comes alive, as the alarm vibrates through the forest shell, calling the various factions to gather at the rallying place. During the first weeks of June the fort at the Great Meadows was Britain's place in the Ohio Valley. The few scattered families of pioneers slipped through it, seeking the new road back over the mountains to safety. Traders, their unsold goods strapped on their packhorses, passed quickly by the drilling squads and on up the old blazed trail, rutted now by the wheels of Washington's wagons.

Up from their towns on the banks of the Beautiful River came those Indians who were loyal to Britain's king. The women quietly made their camp, where their hungry children could watch the soldiers eating while the chiefs sat in conference with the young colonel. Washington knew these Indians: Tanacharison, the half-king, viceroy of the Iroquois League in the Ohio Valley, who adhered to an old loyalty to England; Alliquippa, the Delaware queen and her son Shingass, called "Colonel Fairfax," subject to the Iroquois, loyal to George II, but with their home where they could smell the cookfires at the new French fort; Monacatootha, the Mingo, as the Iroquois dwelling in the Ohio Valley were called, who had carried the raw French scalps from the glade to the Wyandots in proof of Britain's intent against the French. In the Europeans' struggle for the Ohio, the Indian Nations quite reasonably sought to ensure their own survival by alliance with the strongest. Washington, mustering his Indian friends to his fort, strove to keep them loyal and to impress them. Should he fail in persuasion or in war, he knew that the Indians, to please their new French ally, would descend on the border settlements with tomahawk and fire.

The Alleghenies had never been a barrier to the Indian war parties. Now, in the spring of 1754, Washington's raw tunnel to the Great Meadows drained the terror of the mountains from the well-fed soldiers of the Atlantic coast, who thought in terms of sieges and forts, battlefields and supply lines. With the road to Virginia open, Colonel Washington waited for reinforcements, and daily, he waited for his relief from command and its complexities. The relief never came. Instead, word came that Colonel Joshua Fry of the Virginia Regiment had died east of the mountain, and that Washington must continue in over-all command until Colonel James Innes could come up from Carolina with 300 men of that colony. On 10 June, the day after Major Muse brought the three other companies of the Virginia Regiment to the Great Meadows, the complexities multiplied for the young colonel.

On that day Captain Aeneas Mackay arrived at the head of 100 good soldiers, members of the Independent Company of South Carolina. These men and their captain were regular soldiers on the permanent establishment of the British army, which paid them and directed them from London. This was in direct contrast to the Virginia Regiment, which was local to the colony. In contriving aid for his expedition to the Ohio, Lieuenant Governor Robert Dinwiddie had asked London to release to him the Independent Company of South Carolina and the two companies from New York. This was done. Though Captain Mackay was an amiable gentleman, he was a captain commissioned by the king, an appointment which prevented him from serving under a lieutenant colonel commissioned by a mere colonial governor. George Washington, an equally amiable gentleman, could not in honor serve under a captain, nor could he, in good conscience, turn over to a Carolinian the command of his Virginians. With courtesy and impeccable manners, the two gentlemen stood adamant until a temporary compromise was reached. Mackay and his company remained at Fort Necessity, and Washington took his men back to building roads.

Through the hot days of June, with lightning and thunder crackling and rumbling through the mountain gorges, the Virginia Regiment cleared and leveled the road as far as Gist's place. There, on Chestnut Ridge, Washington and his 300 Virginians were thirteen miles beyond Fort Necessity and Mackay with his 100 soldiers. Colonel Innes was still east of the mountains at Winchester, while the Independent Companies from New York were even further away. Moreover, it was rumored that 800 French and Canadians, with 400 Indians, had sallied out of the French fort. Captain Mackay came forward for a conference with Washington and the veteran Major Muse, and it was decided to fall back on the expected—the hoped for—reinforcements.

The retreat from Chestnut Mountain was hurried. Short of transport, Washington and the other officers led their own horses, with the swivel guns lashed to the riding-saddles. No time was taken out for rest, and as the march in-

creased its momentum, no time was given to stop for food.
Men in the line of march stumbled, cursing the stumps of
roots that tripped them. The murmurs from the woods grew
more insistent as the pulse of fatigue and hunger beat louder
in the ears of the hurrying men. The raucous scream of a
blue jay rising on an adjacent slope warned of imminent
danger. A frightened deer ran toward the column moving
slowly on the new-made road. A mountain cat might have
started the deer—or a French Indian.

On 1 July, the second day of the retreat, the army
reached the Great Meadows, panic close at the shoulder of
fatigue. Washington called a halt and ordered a stand in
the familiar place of their victory over the mountain, under
the walls of the tiny fort they had built.

In the open doorway of Christopher Gist's big log shed
on Chestnut Ridge there was shade from the afternoon sun,
and a little coolness seeping out from the dark interior. On
the doorsill sat Louis Coulon de Villiers, captain in the Marine, and half-brother to Ensign Coulon de Jumonville, now
dead, scalped, and buried in the glade.

Coulon de Villiers had come from Montreal to the Ohio
in the spring. He had traveled fast, followed by twenty
Frenchmen and 125 Indians of the St. Lawrence. Striding
through the new gates of the rapidly rising Fort Duquesne,
he had demanded revenge for his brother's death. Contrecoeur, the French commander on the Ohio, had been slow
to react to Jumonville's massacre, preferring to impress the
power of the Lily of France upon the Ohio and its Indians
by the solid walls of an enduring fort, rather than by a
problematic punitive encounter in the forest. By the end
of June, however, the big fort was there for all to see. He
could now turn his attention to the 400 Englishmen building up their strength at the Great Meadows.

The force to go against Washington was ready to Vil-

liers's hand on 26 June. Captain Mercier, the architect of
Fort Duquesne, who had been designated commander,
yielded to the seniority of rank and to the fire of "le grand
Villiers's" thirst for revenge. Two days later, 500 Canadians, soldiers of the Marine militiamen, with 400 Indians,
filed out of the fort and took the trail up the Monongahela.
Villiers reasoned that Washington would continue his road
in that direction.

Arriving at Gist's on 1 July, Villiers saw that he had been
right, but too late. A palisade had been begun but never finished. There were half-dug trenches, and tools and some
heavy stores were strewn in disorder on the ground. The
Virginians had gone, leaving every indication of a precipi-
tate retreat with enough momentum to carry the army
back over the mountains to the coast. Further pursuit
seemed futile. Captain Coulon de Villiers issued the order
to return to Fort Duquesne.

The Canadians moved slowly in the oppressive heat of
July. From the doorway of the shed, Villiers watched his
soldiers make their preparations for the march. A line of
men waited to fill their empty water bottles, and wrangled
until the sergeant brought order. At the far edge of the
clearing, a patrol of Indians broke out of the woods. From
the crested fashion of their hair, Villiers judged them to be
some of those he had brought from the east. With them
was a stumbling figure in a red coat whom the Hurons
pushed contemptuously up to the doorway where the captain sat. The deserter whined of hunger as he told of the
wretchedness of Washington's command, unable to move,
waiting at the Great Meadows for promised aid that did not
come. Villiers rose quickly and shouted for his officers.
Even before the order to pursue, the soldiers in Gist's clearing were hastening their preparations to move out, their
eyes turned eastward to the green ridge of Laurel Mountain.

Shortly after dawn the French made contact with their

enemy. The point man of Villiers's advance saw a man cut
from behind a big tree and run down the road. The Frenchman fired, but the Englishman ran on. When Coulon de
Villiers came up, the point man could show him, on a
gray stone, a rain-thinned spot of English blood. The wound
had only made the English scout run faster; he had four
miles to cover before he reached Fort Necessity.

At ten o'clock, Coulon de Villiers inched his head up
over a rotting log and, through the lower stems of a leavy
bush, looked out over the Great Meadow. He saw that
Washington's 300 Virginians were drawn up in ranks in
the open, in a brave display to meet the French charge. The
ranks shifted and moved in the wet, drizzling rain. The men
held the locks of their muskets under the tawny red of their
coattails. The trenches, which Washington had built in an
elongated diamond shape around the stockade fort, were
manned by the regulars from South Carolina, who crouched
purposefully in a wallow of mud. Swivel guns were
mounted in the fort. Washington, whom the French captain could see standing with his drummer beside another
officer, was inviting the French to attack.

Slowly, Villiers let his head slip down behind the log,
and edged his way carefully back into the bush. Then,
standing erect, he beckoned his waiting officers to him. He
refused with disdain the British invitation to attack. One
by one, he sent his companies around the clearing and
through the woods to the commanding ridge that he had
observed. From that position he could shoot with muskets
down into the trenches, and from the other slopes his fire
could drive the English back into the pen which they themselves had made. Before the last company had moved, firing
broke out from the English trenches. Some of the Frenchmen, hurrying to their position, had exposed themselves to
the aimed fire of the South Carolinians.

The English fire stopped suddenly, as though on an

angry order from an officer bent on saving ammunition. French muskets were now beginning to fire in a wide arc around the British camp. When Villiers again looked out through the leaves, Washington had taken his troops back into the outworks and into the narrow space between the log hut and the pickets of the fort. Villiers's own troops were firing spasmodically down into the British sheep-fold. A man in the trenches was hit and was quickly carried into the fort. A soldier of the Marine, lying beside the captain, took slow aim and squeezed the trigger. The hammer fell, jerking the frizzen forward, but without spark. The soldier cursed and went after the wet charge with pick and worm. The rain poured down through all the long after-noon. From the ridge, Coulon de Villiers could count almost every casualty the British took. While he watched, more than forty men were helped or carried from the exposed firing line.

In the leaden dusk of the rainy evening, Coulon de Villiers called upon the enemy to surrender. Short of everything but casualties, Colonel Washington accepted, sending the French-speaking Captain Jacob van Braam to treat for terms. Three times the agile Dutch fencing master (such was his profession) climbed the ridge to the French captain's campfire. Back at Washington's ill-lit headquarters against the wall of Fort Necessity, van Braam translated to his former pupil-at-arms the French words that he had won in blunt negotiations. As presented to the young colonel, the terms of surrender offered an honorable defeat: at the head of his men, bearing the regimental colors and drums beating the step, Washington could leave the fort, its flag still flying; only the men's muskets would be forfeit, and one of the swivel guns could be carried away as a token. Even the article dealing with the ambush in the glade where Coulon de Villiers's brother had died sounded mild, as van Braam translated the French word *assassination* into "a logical death in battle." The soldiers of Jumonville's party who had been sent as prisoners to Virginia were to be returned, against which two British officers were to stay behind as hostages. Van Braam volunteered for this honorable duty. Captain Robert Stobo, a Scot and a military engineer, stepped forward into the light of the single candle to offer himself as van Braam's companion in exile. So the surrender was signed, Captain Mackay of the Independent Company (the question of seniority unresolved but compromised) writing his name on the document beside that of George Washington.

At first light on 4 July 1754 the dual army marched off. Only a few men were in ranks behind their flag and their colonel. The rest were gently carrying the litters of the wounded in a slow-moving tail behind the drums. No one in the colonial army or among the regulars had had sufficient energy to carry away the gun of honor; it lay, forgotten, against the wall of Fort Necessity.

Captain Stobo watched as the army crawled into the hole of the road that it had built. Villiers's Indians were crowding in on the departing Virginians and South Carolinians, snatching loot from the weary, burdened, hungry men who had been Stobo's comrades. Canadian soldiers watched the passage of the enemy out of the Great Meadows for a while, then turned away in boredom. Finally, the last man disappeared under the trees. Captain Stobo stood alone through the first long minutes of his exile. Captain van Braam had already gone into the fort for the breakfast which was due him as an honorable hostage.

A band of Indians came out of the mouth of the road, each carrying his own personal piece of plunder. The British had gone from the Ohio Valley, but their road remained.

III

Captains Take Notice

In the eleven weeks that he had been on the point of land formed by the confluence of the Allegheny and Monongahela rivers, the Sieur de Contrecoeur had transformed the terrain. Where he had taken possession of a tiny stockade surrounding a single log storehouse, Fort Duquesne sprawled over the land.

In itself, the fort was neat, tight, and formal in the great French tradition of military engineering. Constructed of logs, readily available in the locality, Fort Duquesne was square, with an exactly angled spearpoint bastion at each corner. Within the walls were gathered the vital structures for a defensive siege: a well of water, a powder magazine dug deep into a bastion, bake ovens, a smithy, storehouses, and cells. Flanking the main gate was the guardhouse and the house of the commandant, the Sieur de Contrecoeur himself. As the danger was from the land, the two sides and three bastions which lay between the arms of the rivers were cradles of squared logs, filled level with earth to form a gun platform behind a barricade. The walls of the fort which faced down the Ohio were formed of logs set upright into the ground and pierced with musket slits. A detached demilune constructed of flat-roofed log houses pointed up the Monongahela, to add fire power in the direction from which the British would come.

The demilune had not yet been completed, nor had the fill been brought in to form the smooth uphill approach to the fire positions of the covered way, when on 15 June Fort Duquesne was deemed defensible. Beyond the survey stakes marking the end of the approach slope, a palisade of foot-thick logs enclosed the whole works. During that first summer of Fort Duquesne's existence, the space between the palisade and the wattled wall of the covered way was scattered with bark huts in which the soldier-builders lived. Beyond the stockade wall, untidy stumps and the gray ashes of smoldering brush piles pocked the land to the forest edge, more than a musket-shot away.

There was a river gate in the stockaded wall of the fort, but the main gate was cut through the northeast curtain wall. It was by the main gate and out over the drawbridge which spanned the deep-dug water trap that Coulon de Villiers marched on 28 June to avenge his brother's death, and it was through this guarded way that the two British hostages entered, after the surrender of Fort Necessity.

During the days that he was kept at Fort Duquesne, Captain Stobo observed all its details. As he walked about in the idle waiting of exile, the quiet Scottish engineer casually noted the number of his steps, crossing the inner courtyard. His walks took him past the nine unmounted cannon of small caliber, and tiring, he rested in the embrasures cut into the bastions, while admiring the view along the angle of fire. By leaning against the retaining wall of the covered way to watch the builders pass with their hand-barrows, Captain Stobo, with an experienced eye, could measure the height of the wall. At night, alone in his quarters, he incorporated all he had seen and learned into a carefully drawn map of the French fort.

Beyond the palisades, the Sieur de Contrecoeur had built

huts for the Indian leaders who came out of the forest to
receive gifts and to reappraise their loyalties. In the Indian
encampment, Stobo found one man whose loyalty to the
British was still intact. To him the Virginia captain entrusted the map, with an accompanying letter of intelligence, for delivery to George Washington. The Indian
courier left the forks of the Ohio at the end of July.

By the time Stobo's packet, grease-stained and smudged
by many hands, reached Washington at his family seat at
Mount Vernon, the information it contained was obsolete,
and Governor Dinwiddie's intentions had changed. The
map of Fort Duquesne, however, lay open on the table at
every conference at which the new campaign for 1755 was
under discussion.

Dinwiddie had wanted to turn Washington and Mackay
around at once and send them back to the Ohio. Colonel
Innes and his regiment, together with the New York Independent Companies, were at the Will's Creek end of the
mountain road. But there was no transport. Furthermore,
the Virginia House of Burgesses rose from the summer ses-
sion without allotting money for supplies or for the pay of
the officers and soldiers who that summer already had
crossed the mountain and returned.

Aside from this, Colonel Washington himself was disaf-
fected. Though he was praised and thanked by all those in
high places, his honor was betrayed at every level. To a
commander who was responsible to his men, the withholding of their pay was a repudiation of his obligation as their
colonel. And when the surrender document was translated,
George Washington discovered that he had signed an acknowledgment to the "murder" of Jumonville, not (as van
Braam had led him to believe) to that French officer's regrettable death in fair fight. Washington's friend and in-
structor in the honorable code of fencing had tricked him
by misinterpreting a key word in the French document.

Step by step, the treads of George Washington's dishonor were mounted. By a clerical contrivance, Governor Dinwiddie repudiated the clause in the surrender in which Washington had pledged the return of the prisoners taken at the glade. By this action the hostages—the false van Braam and the staunch Captain Stobo—were abandoned. But the final affront came in the autumn from the Crown itself, which judged that any grade of regular officer outranked any mere colonial commission. As though to underline his personal degradation, Washington was offered a captaincy in an Independent Company in lieu of his colonelcy of the Virginia troops. Betrayed by his friend, his homeland, and his king, George Washington resigned from the service and withdrew to the dignity of his private stature and his honorable estates.

On the colonial frontier, now drawn back to Will's Creek in the eastern foothills of Laurel Mountain, Colonel Innes was in command. There, the wrangle over rank continued, now coupled with inter-colonial rivalry. Innes, secure with a king's commission in his pocket, commanded an army comprised of his fellow North Carolinians, the Independent Companies from New York, the remnants of Washington's Virginia Regiment, and Captain Mackay's regulars from South Carolina. With this mixed and variant force the able colonel contrived to erect Fort Cumberland, named for the king's second son, who commanded the British army. This fort was a stockaded affair, built in two attached parts: a bastioned citadel and a compound containing winter quarters for a garrison. Located on the north shore of the Potomac to dominate that river, Will's Creek, and Washington's mountain road, Fort Cumberland stood on Maryland soil. This gave pretensions of seniority to the captain of thirty Maryland militiamen who had joined Innes's army, particularly as the governor of the host colony was the newly designated commander in chief in North America.

The military appointment of Governor Horatio Sharpe of Maryland was based on his rank as lieutenant colonel in the British army, and was a temporary step until a suitable officer of higher rank could be found and sent out from England. The governor, an honest but uninspiring man, kept his additional responsibility as commander in chief for only three inactive months. In December of 1754 Lieutenant Colonel Sir John St. Clair landed in tidewater Virginia with the advance party of Major General Edward Braddock's headquarters. The general himself arrived in February to take over from Sharpe, and was quickly followed by his two regiments of regulars.

With redcoats on the quaysides and white sails on the horizon, the British colonies awoke to a war. They were like a house of fourteen rooms, in each of which there lived a separate family. Suddenly a back entrance was wrenched open, and out of Canada a chill wind of fear circulated through the corridors. Fourteen proprietors looked up in concern at their own doors and windows. Some, like the Pennsylvanians, remained calm and benign in the plain hall of their peaceful Quakerdom. Braddock and his regulars came quickly from the parent house to bar the door, thrown open by Dinwiddie. The military governor of Nova Scotia looked to the canvas sails of men-of-war to fill the cracks in his side entrance, while in New York Colony, William Johnson braced the double door opening onto New France and loudly called for help. From the big room of Massachusetts, William Shirley hastened to the aid of his neighbors.

In New York City, Goldsborough Banyar, agent to William Johnson, scurried through the wintry streets, seeking news in the offices of the great and gossip in the taverns. Faithfully, the little man reported to his master on the Mohawk River all that he had heard—and overheard.

William Johnson was a man big in stature, big in concept

and ambition, and big in voice. He was also a shrewd man in business, diplomacy, and politics. Ever since the Congress on Indian Affairs held in Albany from 9 June 1754—the same congress at which the sage Pennsylvanian, Benjamin Franklin, digressed to urge that the British colonies "unite or die"—Johnson had been waiting for his Crown appointment as sole Indian agent in the north. With the authority of that post, and its enabling means, he could hold the fidelity of the western Iroquois and of the Nations of the Ohio in fief to them. The commission from the Crown was slow in coming, even though from his listening post Goldsborough Banyar assured Johnson in flattering terms that he would have it.

All summer long, bad news came to Johnson's ears. Banyar wrote of Ward's expulsion from the forks of the Ohio, and of Washington's having been "banged" at Fort Necessity. Even "King" Hendricks of the Mohawks, kinsman to Johnson through intimate family ties, prophesied that the French would turn the English out. Alarms, too, frightened the frontiers of New York and New England. On 27 August, the settlement at Hoosick fell to a French and Indian raid, and twenty persons disappeared in the smoke of their homes or as slaves in the train of the marauders. Panic seized the outer frontier. The governor of New Hampshire claimed that thirty new townships were abandoned as a result of the raid on Hoosick. Still Johnson did not have permission to react with the decision and violence necessary to win back the respect of the Indians; all he could do was to put the local militia on defensive alert.

In December, Goldsborough Banyar gleaned a crop of news to fill Johnson with hope. Braddock had received the command in North America. Sir John St. Clair, his deputy quartermaster general, had landed in Virginia, and James Pitcher had arrived in Boston, there to begin a muster of 3000 colonial men into the regular British army. Two new

regiments of 1000 men each were to be raised in North
America and numbered the 50th and 51st of the British line.
Their colonels, wrote Banyar to William Johnson, would
be Massachusetts men: Shirley, the governor and newly
created major general, second-in-command to Braddock,
and Sir William Pepperrell, the relict of the 1745 campaign
against Louisbourg. Of the remaining 1000 recruits, 400
would go to fill out the 44th and 48th regiments, coming
out at half strength from the Irish garrison. It was assumed
in the taverns that the last 600 of Mr. Pitcher's muster would
be Independent Companies, found among the tough, hard
rangers along the forest frontier.

With the movement of events surging toward a great
campaign in 1755, William Johnson found it politic, in
February of the new year, to make the difficult winter journey from the Mohawk Valley to New York City. There
the colonial government was sitting to hear, and to signify
approval by a cash allotment, a report of the military affairs
of the northern frontier. The year 1755 was one in which
the handle of opportunity was the hilt of a soldier's sword.
Johnson, clutching the haft of the Iroquois tomahawk in
one hand, reached for the bright blade with the other. But
Governor Shirley of Massachusetts had grabbed first.

Since 1745 William Shirley had conceived himself a general. In two terms as governor, he had convinced himself,
several other New England and adjacent colonial governors,
and the lords of Whitehall that he was, indeed, the grand
strategist for North America. When the map-readers in
London sent General Braddock to recapture the forks of the
Ohio, they acknowledged Shirley's pretensions and made
him a major general, charged with the security of the other
fronts which were threatened by French encroachment.
With the commander in chief assigned the sweet duty of
bringing down retribution on Fort Duquesne, it is no wonder that Shirley took for himself the field command of the

expedition to capture Fort Niagara. As every strategist in North America knew, this place was the neck noose of New France's far western lands, as well as the Ohio River way to the Mississippi. If, by the end of the summer of 1755, Shirley himself with his two regiments, the 50th and 51st, could meet General Braddock on the parade ground (Niagara was Braddock's second objective) it would be a glorious reunion for England, and a rewarding one for Shirley. A victory-at-arms was worth a knighthood to the commanding general. This Shirley knew, for such had been the reward to William Pepperrell, whom the governor had sent as field commander to Louisbourg ten years before.

Shirley's road to Niagara led through Iroquois lands in the colony of New York. During the winter of 1755, the governor of Massachusetts had faced and solved the political problems which this involved. With his political astuteness backed by his major general's commission from London, he had rallied the governors of New Hampshire, Rhode Island, Connecticut, New Jersey, and New York to support, with men and matériel, yet another campaign for the summer of 1755. This all-colonial venture would move north out of Albany and would build a fort on Lake Champlain to dominate and neutralize the French Fort St. Frédéric at Crown Point. In appointing William Johnson to be the general in command of this northern thrust, Shirley not only acknowledged New York's political rights to command in its own province, but he brushed "Farmer" Johnson from his own path to Niagara while assuring himself safe passage through the lands of Johnson's Iroquois friends.

The "Old Gray Bear" of northern colonial politics had done well for himself in the preliminaries of the 1755 campaign. He had also heavily committed his own colony of Massachusetts. Apart from the men for the two new regiments of regulars, other men from the Bay were rolling their blankets to march with William Johnson, while ships

and schooners were gathering in Boston Harbor to carry
yet another 2000 God-fearing Massachusetts soldiers eastward to Nova Scotia. On Governor Shirley's eastern flank,
the military governor of Halifax was calling for help against
Fort Beauséjour, the source of agitators who were stirring
unrest among the Acadians, consigned by the Treaty of
Utrecht to dwell in Nova Scotia as faithful subjects of the
English king.

Four expeditions against New France were now scheduled for the year 1755, and the American colonies waited
only for the snows to melt and the mud to dry. The men
prepared to "go for soldiers" against those evil men in Canada who ate frogs, worshipped statues, and, most reprehen-
sible of all, referred to the noble Britons of all the colonies
as "*les Bostonais*."

In April, Shirley passed through New York on his way
to the conference of governors, called at Annapolis in
Maryland by the commander in chief. At the conference,
all plans were approved, and Governor Shirley, in scarlet
and white, rode north to take over his command. Braddock
stuffed the plans for 1755 into his field desk and went into
conference with his quartermaster on the question of securing transport to carry his army over George Washington's
mountain road. For his own comfort, Braddock had pur-
chased from Governor Sharpe an elegant chariot.

For William Johnson, too, it was a season of travel. From
New York, he had returned to Mount Johnson to forge the
poor sword he had received into a proper weapon for his
ambition. Almost immediately, however, he was summoned
to wait upon General Braddock at that gentleman's headquarters in Alexandria, Virginia. There, Johnson received
at last his long-awaited commission as agent to the Six Nations of the Iroquois League. There was so much to be done
in Albany! Guns must be found, boats must be built, stores
of food and of powder must be gathered, while his Indians

must be cajoled, inflamed, and recruited. All this William Johnson accomplished that spring at Albany, on the upper Hudson, and one day he wrote to Messrs. Colden and Kelly, Merchants, to send him some "thin green velvet," and enough silver lace, one inch in width, to bind his two uniform coats. General Johnson had made ready for war.

On 9 April, while governors and generals bowed over their desks, Captain Abijah Willard formed up his company on the square in Lancaster, Massachusetts. He faced the stiff ranks of his command as a hush fell over the crowd of women and children gathered nearby. He knew the sequence of commands to be given. He had heard his father give it ten years before, when he, Abijah, had been a private soldier of the company. Quickly, his voice gave the order, and the men of Lancaster marched away from home to capture Fort Beauséjour.

IV

Many Sails Quit Many Ports

The "great press" of 1755 ran hot through the streets of English seaport towns. Thirty-five ships of the line had been ordered commissioned for sea duty. Thirty-five man-hungry ships' captains pounded their cabin tables in their impatience to sign on a crew fit for sea. To the searching, hustling press gangs it was a matter of indifference whether a man's hands were stained deep with rope tar or were big with calluses from a dung fork. Four limbs and a body with a lash for the tail made a landlubber into a man-of-warsman before the first gale in the Bay of Fundy, or the guns of a broadside were run out to deny a "M'sieur" his right to be afloat.

At the quayside in Brest, where Brittany's peninsula points westward to Canada, six good regiments of the French king's army were lined up, ready to embark. One by one, the companies filed down the worn stone steps to the waiting boats which would row them out to the warships, anchored in the roads. Men from the southern plains of Guyenne and from neighboring Béarn, on the Spanish border, and the harsh-voiced men of Languedoc, climbed unsteadily up the bulging wooden sides of the ships whose destination was Quebec, in the cold inland of New France. With the regiments of Béarn, Guyenne, and Languedoc went the regiment La Reine, proud favorite of France's queen. In other boats to other ships, the regiments of Artois, in the far north, and Bourgogne, of the vineyards, were going to the bleak, misty rocks of Louisbourg. Each white-coated regiment counted a full 500 soldiers; each had its presaging shadow of forty replacements.

The Sieur de Rostaing, second-in-command of the troops, had supervised the embarkation. His own baggage safely stowed in his cabin on Captain Hocquart's *Alcide*, Rostaing waited on the empty quay to make his report and to bid *bon voyage* to his general. Major General Ludwig August Dieskau was sailing out to Canada aboard the flagship. For the aging German veteran of the French army it meant third-best quarters, but it offered an opportunity to plan and concert his campaign with his shipmate for the voyage, the new governor general of New France. Duquesne de Menneville, the able sailor-governor, was giving place to the Canadian-born Pierre Rigaud, Marquis de Vaudreuil-Cavagnac. Born in Quebec, Pierre de Vaudreuil had been but five years of age when, in 1703, his father had begun a long, twenty-three-year term in the governor's palace overlooking the St. Lawrence. The young marquis had followed in his father's footsteps. For ten years he had been governor of Louisiana. Now, after two years in France, he was returning to his birthplace, viceroy of his own heritage.

With a gesture of graceful elegance, the governor general acknowledged the sweeping bow of Rostaing, whom Baron Dieskau had presented at the head of the stone steps. While all the fleet waited, Vaudreuil took dignified leave of the officials of Brest and of Admiral de la Macnamara. The latter, with nine ships of the line, would see the Quebec fleet past the narrow waters where, it was believed, the British blockade fleet lay in wait. Then, with General Dieskau and

Admiral Du Bois de la Motte, his shipmates for the voyage, the Canadian marquis stepped into the longboat, made room on the cushioned seats at the stern, and began the journey home.

In London and at Versailles, the French and British ambassadors made their respective calls of regret and explanation which each government accepted but did not believe. The Duke of Newcastle, in his fuddled way, hoped that his opposite number in the cabinet adjoining Louis's study would not hear about the general and the two regiments he was sending to Virginia, a move of which the French minister, of course, was well aware. The British ambassador, Lord Albemarle, was put to some pains to persuade the French minister that Braddock's army was purely a defensive one. It then resolved upon the French minister of war to find a general and six regiments to send to New France, to defend against Britain's defense! Dieskau sailed with a French war fleet on 15 April 1755. His orders, and those of the Du Bois de la Motte, were to avoid conflict.

Britain picked up the next stone to throw, wrapped it in orders to attack the French fleet landing French troops in North America, and sent the stone skipping across the North Atlantic in the form of Admiral Edward Boscawen and eleven ships of the line.

At his home in London, the French ambassador, Mirepoix, gave a small dinner-party, for which the most important guest, diplomatically speaking, arrived somewhat late. The Council of State had sat well beyond the dinner hour. But Sir Thomas Robinson did manage to arrive, to eat and drink and to wipe his lips upon the fine napery of his host. In the rare, warm fellowship of the port, Sir Thomas could still baldly reassure Mirepoix that Boscawen's intentions were peaceful. Gaging the state of his guest's mellowness, the Frenchman held to the opinion he had formed on the reports from less accomplished and exalted sources: England was acting toward France in a most warlike way.

In the second week of June, Admiral Boscawen's warships lay fogbound on station off the strait between Cape Breton and Newfoundland. The British fleet had made a fast passage from England and, by every calculation of experience, had beaten Dieskau and Du Bois de la Motte to the narrow entrance to New France.

A light surface breeze, rising with the sun, stirred under the canvas, lifting it yardarm by yardarm to the mast tops. Lookouts, stationed at the quarters of *Dunkirk*, called out one by one as they took shape out of the retreating fog, the names and location of the ships of Boscawen's fleet. On that morning of 8 June, there were fifteen ships of the line and one frigate, Francis Holburne's squadron having joined forces with the admiral. Each vessel was a familiar silhouette to the sea officers of Captain James Howe's *Dunkirk*, so the call to action stations went out before the count had come to nineteen, and sails were trimmed for pursuit to leeward, where three strange hulls were taking form.

Six bells of the morning watch had been sounded before *Dunkirk*—and, close astern, *Torbay*, flying Boscawen's red signal flag to "Engage!"—came within hailing distance of the largest of the three French ships. She was *Alcide*, and her Captain Hocquart spoke first, asking politely whether England and France were at war. Captain Howe, bellowing in French through his megaphone, identified his ship, himself, and his admiral, and announced his intention to take *Alcide* his prize. Hocquart, in crossing the deck to his battle station, found time to pause where the Sieur de Rostaing stood with a group of his army officers, to mention the fact that the British admiral was an old acquaintance.

Through the after-gun ports, the division captain saw *Dunkirk* overhaul, to ride gently in the swell over the bell muzzle of his long black cannons. As he lay the last gun true, flame-shot smoke bellowed from the Britisher's side. The round shot were still in the air when Hocquart gave the order to fire, and the linstocks fell on the primed touchholes of *Alcide's* bearing battery. The shock of recoil and the shock of *Dunkirk's* broadside were one, as the Frenchman's deck dissolved into an eerie place of acrid smoke and hurtling splinters, of snapping stays and crashing spars, lanced through by screams, until silence gave room for groans.

For *Alcide* there was little hope of victory or escape, though the French captain could see his own shot striking home on *Dunkirk*. The bow guns of *Torbay* were dropping their shots close alongside when Hocquart turned to make the lonely walk to the counter where the flag halyard was secured. The distance was but a few steps, but it was a long way around the torn body of the Sieur de Rostaing, who lay with the other dead, sprawled shapelessly on the quarter-deck. His head bared, Captain Hocquart raised his eyes as he sorted out the double strands of rope. For a moment he let the big white flag hang free, while a light wind shook out the folds hiding the golden lilies of France, then he allowed it to sink by its own weight to the quarter-deck of *Alcide*.

To windward, a cheer went up from the deck of *Dunkirk*. To leeward, *Torbay* swept by, her open gun ports a wide menace, in the last minutes of her pursuit of the little *Lys*. The third French ship sighted that morning by Captain Howe had regained the fog cover and made good her escape, as had all the other ships of the French fleet. Now they were safe; Du Bois de la Motte's squadron sailed through the Cabot Strait, on course across the gulf, bound for the St. Lawrence River; the three ships carrying the regiments for Louisbourg closed the narrow mouth to the harbor behind the fortress guns.

Not until much later that summer would Baron Dieskau

learn the fate that overtook his second-in-command, the Sieur de Rostaing, or what became of the 400 soldiers of La Reine and Languedoc aboard *Alcide* and *Lys*. When London heard of Boscawen's action in the lifting fog, a querulous elder statesman mumbled about "a European war for a bit of North American muck." At his embassy, M. Mirepoix packed his table linen and silver in his traveling-box, in response to a recall to France. All along the English coast the newly commissioned ships of the line were putting out to sea, as Admiral Hawke set up a close blockade of the port of Brest. At Versailles, King Louis still preferred peace, as he wrote his letters to those two ladies of Europe: the Empress Maria Theresa of Austria and Elizabeth, Empress of all the Russias. In another part of the palace, where the king would visit her later in the day, the Marquise de Pompadour, too, was writing to those same gracious ladies in positions of power.

The Abbé le Loutre was awakened early on the day the British came to capture Fort Beauséjour. So urgent had been the governor's call that the priest was still buttoning his cassock as he ran up the stone steps of the bastion where Vergor was waiting and watching. Through habit, Le Loutre had put his pipe in his mouth.

Far to the southwest, across the mud flats of Beau Bassin, down the dark waters of Chignecto Bay where it opens into the Bay of Fundy beyond, a British fleet rode at anchor. As the priest and the governor watched, sails broke out on a distant mast. A French officer with a telescope was counting aloud as the British sloops and schooners followed the three frigates up Chignecto Bay on the rising tide. There were forty vessels in all, each, Vergor knew, filled with soldiers coming to attack his quiet and profitable fort. To him, they came as a complete military surprise.

The English came to Fort Beauséjour on the day (2 June)

marked in the calendar of the Roman Catholic Church as
sacred to the memory of the "martyrs of the Gauls." For
the Abbé le Loutre, this was peculiarly apt. No pagan Gaul
of the second century devised for a martyr more ingenious
physical torture than that which Le Loutre took pleasure in
inflicting on his English captives. In a single two-year period, during the eighteen years that he scourged the countryside surrounding the Bay of Fundy, "in the Name of
God, for St. Louis of France," the abbé paid out 1100 *livres*
in scalp bounty.

Joseph Louis le Loutre was born in 1710 at Morlaix, in
Brittany, the ancient motto of which ("Si les Anglais te
mordent, mordes-les") may be translated to read, "If the
English bite you, kill them." As vicar general of Acadia, Le
Loutre lived by the motto of his birthplace, with which he
coupled a useful fanaticism evolved by his own nature out
of his Roman Catholic teachings.

Acadia, in the abbé's time, encompassed only the north
shore of the Bay of Fundy from the Kennebec River in
Maine to the Gulf of St. Lawrence, including the large
islands of St. Jean (Prince Edward Island) and Cape Breton.
Nova Scotia, with the French Acadians living there, had
been bitten off by the British at the Congress of Utrecht
which ended the wars of Marlborough's victories. Assum-
ing the severance of Nova Scotia as a personal stigmata, Le
Loutre killed Englishmen with all the savagery of a crazed
otter in a school of fish.

Directed against such a natural enemy as the Protestant
British, the abbé's fury had the logical consistency of a patri-
otic national policy. His iniquity showed as a stain when it
splashed onto the work clothes and church dress of the
Acadians who were his parishioners. By withholding the
sacrament and threatening eternal damnation, the vicar general scourged the devout Acadians out of their parish
churches around the Minas Basin, Annapolis Royal, and

other Nova Scotian communities. He even burned one of his own chapels because it seemed likely to be included in British territory. With the Micmac Indians (also his parishioners) as his "imps of the Lord," Le Loutre in buckskin drove the simple farmers from the good land of their ancestors onto barren ground to starve, for no other reason than to spite the presumption of the English.

There were 1200 sullen, terror-bound Acadians around Fort Beauséjour on the morning of that day, holy to the martyrs of the Gauls. They were employed in building a dyke along the Rivière au Lac, north of the fort. This project was a whim of the Abbé le Loutre, and, his pipe in his mouth, he took pleasure in working on the dyke with a mattock.

Jacot de Fiedmont, the acting engineer officer at Fort Beauséjour, had begged for the Acadian labor to complete the defenses of the fort, but that idea had not appealed to the vanity or purpose of the priest. Nor would the governor test his own strength against that of the vicar general by exercising his prerogative to call up the Acadians as a labor *corvée*. The governor, who also was working for his own ends, knew enough of practical politics not to encroach on another's preserve.

Louis du Pont du Chambon, Sieur de Vergor, arrived at his political stand and his governorship by the same route. His father had been governor of Louisbourg when it fell to the Massachusetts men in 1745, at the time that François Bigot, as intendant, managed the finances of the fortress city. The governor's son had learned little from the siege, but he had learned much from the intendant. Bigot had found Vergor a likely lad and had carried him along as he himself climbed above the mere plundering of a city to the limitless opportunities for graft as intendant over all of New France. The younger man became adept at perfidious connivance with his master.

In 1754, Bigot gave his faithful assistant his own chance to prosper. Vergor was made commandant and governor at Fort Beauséjour, but within a year of his taking up residence the Massachusetts men came to invest his city as they had come to that of his father. This had not given Louis enough time to amass even a modest fortune in graft, or to realize his ambition to purchase an estate in France adjacent to that of his friend François Bigot.

On the day they entered Chignecto Bay and on the following day, the British were busy landing at Fort Lawrence, across the Missaquash River from Fort Beauséjour. There were 5100 men with guns, stores, supplies, and equipment to be put on a shore which, to soldiers carrying, pulling, or pushing the loads, seemed interminably remote across the wide mud flats. While they labored, cursing the army, their commander, Colonel the Honorable Robert Monckton, second son of an Irish viscount, held a council of war in his dry quarters at Fort Lawrence. With him were the colonels of the two regiments of regulars (the 40th and 45th) which had been assigned to the expedition from the permanent garrison at Halifax, the capital of Nova Scotia. Broome, the gunner officer, was late in arriving, his boots squashing mud, having supervised the landing of the squat, brass, 13-pound siege mortar. Also present were two Massachusetts lieutenant colonels: Scott, of the 2nd battalion, and John Winslow, commanding the 1st battalion of his regiment. Winslow, second-in-command of the whole expedition, sat at the council table beside the portly Irish gentleman. Between the British and colonial factions which composed Monckton's army, neat and trim in the blue coat of the Royal Navy, was Commodore John Rouse, captain of His Majesty's frigate *Success*. When the sailor spoke at all, it was in the flat tones of one brought up on the Massachusetts coast. As a privateer, Rouse had carried to London

the news of the capture of Louisbourg in 1745, and as his
reward, he had returned to his native Boston a post captain
in the Royal Navy.

Vergor, too, a military role suddenly and unexpectedly
having been thrust upon him by Monckton, was getting
ready for battle. His preparations consisted of loud wails
for help to Drucour at Louisbourg and to Duquesne at Quebec, while he endeavored to remove from possible danger
the cargo vessels lying just across the isthmus at Gasperaux,
on Baie Verte.

Though himself a captain in the Marine, Vergor left all
purely military preparations to the fourteen other officers
of the garrison. They had 150 soldiers with which to make
do, plus some Indians and Canadian *coureurs de bois*. With
an opportunity to fight the British, the Abbé le Loutre also
came to their aid. He marched his Acadian refugee laborers
up from the dyke to de Fiedmont for work on the fort,
where they were mustered into the militia. The Acadians
took up their issued arms with reluctance, being British
subjects by oath, and disinterested by temperament. Having hidden their women in the woods, however, they appeared to be an army of 1200 stolid, blank-faced soldiers,
ready, in hopelessness, to do as they were told.

On 4 June, the Massachusetts-British army marched up
the Missaquash to make a crossing at Pont à Bout. An assault
force of 250 regulars led out. Surgeon John Thomas of the
1st battalion heard the firing break out from the French post
across the bridge, and, running forward, he soon was tending his first wounded. As he dug partridge shot (the charge
of a swivel gun) from the arm and side of a private of the
45th, he could hear the Indians howling across the stream.

The action at the crossing was of short duration; the
French burned their blockhouse before running off after
their Indian allies. Later, when the colonial regiment crossed
the river on the repaired bridge, young recruits from peace-

ful Massachusetts hamlets saw their first dead man. He had
been a sergeant of the regulars. Now he lay flat beside the
trail, the tails of his long coat tipped up over his head to
cover the death look on his face.

Step by calculated step, Monckton moved his battalions
across the river into positions on the high ground east of
Fort Beauséjour. Daily and hourly the incidents of battle
accumulated to make up the campaign.

Captain Rouse sent Salvenus Cobb to work a gunboat
up the Missaquash, and the French who contended the passage were driven away.

When the church and town outside Fort Beauséjour were
burned to make a field of fire, the British regiments which
moved in quickly got much useless plunder. A Captain
Adams of Massachusetts, on a scout with the rangers, returned driving a very handsome coach which he presented
to Captain Rouse. The commodore had it fetched aboard
Success.

On 8 June, Lieutenant Alexander Hay, while walking
back to Pont à Bout, was snatched away by a party of Le
Loutre's Indians. He was spared the torture, to be given
over to Marine officers who lodged him in the safest casemate in the fort.

The more imaginative of the reluctant Acadians began
slipping away to seek their women. Boasting bravely, Vergor led out a "do or die" sortie. From behind stumps the
French fired at extreme range on the British, who were
building trenches, until the governor led all the men back
into the fort. That same night, Captain de Bailleul took out a
French patrol from the Marine. His anger and frustration
carried him headlong into a skirmish, and while fighting his
way back through the British outposts he fell, wounded.

On 14 June, Vergor received word from Louisbourg that
no help could be expected from that source. He intended

to keep this news secret, but his servant read the message and told his wife. Shortly thereafter the Acadians developed an acute fear of the plague, and wished to leave the fort—a considered preference to being caught under arms against their legal king and hung.

Early in the morning of 16 June, the big British mortar lobbed a bomb high up into the air above Fort Beauséjour. Watching the trajectory, Captain Broome and his gunners saw the 13-inch shell hover for an instant, then, as gravity overcame impetus, plunge into the fort. The bomb fell onto the curtain wall beside the main gate and penetrated into the "safe" casemate room which sheltered Lieutenant Hay of the 40th, in company with several French officers. There the shell exploded. Hay, the Sieur Rambaut, and the Indian interpreter Fernand were killed at once. Rescuers found two other officers, wounded and shocked, in the debris of the collapsed room. Vergor's morale collapsed with the curtain wall. As the surviving officers of the Marine turned in disgust from the governor to the wine store, while Le Loutre screamed for "a fight to the death," Vergor sent out a flag and a drum to ask for a parley.

Shortly before the hour of ten, as the embassy set out, the Abbé le Loutre deserted the fort and its craven governor. Within four hours Le Loutre, "the Otter," had gathered a congregation of his Micmacs for a final slash at the British flank down by the new dyke. Then the vicar general of Acadia retired into his sacristy, the impenetrable forest.

Throughout the afternoon the French ambassador shuttled between the fort and Monckton's field headquarters. On each successive journey he appeared more disheveled of dress and unsteady of gait, until at last Colonel Monckton made good his threat to walk in at precisely seven o'clock that evening. Fort Beauséjour had fallen into a state of drunkenness, its dead defenders abandoned without burial, its survivors shattered into fragments of greedy, brandy-sodden looters, the followers of Governor de Vergor.

Within two days, Colonel Winslow received the honor-able surrender of Fort Gaspereau and its twenty soldiers, and the whole isthmus was in British hands. When he re-turned the fifteen miles from the Gulf of St. Lawrence to the Bay of Fundy, Fort Beauséjour was no more. The Brit-ish Jack was flying over Fort Cumberland.

V

Redcoats on the Ohio Road

The main British army in North America was beyond the *other* Fort Cumberland, in Virginia, on the day Fort Beausé-jour's name was changed. Major General Edward Braddock was on the wilderness road to the Ohio, the road George Washington had built as far as the Great Meadows and Fort Necessity.

The commander in chief in North America had left his chariot and other comforts behind at the base camp on Will's Creek. Braddock himself rode horseback, as did his staff and escort of Virginia Light Horse; all other regular officers walked the trail with their men. They had been presented with mounts by the governor of Pennsylvania, but when the scarcity of horses became acute they had relinquished them to the pack train and the artillery teams. Only through the influence and efforts of Benjamin Franklin in Philadelphia had a sparse muster of horse transport been assembled to permit the expedition to move out at all.

On the day that Colonel Monckton took the surrender of Fort Beauséjour, General Braddock stood beside the road in a dark pine wood called "The Shades of Death," watching his train file by. Already the beasts appeared tired after their traverse of savage mountains. A chain of pack horses

45

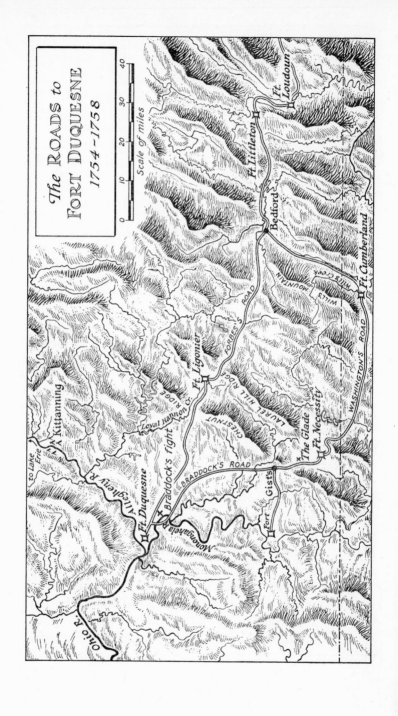

The ROADS to
FORT DUQUESNE
1754–1758

Scale of miles
0   10   20   30   40

to Lake Erie
Kittanning
Allegheny R.
Ft. Duquesne
Braddock's fight
Loyal Hannon Cr.
Ft. Ligonier
FORBE'S ROAD
CHESTNUT RIDGE
Braddock's Road
BRADDOCK'S ROAD
LAUREL HILL RIDGE
Monongahela R.
Fort Gists
The Glade
Ft. Necessity
WASHINGTON'S ROAD
Bedford
WILLS MOUNTAIN
Wills Creek
Ft. Cumberland
Ft. Littleton
Ft. Loudoun
Ohio R.

with heads hung low shambled by where the immaculate general in red and white stood with an aide as spruce as himself. The drivers of the gun teams and the artillery wagons were heavy with their whips as they hurried past, trying to gain momentum for the rise in the road ahead. A tall young carter cursed and hauled at the bit of his dray horse as he came past the general. The young man was Dan Morgan, giving absorbed attention to his horse so that he need not recognize the haughty British officers standing beside the road. He had struck one such Englishman a few days before, and his back was still raw from the flogging he had received for it. Before the drove of horned cattle came up to him, Braddock mounted, and with his troop in file behind him, rode the three-mile length of the supply train. Those at the head of the column were already making their bivouac fires when the general passed them. Darkness had fallen when he rode up to his own tent and dismounted.

Edward Braddock had done well to get his army on the road beyond Fort Cumberland in the second week in June. From the spearhead of his marching army, where the axemen and carpenters and rangers worked at widening the road, to the last squad in the rear guard, Braddock's force was fighting fit. In the weeks before departure all the frills of the army had been shorn, the plan of march and siege carefully studied and set, and the key officers of staff and command had been selected with the care and attention that Braddock gave to a hair ribbon on the morning of a Royal review. At Fort Cumberland, Colonel Innes commanded the base camp, Lieutenant Colonel Ralph Burton of the 48th Foot having tactfully replaced that somewhat superannuated officer in over-all supervision of the colonel troops, both militia and Independent Companies. At Fort Cumberland, too, were left the "odds and sods," and a hospital under the charge of a forthright lady of capable courage, Matron Charlotte Brown. Sir Peter Halkett, seconded by Thomas

Gage—both men of initiative and daring—commanded the
44th Foot. There were some reservations about Colonel
Thomas Dunbar, whose regiment, the 48th, marched with
the baggage train.

In the selection of his own staff, General Braddock was
both wise and diplomatic. Captain Robert Orme, an old
friend and protégé from the Life Guards, had come with him
from England. Two young men from the colonies were
asked to join the general's staff family: the son of the governor of Massachusetts joined as secretary, and as a volunteer
without military rank there was George Washington, who
knew the road and was familiar with the wilderness and its
people.

Close to the staff were Gist, the woods pilot of the Ohio
company, and George Groghan, the keeper of Pennsylvania's Allegheny marches. Groghan had brought his Indians
with him, but they had not been acceptable to the British
general as comrades-in-arms. They expected to attach their
numerous relations for rations, and there was potential danger to the peace of the army in the enthusiasm shown by the
British officers for some of the Indian women. A war party
of Cherokees from the mountains in the western Carolinas
had been expected, but the warriors of that Nation turned
back in disgust at the hostility they encountered from the
settlers along their line of march. For the tight control of
his army, General Braddock was well free of Indian auxiliaries. He even repudiated the services of "Captain Jack" and
his small band of vengeful white Indian-killers. That there
were Indians in all the woods around him Braddock knew,
for he had seen the scalps brought in by those friendly to
the British, and on occasion he found the scalps of his own
men, stragglers and scouts, nailed to the trees. But of his
army there were only eight painted warriors, members of
the party of Washington's friend Monacatootha, half-king
of the Mingos in succession to Tanacharison.

In his planning of the expedition, in which colonial rangers of the Independent Companies would do the scouting, General Braddock had foreseen the problems that lay ahead. Not only did he have his cavalry troop for contact couriers and as a mobile arm of opportunity, but he had the nucleus of a navy in thirty seamen from HMS *Garland*. These men marched with the van, where their carpenters' knowledge of tools and their seamen's skill with tackle served the expedition well in shaping bridge timbers and clearing windfalls along the road. When the army came off the rough mountain road it would take over the French riverboat transports, and on the Great Lakes the naval contingent would build boats to sail again on wide waters.

In the schedule of Braddock's campaign, Fort Duquesne was a three-day siege. After that the British army would roll up the French line of communication like a ball of tarred string, unraveling, as they came to them, the knots at Presque Isle, at Fort Niagara, and if the weather held, at Fort Frontenac.

The British-Colonial army, marching through the hot days of a dry June, was a tightly packaged affair, with no loose ends in its organization and its route—by land, by water, and in battle—carefully planned. Edward Braddock was that kind of soldier.

At the age of fifteen he had entered the 2nd Foot Guards, where he learned the smell of dry pipe clay before he learned how to pinch snuff from the mull in the anteroom. He had neither the great wealth nor the great patron necessary for rapid promotion, and long years as a company officer gave him time to study and to practice the new precision drill, invented in Anhalt-Dessau, perfected by the two great Prussian Fredericks, and so much admired by the Hanoverian King of England. A long career preoccupied with the niceties of dress and drill paid off at the Battle of Fontenoy in 1745. Braddock led his guardsmen, their dressing true and their discipline as bright as their buttons, through the French guards and into the heart of the French army.

Fontenoy and the detail-minded Royal Duke of Cumberland's promotion to commander in chief gave impetus to Braddock's lagging career. In the ten years following, he passed through the difficult grades of lieutenant colonel to attain the rank of brigadier. Though he was abroad in Gibraltar, where a guardsman could live on his pay while his competence accumulated, Braddock was not forgotten when a commander in chief was required for North America. The duke called him home, made him a major general, and sent him off to Virginia, where, still safe from his creditors, he had a chance at fame, fortune, and a knighthood.

Braddock was eight days on the forest road from Fort Cumberland to Little Meadows, a distance of only twenty-four miles. Great Meadows was as far away again, and the confluence of the Monongahela and Allegheny rivers was many miles beyond that point.

Information about the enemy brought pressure on General Braddock to hasten his advance, which had been slowed by the weakness of his horses. His spies told him that 900 French soldiers were coming to reinforce the garrison of fifty men he believed to be at Fort Duquesne. In the race for the fort which now appeared to be developing, the weather favored the British. The unusually dry June which gave them good roads for boots, hooves, and wheels, was, to the French, a drought which left no water in the rivers to float the keels of their water-borne transport. Nevertheless, Braddock decided to press forward a flying column. On 19 June, he split his column into two divisions. General Braddock himself took the first division forward at a hard pace. It was the elite division. Twelve hundred of the "choicest men" made up its complement, and the best horses in the army pulled the guns and thirty wagons of the divisional artillery. The strongest pack animals carried thirty-five days' provisions on Braddock's dash to the Ohio.

George Washington did not go with his general. He lay aflame with fever in the back of a cart in the middle of Colonel Dunbar's slow-moving second division. He was sitting up when the cart brought him to Great Meadows, and as the doctor helped him down he could see the fireweed growing where Fort Necessity had stood. Though weak and spent, he left the Meadows on the following day. It was the first anniversary of the siege.

Washington did not catch up with the first division until the afternoon of 8 July. He found the staff and commanders in a council of high good spirits, planning the next day's march. On the following day they would move up, ready to begin, on the tenth, the siege of Fort Duquesne, which, from Gist's and from Indian reconnaissance, they knew had not been reinforced.

With the map spread out before him, Braddock gave his orders. Because of difficult and dangerous ground ahead on the right bank of the Monongahela, on which the British army marched, he would cross over and back at the fords. Without looking down, Braddock twice jabbed at the map with his fingers. The officers' eyes did not waver from the eyes of their general; later, each one would examine the map. Having made the second crossing, the army would climb up onto the high ground parallel to the river and march down the road to the French fort. The order of march would be as usual. Lieutenant Colonel Thomas Gage would lead the advance party. Braddock looked at Gage, who nodded his head. The main body of the army and the convoy would follow immediately behind, led by the Light Horse (Braddock paused until Captain Stewart, who was scribbling notes, looked up), who would detach six horsemen to ride with the point of Gage's advance party, to bring back warning of contact. The disposition of each company, each gun, the pack horses, and the flanker scouts was given out, until the full picture of the march began to focus in the eyes of the British and Virginia officers. Gage was to be ready and to move out before the early dawn. The orders group was ending, but there was one additional item: at Frazer's house, across the second ford, colors were to be uncased and field music was to play the army down the last stretch of road to Fort Duquesne.

In Fort Duquesne the French flag hung limp before the home and headquarters of the dispirited commander. The scalps of three British stragglers lay on a table beside the still-open cash box from which he had counted out the coins to the Indians who had brought them in. They offered no hope, as there were so many more scalps, the hair neatly tied and queued, on the heads of the British army not two days' march from the French fort. To meet the enemy, Claude Pierre Pécaudy, Sieur de Contrecoeur, had less than 100 soldiers of the Marine and but 200 Canadian militiamen, in a fort still unfinished and unprepared for a siege. His reinforcements—300 soldiers—were stranded on the banks of dry rivers far to the north, but even their arrival would scarcely match the strength of the British, whose numbers had awed the Indians watching them all the way from Fort Cumberland.

In spite of the three hanks of hair on the commander's desk, the Indians eating French rations on the Ohio remained neutral. Even the zeal of their trusted friend Captain Beaujeu had failed to rouse them to go with him to an ambush in the broken country up the Monongahela. The best they would promise the ardent young seigneur was a council, and their answer on the morrow.

On the morning of 9 July, Daniel Hyacinthe de Beaujeu stepped through the outer picket gate to hear the answer of the chiefs. Solemnly, the representatives of ten Nations approached the slim figure awaiting them. Athanasius, the Huron from the Mission of Lorette, and all the chiefs and warriors he spoke for, noted at once that Beaujeu himself was dressed in the Indian fashion for war. Only the cold metal eye of a French officer's gorget lying on the wide naked breast of the young Canadian linked him to the government of New France. In a short, sonorous oration, Athanasius declined the invitation to waylay the redcoats. There was silence, while a curl of scorn formed slowly on the lip of Captain Beaujeu; when he spoke, it was of shame. Then his voice, pitched high over the heads of the chiefs to drench the warriors beyond, lapped tauntingly around the barren word "coward." A man of the Beaujeu blood had led the armies of France as constable; another had fought for the true religion as Grand Master of the Knights Templar; now, on the banks of a forest river, the voice of a third Beaujeu assumed the heritage of leadership. With measured insolence the French captain flayed the stolid mass of listening Indians with raw words. Deliberately he taunted them to anger. The silent indifference of the warriors crumbled before the scathing voice, first as a whisper, then as a murmur, finally as the first bellicose whoop of Beaujeu's war party.

It was noon before the frenzy stirred up by Beaujeu could be controlled and directed down the path on which the British were approaching. By then, the Indians had danced out their boasts and streaked themselves with the fierce colors of war, amulets to luck and courage. At last they were gone, more than half a thousand Indians, jogging the trail, silent now that they were in the woods, following their young leader and half their number of Canadian militiamen and marines. Almost alone at his fort, Contrecoeur turned and went through the gate. Unseeing, he walked by an English prisoner seated in a patch of shade, watching in wonder an ant, as it climbed tirelessly down a stick which the man turned idly in his hand.

The senior naval officer was the first of the British column to see Beaujeu. Mr. Engineer Gordon looked up from the theodolite that he was leveling to see the Frenchman, naked as an Indian, 100 yards down the trail and waving his hat to right and left to give direction to other men, running up behind him. Shouts and calls from the woods told the sailor that others of his men now saw the enemy, so he grabbed his instrument and ran for the companionship of the road-building party and of the guard of grenadiers, forming a firing line across the narrow road. Mr. Gordon veered to the right, and the first hurried British volley chased up the trail along which he had run. Two hundred yards away, the young French officer was still directing his men into the bush.

Colonel Gage had come up, a horseman had been sent back to the general for orders, and the two companies of grenadiers had jostled into line before the third deliberate volley was fired. With it, Beaujeu fell. With his fall, the progressive fire from the woods, which was licking down the sides of the British column like waves along the bow planks of a frigate, gradually lapsed into silence. When it started up again as Beaujeu's lieutenants took hold, the French fire had a more earnest tone, reached further back along the flanks of the British lining the road, and showed in the staggering fall of a grenadier or the plunge of a horse to its knees.

Spurring his horse through the press of men, General Braddock came up with his staff and escort behind him. With Gage, he got the 250 men of the advance guard into line, facing right and left by companies. One of the two guns with Gage came into action. Its roar had the reassuring voice of authority, and the familiar sound of battle steadied the British regulars. A shot from the woods took

Braddock's horse, the first of five to be shot from under him that afternoon. A cavalry horse was brought, and the general swung up into the saddle. From his high seat he could look out over the heads of his foot soldiers to the strange field of battle in which there were no ranks of the enemy to charge, only a welter of untidy tree trunks and brush diminishing into a distant wall of forest.

Without a Frenchman in sight, Braddock was forced to fight his battle by sound alone. All along the British column the guns, he could hear, were in action—but without targets. Sir Peter Halkett's troops were coming up to join on behind the stand of the advance guard. Enemy fire on the left appeared to be sparse, coming from the edge of the high ground above the river. Braddock saw that Gage had executed the order to form and fire by platoons. Only the New York companies, and some Virginians who had come up, were out of ranks, skulking away behind trees and crouching in the bushes. Braddock turned to Shirley, riding at his crupper, but, seeing the saddle empty, called out to Burton to have those gormless colonials in ranks.

Now the main French fire came distinctly from some high ground to the British right. Braddock put a company into the charge for that key position. High, red mitre caps slanted off through the trees in a ragged, broken line. Somewhere out of sight the drum stopped beating, and the irregular French fire from the hill quickened. The charge came stumbling back to the companionship of the road, where a man could look up to the open sky, and could feel a shoulder touching his. No officers returned with the grenadiers from that first charge, and not many of the men. A second charge was organized and launched. Like the first, it, too, came back officerless, shattered, but with a difference: its men had seen the mutilated bodies of the dead and wounded of the first charge, lying out there in the woods. Word of the Indians' work spread up and down the British firing line.

Imperceptibly at first, the British fire quickened. As they heard the changing tone, experienced officers began shouting to their men to steady down.

While waiting for yet another horse to be brought to him, General Braddock ordered Gage, whom he saw to be cut and wounded, to withdraw on the wagons. Then, moving back along the road, his horse picking its way among the dead and wounded, Braddock sought out Colonel Halkett. That officer was dead, and the general ordered Colonel Burton into a final covering charge. A hundred men, colonials and regulars, went forward behind the colors in the colonel's attack. It failed when Burton fell and was carried back, protected by a screen of fire put up by Virginians and British alike from behind trees and cover where they found it.

Platoons, led now by sergeants and corporals, walked back in file away from the cluster of dead which marked the point of the army's advance. Mr. Gordon's theodolite lay with them, and with two of his midshipmen, far from the sea.

General Braddock sat his horse, watching, gaging, judging the drift of battle and the temper of his soldiers at the crucial moment that a withdrawal brings on. He was alone. Of his official family and senior officers only Washington, off now commanding the remnant of his Virginians, was unwounded. Captain Stewart rode with the general as escort.

The ball that took Braddock struck him in the right arm, crashed through the rib cage, and spent itself in the soft tissue of the lung. Stewart, leaping from the off side of his startled horse, caught the general as he fell. For only an instant did he lie on the ground, a toppled monument to order in the eddies of an ebbing rip tide. Then he was picked up and carried along with the retreating army.

General Braddock crossed the first ford in the back of a commandeered wagon, the remnant of his first division with him, but without their equipment. On the high ground above Frazer's house lay the dead, the guns, wagons, equipment, even muskets, scattered along the road. Deserted pack animals browsed where they could find grass. From both sides of the road, marines and Canadians cautiously approached, their muskets loaded, primed, and cocked. The Indians, too, drew in.

From the far side of the ford, George Washington watched with a mixed group of provincials. When no pursuit developed, he withdrew with his men for a quarter of a mile, where he came up with Braddock. The general had had his wound dressed and, giving orders the while, was attempting to mount a horse. The effort was too much; Dr. Craik finally persuaded him to get into a hastily made litter, and the retreat of the wounded began once more. No soldiers were left with the general, only the sore-wounded in the carts and the walking wounded, still under arms.

Washington took a horse and rode on at a canter to Dunbar's camp. On the road he met the wounded Gage with eighty men in ranks, hurrying to rally to the general. There was little to cheer Washington at the camp of the second division. Everyone, from Colonel Dunbar to the drummer boy, had caught the infection of defeat and retreat. Some units were already moving out for Fort Necessity and beyond. It was with difficulty that the young Virginia volunteer rounded up wagons to return for the wounded who had been left with the general between the two fords. There still remained some daylight in the crowded hours and minutes of that day which had begun with flags and music and the sound of many feet splashing through the waters of the ford.

Five days later, Edward Braddock died of his wound. As a member of the general's official family, and because the chaplain was a casualty, George Washington read the funeral service. He stood beside the grave while the earth was filled in; then, while the mound was patted smooth, he called to the waiting wagons. One by one they came, hesitating as they bumped over the mound in the middle of the road. By the time Dan Morgan's turn came to cross the grave, the mound was flat. He flapped the reins on the flanks of his big brown horse and drove on. Around the next bend in the road, or perhaps the one beyond, he would get a glimpse of the Great Meadows.

VI

War Over the Land Bridge

Captain Jean-Daniel Dumas of the Marine, successor to the command of Beaujeu's Canadian-Indian force, returned to Fort Duquesne after nightfall. There were lights in the fort, and many people were passing in and out of the wide-open gate in the picket wall. Down by the Indian encampment bonfires blazed, and at each fire a shouting, drumming dance was in progress. Dumas was the victor over Braddock. It was he who had steadied the Canadians and, with the half-breed Langlade, had rallied the Indians after Beaujeu had fallen to the British volley. He had organized the mile-long gauntlet and had held it firm through the three long hours of the incredible battle, until at last the British discipline broke. With the flight of the British, the French "army," too, was shattered, disbanded, dispersed, gone out of all control, on a rampage of looting and pillaging born of its own unexpected success. So Captain Dumas returned to Fort Duquesne, not at the head of his victorious soldiers but virtually alone, leading a two-wheeled English cart.

For the thirty-odd Frenchmen and Indians killed, there were more than 400 British dead, lying along the road and in the underbrush. Though at that count there were not enough scalps to go around among the Indians engaged, let

alone the Canadians so inclined, there was much else to
catch the fancy of the eager scavengers. There were red
coats, white breeches, shoes and gaiters, pipe-clayed belts
with shiny brass buckles, caps and hats, blankets, pouches,
and all those curious little things that a man keeps by him in
his pockets. There were practical things for the taking:
lengths of chain and wooden buckets from the gun carriages,
tools and utensils, even a theodolite. From the dead horses
one could take hooks and hasps and the leather from harness,
or a good, strong saddle. In the carts were tents and food
and even rum, and of course there were the carts themselves.
Things such as these did not comprise all the booty at the
scene of Braddock's rout. There was a herd of pack horses,
and, trying to hide in the woods, a few refugees, mostly
men but some women followers of Braddock's army. When
taken prisoner, the refugees could carry great loads of their
captors' loot, and later, in distant Indian villages, they could
be made slaves. At the site of Braddock's defeat there was
booty for all.

Captain Dumas's treasure was in the single cart whose
horse he led in by the bridle, through the gate of Fort Duquesne and up to the commandant's door. For want of
horses, he had been forced to leave on the battleground the
fifteen pieces of British artillery with all their stores. But
in the cart were the files, documents, and papers of the
British commander in chief in North America.

Quickly found among the documents in General Braddock's field desk was the detailed map of Fort Duquesne,
drawn the year before by the hostage, Captain Stobo. That
the British had this map was of little interest to the two
Frenchmen, Contrecoeur and Dumas, as they puzzled
through the unfamiliar English words by the light of candles on the night of the victory celebration. The map, when
it reached Montreal, would send Stobo (still a hostage and
still a British agent) to jail. But that document gave the key

to the intelligence value of the other papers captured with the baggage of the defeated British army. In the morning, General Braddock's field desk was on the way to the governor general of New France.

Vaudreuil was at Montreal when Braddock's papers were brought to him. Since his arrival in Canada a month previously he had been busy. With all the pomp and ceremony with which he surrounded himself, he had taken over the government from the Marquis de Duquesne, and had immediately sent letters to France, deprecating the work of his predecessor. There was nothing that the new governor general could do about the loss of remote Fort Beauséjour and the plight of the Acadians. His forces—regulars, colonial marines, and militia—were on the St. Lawrence, or, in the case of the latter two, were committed to the river forts and to the upper lakes. The threat to New France lay at Fort Duquesne, at Fort Niagara, and at Fort Frontenac, at the back door of Montreal. As everyone in Canada could see, the British post and little fleet of gunboats at Oswego on Lake Ontario was the menace to the Canadian west. Further, the little fort was the fist and the bountiful hand by which the western Nations of the powerful Iroquois were held in check and placated by the British. The Marquis de Vaudreuil was determined to have that place, and with it the Iroquois, before the summer of 1755 was over. To that end, he began the movement toward Fort Frontenac of the four regiments of French regulars which had come with him from France. At that fort they would gather for a spring on Fort Oswego. To control the move, and to keep closer watch on the army general, who was under the governor's orders but who reported directly to France, Vaudreuil took up his official residence in Montreal.

He was there, watching the white-coated regiments embark for the voyage upriver, when the canoe turned into shore with its courier from the Ohio, bringing the news of

Dumas's victory. Vaudreuil was at his big desk, with the
Baron Dieskau at his elbow, when the vital document from
Braddock's luggage was brought in. It changed his entire
plan of campaign.

Before Vaudreuil and Dieskau lay exposed the plans of
the four British campaigns against New France for the year
1755. They knew the story of the expeditions to Fort Beauséjour and Fort Duquesne, the final pages of which had now
been written. They had divined the intent and importance
of Governor Shirley's move to Oswego. What the governor
and the general did not know, until they read of it in Braddock's battle orders, was the fact that William Johnson's
expedition against Fort St. Frédéric was an offensive, rather
than merely a diversion. In Johnson's fist were men and
guns enough to shatter the small French force of observation at Crown Point. At Johnson's command was a fleet
of transports and armed vessels, to carry his army across
Lake Champlain to the back door of Montreal. The commercial capital of New France was menaced. With the
French troops gone west and without walls of defense,
Montreal lay exposed and unready.

Vaudreuil and Dieskau acted quickly in response to the
threat that Johnson suddenly presented to them out of
Braddock's papers. The governor gave up his plan to attack
Oswego. A reappraisal of Shirley's position showed him,
with Braddock gone, to be an ineffectual tentacle, rather
than a pincer threatening Niagara. Indeed, with French
troops at Frontenac and colonial troops now uncommitted
on the Ohio, Shirley's regiments on Lake Ontario were
themselves squeezed between the jaws of French pincers.
The general undertook the defense of Fort St. Frédéric.
But to a soldier of Baron Dieskau's temper and training, the
ends of defense were best achieved by attack.

The baron, however, needed troops beyond the number
and above the quality of those then holding the Lake Cham-

plain line. Of the baron's four regiments of regulars, two—Guyenne and Béarn—were beyond recall at Fort Frontenac. La Reine and Languedoc were moving up the St. Lawrence on their way to join the others, and could be turned around. Messengers set out at once. Dieskau himself did not await their return to Montreal, or the completion of Vaudreuil's desperate roll of the muster drum among the militia and the Indians of eastern Canada. With the leaping bound of imagination, he hurried to Fort St. Frédéric, to the 1200 troops there, and to the watch on the enemy approaching the as-yet-unknown place of battle.

On 16 August, the Chevalier de Montreuil saw the last of the French troops through Montreal on their way to Dieskau. The chevalier was the army adjutant general, and, since Rostaing's death aboard *Alcide*, second-in-command to Dieskau. As the senior staff officer, it had been his duty to stand at Montreal, gathering in and dispatching south to his general every man on whom he could lay his hands. He had done well. In a three-week period, 1800 soldiers, militiamen, and Indians had taken the route up Lake Champlain to Fort St. Frédéric. Now the Chevalier de Montreuil was ready to go as second-in-command to his general at the front, where the fighting and the glory would be. There was need to hurry, as time was running out.

The news of Braddock's defeat, which rang through the streets of Montreal on the peal of church bells, slithered into Albany on the tail of rumor. With two independent armies staging there, the report of disaster spread, grew, and flowered with detail. The two army generals, William Shirley and William Johnson, who mistrusted each other on sound civilian political grounds, anticipated the confirmation or denial of the rumors, each according to his own best interests.

General Shirley, who, if Braddock *were* dead, was by succession the supreme British commander in all of North

America, reached out with his assumed authority to seize control of Johnson's campaign. On 26 July, he issued a cautionary order to "that farmer," Johnson, which would tie his army to a passive defense. Having curbed his rival's ride to glory, Shirley dashed off to meet his own high destiny at Oswego and Niagara. With Braddock dead, all the reward for capturing Fort Niagara would fall to the old governor of Massachusetts. It was almost worth the loss of the son and heir who lay dead and mutilated on the bank of the Monongahela. Another son rode westward with Shirley to be heir to the hoped-for coronet.

William Johnson was a general for half a year before he became a soldier. For six months, the "Squire of the Mohawk River" was a business man, a politician, and a diplomat-ambassador, while his major general's commission lay with his fine new sword on the table beside the door which opened on the meadows of war's opportunities.

As a man of mercantile affairs, Johnson had assembled at Albany the vast pile of stores which his army would use on its campaign north to Lake Champlain. Not the least of his purchasing achievements had been the ordering and the delivery of two fleets of bateaux: one to ply the rear link of his route from Albany to the head of navigation on the Hudson River; the other to float his army down Lake Champlain to attain its objective, the capture of the French Fort St. Frédéric. In addition to the boats, a train of wagons was hired to transport matériel, including the whole second fleet, over the land bridge that divided the two waterways.

It was Johnson the politician who had to keep six colonial governors to their promise to furnish the regiments for his campaign. If the governments of Massachusetts, Connecticut, New Hampshire, Rhode Island, New Jersey, and New York had fallen short by twelve hundred of their quota of 4700 soldiers, well, Johnson, too, failed in his guarantee to put a thousand Indian warriors into the woods.

At a long Indian conference held at Mount Johnson, his home, William Johnson, the Indian agent, had used all the devious diplomacy at which he was so adept in an attempt to rouse the Six Nations of the Iroquois against the French. But the western chiefs, particularly the numerous and warlike Senecas, were as hesitant to commit themselves to the British on the Hudson as they had been to ally themselves with the French on the Ohio. Even the "cannibal" Mohawks, with whom Johnson lived on intimate terms of family and clan, were reluctant to take up the hatchet for fear of fighting against their blood cousins, the Caughnawagas, the "praying Indians" whose church was in New France. In the end it was only because the senior chief of the Iroquois, King Hendricks—who was Johnson's father-in-law by a Mohawk marriage—joined the northern army, that the chiefs consented to let their warriors go. The long conference was ended with solemn dignity, and "General" Johnson bade his guests farewell. There was little that the brown girl who presided at the foot of the table at Mount Johnson could serve for supper that evening; the guests, 1200 Indians who had come to the conference, had eaten everything. But William Johnson had no time for meals or comforts. The army in Albany was in tatters because of his neglect.

The troops had begun to arrive in Albany early in July. The contingent of each individual colony carried with it the chips of its own convictions and prejudices. These were flaunted like epaulets before the strangers of the camp and of the town. Albany itself was put off limits. Colonel Ephraim Williams called down the wrath of his Massachusetts God upon the wicked and profane soldiery, particularly the roisterers of New York and the schismatic Rhode Islanders. Phineas Lyman, next to Johnson in the line of command, fancied himself a military genius in the image of the great Turenne, a role which his Connecticut Regiment boisterously proclaimed. Colonel Joseph Blanchard, with his regiment of Episcopalian New Hampshire men, never did arrive to add their backwoods independent attitude to the seething inter-colonial camp at Albany. Colonel Schuyler's good regiment of New Jersey "Blues" had come and gone, snatched away from the northern army by a loud rattle of seniority in rank on the part of William Shirley, bound westward for Oswego. The "theft" of the New Jersey men left Johnson indignant and his army the poorer by 500 of his best soldiers.

At the end of July the northern army sat, disjointed and truculent, amid its great concentration of goods and guns and transports. At last, the force that was to unite it seeped into camp as a mere rumor. No one believed that Braddock's army, with its two regiments of British regulars, had been, *could* be, defeated. But in the rich soil of an idle, discontented army, the tale took root. On 27 July, General Johnson, for the sake of morale, had to brand the reports of disaster as "false, treacherous, and groundless." Three days later he ate his words.

All of the rumors were true, even to the details: the main campaign of the year had been shattered and abandoned. In all the long catalogue of woe there was but one morsel of consolation. The colonial soldiers of Virginia had done well in covering the retreat with a steadiness that had been expected, but not found, in the regulars.

To the men of New York, Massachusetts, New Hampshire, Rhode Island, and Connecticut, the conduct of the Virginia colonials was sufficient foundation on which to rebuild their shattered confidence. From the menace, now brought to an imminence by the failure of the regulars, the men of Johnson's army made a mortar that bound them together into a wall of common purpose. This was to defend their own frontier in Albany, where a year before Benjamin Franklin had tried, and failed, to persuade the British colonies to unite. The shock and the threat of a common disaster now created a completely unified army of colonials. After an awful moment of hesitation, the northern army began its move to the ground where it would fight.

Johnson's army did not move with the alacrity with which Baron Dieskau had turned around his regulars. It moved with the ponderous certainty of a caterpillar.

Phineas Lyman went first, with the advance guard, to the Great Carrying Place at the end of northern navigation on the Hudson River. There, while his soldiers built log-and-bark warehouses for the perishable stores, rangers probed ahead tentatively, seeking the best way over the land bridge that divided the Hudson River from the northward-flowing waters of Lake Champlain. Moses Titcomb of Massachusetts brought on the first division when the river boats had returned from taking Lyman forward. Titcomb had 1100 men, with most of the stores, to move up the sixty miles of river to the Great Carrying Place. Along the shore road, the wagons and cattle kept pace with his boats. Finally the tail of Johnson's army, heavy with its artillery train of twenty-one guns, let go its hold on Albany and inched its way up-river to rejoin the head and body of the army.

General Johnson did not at once accompany his troops into the field. Braddock's defeat, which had united the five colonial entities of his military command, had brought on a new diplomatic crisis for Johnson the Indian agent. Seneca warriors with Beaujeu and Dumas had dipped their arms deep into British blood and loot on the Monongahela. They had gone over to the French, ending the old alliance with the British and shattering the solidarity of the Iroquois League itself. In a last desperate effort, William Johnson asked the Six Nations to remain neutral, at least, until the British could show their prowess in war at Niagara and on Lake Champlain. To this, even the Seneca chiefs agreed. Johnson's own faithful Mohawks went with him into battle. The old King Hendricks, regally uniformed, rode a staid horse beside his white friend. A seventeen-year-old Indian youth often led the old king's horse. He was Thay-en-da-ne-gea, or "Joseph Brandt," who was going on the war party with his friend of the schoolroom, the general's son John Johnson.

William Johnson had slept little and his meals had been sporadic during the tense days of the Braddock crisis. Before that, the problems of the long Indian conference had been compounded with the assembling of his mismatched army and confused by the contemptuous arrogance of his political rival, Shirley, who had stomped through Johnson's army and the Indian camps. Johnson was tired when he reached the Great Carrying Place on 14 August. A guard turned out to honor his generalship, and a flourish of drums and music proclaimed his authority. A little of Johnson's weariness slipped from his wide shoulders. The senior officers, who greeted him with an acknowledging doff of their gold-laced hats, must wait the word they wished to have with him until he had washed and dined—perhaps until he had slept a bit. Here with the army, *his* army, Johnson felt safe, joined in the calm world of common, simple purpose, bound in a single direction with success the only admissible goal.

It was the general's intent to push a twenty-mile road directly across the watershed to the head of Lake Champlain. From a fort to be built there, his army would advance by water down the narrow channel through the Lake Champlain marshes to the Ticonderoga Peninsula. On that most strategic site, Johnson would build his containing fort before continuing on to the investing of Fort St. Frédéric, ten miles to the north. The plan was a deliberate one, taking time, envisioning only minimal opposition on the approach march, and committing the soldiers to the spade rather than to the bayonet. At a council of war on 24 August, the initial direction of the route north was radically changed.

Upon his arrival at the Great Carrying Place, William Johnson had sent four of his most trusted Mohawks to Caughnawaga as ambassador-spies. Their mission was to persuade their Roman Catholic cousins not to join the French in war against their friend Johnson. On 21 August, the four Mohawks returned, their embassy a failure, themselves bemused, baptized, and bearing news of the huge French army marching to smite the English at Armageddon on the portage road. Clan Brother Johnson marveled at the ambassadors' wondrous tale. General Johnson repeated the spies' report to his council, with a less fervid estimate of Baron Dieskau's strength. But the fact remained that since Braddock's defeat, a worthy French force was in the field against Johnson, led by a general who would give battle. Furthermore, if Armageddon was to be an ambush, the most likely place to set it was on the twenty-mile road to Lake Champlain, or in the narrow, marshy stretch of the lake south of Ticonderoga. It was the decision of the council of colonels, now forewarned, to side-step the dangerous ground.

In the next valley to the west of Lake Champlain lay a long, slim sliver of a lake of deep, clear water. For thirty-five miles, high, forbidding mountains bent the shoreline to the lake's outlet, which was a three-mile river, stepping down over falls into Lake Champlain at Ticonderoga. The French priest, Isaac Jogues, who first saw this most beautiful of lakes while taking his initial bloody step to martyrdom and sainthood as an Indian captive, named it for the Holy Sacrament. William Johnson, when he turned his soldiers onto it, blazed it as *the* invasion route of armies and re-named it "George" in honor of the English king.

For three days, the colonials cut and hacked, shoveled and hauled, making their road from the Hudson to Lake George. The first half of the way lay across the floor of the long valley, past the great stone which, according to the French, marked the border between New France and New

York. The second half of the fifteen-mile road climbed gradually up to and through a gap in the mountains, where lay a small, round pond, now parched in the late August heat; then the road followed the side hill down to the shore at the end of the lake. There a soldier could plunge his head into the cool water, drink deep, and curse the army, or he could pray for salvation from torment.

For eight days after they reached Lake George on 29 August, Johnson's army worked. The soldiers made a camp site by cutting a wide swath out of the forest, exposing the knolls and undulations of the land. Into the widening clearing rolled the carts and wagons as they came up with their loads from the Great Carrying Place below. The soldiers cheered the first gun on its limber, as it broke out of the forest and rumbled down the last grade, its gunners at the drag ropes braking the roll of the heavy piece.

Quickly, the convoys off-loaded and turned around for the trip back to the bridgehead for another cargo. Bouncing along easily in their empty carts, the teamsters had time to think how long and lonely was the portage road. Here the road was so narrow that an overturned cart could hold the wagons behind for a massacre; there, under that ridge, French Indians could shoot down on ten teams, strung out along the track. Tobias Hendrikse Ten Eyck, walking behind his team with the reins loose, could understand the fear of Indians that had made his Negro hostler-boy desert.

General Johnson had heard the carters' complaint and their demand for more armed guards. That afternoon of 7 September he had ordered 1000 men, under Colonel Williams, to patrol back along the portage road. There had been a report from the Mohawks of a large party of the French and their Indians loose on the watershed. Williams's fighting patrol was scheduled to set out at six o'clock the next morning, and would investigate the rumor.

Late in the evening of the 7th, Johnson walked over

the ground where his engineer officer had staked out the outline of a big fort. On the top of the bluff where the northwest bastion was outlined, the general stopped while a faint cramp coursed over his abdomen under the braided waistcoat. He could look down the lake, over the water and islands to the high, distant mountains and the wide sky. At that late hour the elements were one, as time gathered them together into the fall of night.

Darkness seeps into a hardwood forest on a blue light that gives to forms moving in the undergrowth the indistinctness of a gray squirrel running out along a limb. Into such a shadowed light, the off-white coats of French infantry blended and were lost, blurring the count of the long line of soldiers as they crossed the beechwood hollow to begin the climb out of the Champlain Valley. There were, in fact, 220 officers and men of the regiments La Reine and Languedoc making the approach march to the new English portage road on the night of 7 September 1755.

These were the men whose arrival at Fort St. Frédéric the Baron Dieskau had awaited with such impatience. When they finally came, the French general had not let them stop to rest. He needed all of them in the deserted land, beyond which he must find and meet and stop the oncoming British, before they tried the rickety door of Fort St. Frédéric, which, once opened, gave access to Montreal. At Ticonderoga, where a French survey party contemplated the building of a new stone fort, Dieskau left some of his travel-weary regulars. At the Narrows, where, ten miles further on, two great rocks all but pinch out the lake channel, he left more platoons of his French troops. They would act as a rear guard while the general dashed on ahead to give battle.

The two companies of La Reine and Languedoc which Dieskau kept by him were the pick of their regiments, grenadiers chosen for their strength, steadiness, and resolve. The

rest of the baron's assault force was a mixed company of
militiamen and Indians, whose value the experienced old officer shrewdly appraised. The 700 Indians from the eastern
Nations were well led by rock-hard, woods-wise Canadians: Legardeur de St. Pierre, Longeuil, St. Luc, and Niverville. Their Canadian cadets who ran with the small war
parties could be counted on to keep the painted warriors up
in the firing line, and after the enemy was broken, the Indians themselves needed no leadership to press a savage pursuit. But the Indians were moody, and strange loyalties
moved them. Though French and Catholic, Dieskau's
Caughnawagas had refused to fight against their British
Protestant and heathen cousins. On the night march of 7
September, the Caughnawagas went first, as guides who
would not fight until the after-battle massacre, when they
could be sure that those whom they scalped were not Iroquois brothers.

The 600 Canadian militiamen who marched up into the
mountains with Dieskau's striking force were untrained
men, loyal and obedient but unreliable, without the discipline or experience to look steadily at the enemy and not see
him looking in return. The baron had never seen an auxil-
iary force such as that made up by his Canadians and Indians which could stand in the face of cannon fire. On the
basis of this military truism, Dieskau chose to make his attack on Johnson's main force at Lake George. From spies,
deserters, and chance prisoners, the French general judged
the British guns still at the Great Carrying Place. On the
shores of Lake George, therefore, Dieskau's Indians and
militia would stand man to man against Johnson's colonials,
on equal status as soldiers. The grenadiers of La Reine and
Languedoc were the weighted balance in the French favor,
for it was another truism of war that auxiliaries, such as
Johnson's Indians and colonial levies were, would not stand
to a bayonet charge by regulars.

It was breaking dawn when the guides showed Dieskau the raw cut of the road where it bordered the little pond in the mountain pass. A cadet on scout to Lake George came running up to the general, and with a correct military courtesy incongruous in view of his painted Indian nakedness, told of having seen in Johnson's camp a force preparing to march by the road. It was all too perfect: the enemy dividing his force, and the French already on the narrow road over which the British must pass. Dieskau had come to his chosen battleground. The day's action would begin here as an ambush, *à l'Indienne.*

Quickly, easily, and quietly, the militia and the Indians found their places on either side of the road. Cramped by their customary precise movement, the regulars more slowly formed their line across the road, making the base of a letter "U" open toward the approaching enemy.

For two hours, the French army sat waiting, each man in his particular "hide." Restlessly, the men began to wander toward a neighbor; the officers called them back. Word was passed that a British ranger had been taken, and that the enemy was approaching. The French settled down to waiting.

Colonel Ephraim Williams, riding straight in his saddle, passed the ends of the French ambush. Beside the Massachusetts man, King Hendricks slumped moodily on his quiet horse. Rounding a bend, the colonel could see his advance guard poised, their muskets half raised, all looking up the hill to their right. Suddenly a doe with half-grown twin fawns dashed into the road clearing, turned onto the road for a few leaps, and then crossed over. A few of the advance guard raised their muskets, tempted to take the shot. Others studied the hillside, wondering who, or what, had started the wild deer on their panic run. A few steps further, they saw an Indian waving toward them from out of the brush. The Mohawks recognized the man as a Caughnawaga. Two shots came from high up on the hill to the British right.

Startled, the British column stopped. The waiting lines of French paused, astonished that their trap had sprung too soon. Then they fired, whooped, and loaded to fire again and again into the havoc on the road in front of them. Both Williams and King Hendricks, on their horses, were down. Old Hendricks, hatless, absurd in his fancy coat, scuttled on hands and knees into the underbrush. Colonel Williams picked up the hat at his feet, recognized it as the old chief's, and hurled it off into the woods. Then he climbed up onto a big rock. He had only a moment to look down on the confusion of his own troops before he was toppled from the rock, dead. On the road ahead, Dieskau's Abenakis and Canadians, who had been robbed of their shot by the exposure of the ambush, poured out into the road. Behind them, their fire masked, La Reine and Languedoc awaited orders to advance to the charge. The orders did not come. As they stood ready, poised for a volley, the sound of battle retreated, diminished, and at last was stilled in the distance.

Some time later, the grenadiers were formed up in column on the road and given the *"En avant! Marche!"* Around a slight bend, the soldiers saw the carnage of the dead. It is difficult for a sergeant to keep his files straight when the pace is broken to step over a corpse. The two companies marched over the battleground and down into the valley below.

The firing up in the pass was audible in the armed camp of the colonials. William Johnson heard it in his tent, where he lay ill with the gripings of a dysentery. He struggled up, put on his coat, and went out to stand at the brush-log-and-stump fence which fortified the camp. A short musket shot came from the edge of the wood. The fire seemed less intense now, but closer. Without waiting on orders, Captain William Eyre, Johnson's artilleryman engineer and the only regular soldier with the army, went off to position the guns. In the camps of the regiment, drums beat the assembly, and the soldiers, listening, dropped their tools and ran to take up their arms. Where Johnson stood, there was the command post. The whole camp became orderly with activity as men found their regiments at the barricade, which each contingent sought to build higher and stronger than its neighbors.

There was a time before noon when near-panic seized the British, when the flood of refugees from the ambush poured into camp and filled the receptive ears of the men with their awesome tales. With difficulty, the officers brought their men back from the brink of fear to useful work on the barricade. Only the Mohawks did not join in the defense. Their great king was gone, murdered by Abenakis at the fringe of battle; some of the women, and four lesser chiefs, were dead with him. It was a time for a great mourning.

The turmoil of near-panic which seized Johnson's army was echoed in the confusion of victory which disrupted Dieskau's forces. What little cohesion the Canadian militia had was dissipated in the excitement of the big killing on the road, while the Nations of Indians were snarling at each other for possession of the few Mohawks who had been captured alive. The French army, after the ambush, was like a pack of hounds loosed in a rabbit warren, so intent on the killing and rending that the big red stag is forgotten. Valuable time was lost while Master Dieskau brought his wild pack to heel. The time of the hunt had come when the mastiff grenadiers should have been uncoupled to bound forward and drag the deer down before he could recover and turn at bay.

It was early afternoon before the grenadiers were marched out onto the field and maneuvered into line, facing the tangled antlers of the colonials' rough barricade. While the amazed New Yorkers and New Englanders watched, the white-uniformed regulars from Europe leveled their muskets. For a long, long moment, the Frenchmen looked hard at the British, and the colonials stared in wonder at

these men from France. The volley of the grenadiers leaped
forward in stabbing flame and billowing smoke. Again and
again, the French volleys roared out. Gradually, with the
surprise that tempts curiosity, the huddled colonials realized
that few of their company were being hurt. A boy, whose
father farmed the Pocumtuck Valley near Deerfield, in
Massachusetts, ventured a look over the log behind which
he lay. He saw, across the stumpy field, a composed, arrogant line of men in white, like those of whom his grand-
mother had told when she would frighten him with tales of
her captivity in Canada. An officer on the right of the
French line looked to be a fair shot to try. The boy from
Deerfield aimed his musket, and was satisfied that, at extreme deer range, he had hit the officer in the right arm.
There were other good targets, and other colonials were
now taking them. Captain Eyre himself was laying his
number-one gun with the gun sergeant while, kneeling by
the left wheel, the bombardier was blowing up a spark on
the linstock match.

In the hospital tent, Surgeon Williams was binding up a
hip wound for General Johnson, whom earlier he had doc-
tored for dysentery. This time the simple, God-fearing doctor from Massachusetts found something to admire in the
great, hulking Irishman from the Mohawk Valley, who
cursed the probe, or the stabbing cramp in his bowels, that
kept him from returning to the guns. They were in action
now, sounding like barn doors slamming in a thunder squall.

The grenadiers of La Reine and Languedoc were taking
the British musket and cannon fire in good order, and steadily returning it with controlled volleys. To their left, the
Canadian militia were firing erratically from inside the edge
of the woods. There was no sign of the French Indian allies.
From his battle station on the left of his grenadiers, Dieskau
had sent the Chevalier de Montreuil (whose right sleeve was
torn and bloody) to organize and inspire the Canadians to

rush the British barricade. It was while his second-in-command was away that the baron was hit, and hit again, and hit a third time. Returning from his hopeless mission—no threat or plea would move the militia out into the open where the cannon's eye could see them—Montreuil found his general propped against a tree, unattended, yelling orders to his grenadiers to charge. But the moment had been lost. Though they had begun a charge, the ensign, who was now the only officer of Languedoc, could not hold his men to it, and Captain Maron of the queen's proud regiment had been forced to swing his company to the right, where the British were beginning to infiltrate. Elsewhere, Johnson's soldiers were starting to move, and all along the barricade columns were standing up to take a clear, unobstructed aim at the white coats. It was time for the French to retire.

Twice, the Chevalier de Montreuil tried to lift his general, first with the aid of two Canadians, but that attempt failed when one of the men was shot dead and the other fled. Alone, Montreuil could not safely move the baron's thrice-shattered leg. Reluctantly, the chevalier left his general in order to take over the command of Dieskau's army in retreat.

Under his tree, wearing his rich, gold-laced coat and waistcoat, his only escort a dead Canadian and the body-servant he had brought with him from far-off Germany, the colonial patrol found the Baron Dieskau. It closed in, stepping cautiously, as though the wounded man were a coiled rattlesnake. Someone shot quickly from the hip, and as the four-times-wounded man writhed with the new pain, they seized him.

The battle of Lake George was over. In the morning it had gone well for the Canadians and their Indians. In the afternoon, all but alone, the French regulars had stood against the rising surge of American confidence, and had been beaten.

The epilogue of battle was spoken at dusk in General Johnson's big tent. The leader of a relief force of New Hampshire men from the Great Carrying Place reported it as he bent over the foot of the wounded general's bed. He told how he had surprised French Indians scavenging among the British dead at the scene of the morning massacre. He had killed many of them, throwing their bodies into the little pond until—he swore it—the water turned red with blood. From another camp-bed in Johnson's tent, the Baron Dieskau faintly heard the strange man's words from the dark forest edge of a drugged sleep.

Outside the tent, the New Hampshire captain shouldered his way through a ring of sullen Mohawks. They were petulant, having wanted the French commander for vengeful torture, only to be refused by their Brother Johnson.

VII

Over the Sea and Out of the Forest

For William Shirley, the death of Braddock was an ele-
vating event. Already second-in-command to the English
general, the events on the Monongahela automatically raised
the Massachusetts governor to the supreme military command in North America. With General Braddock's army
turned back on the convergent road to Fort Niagara, the
importance of Shirley's own expedition to that place increased, as did its leader's opportunity to gain the highest
prize as sole victor, should the expedition succeed. As the
commander in chief outranked the other expedition commanders, Shirley was now in a position to curb the military
ambition of his despised and feared political opponent, "that
farmer" from the Mohawk, William Johnson. The new
commander's first order, given even before the news of
Braddock's death was confirmed, was one which confined
Johnson and his whole army to a purely defensive role. A
defender is thanked, while a conqueror is pitched onto high
plains of glory.

Shirley's lunge for fame had carried him as far as Oswego
by the time Dieskau thrust through to the portage road to
Lake George. For a month, the British Niagara army had
been poised on the shore of Lake Ontario like a hesitant

diver on the edge of a dock. Nine days later it was still
there, going nowhere because it was looking back over its
shoulder, when the express messenger brought to General
Shirley the news of the Battle of Lake George.

General Johnson's success in repulsing Baron Dieskau's
attack was duly and ceremoniously cheered at Fort Oswego. From the right of the parade beginning with the
50th, the fire of the *feu de joie* coursed along the files,
through the 51st Foot and down the blue-clad New Jersey
Regiment. Five condemned deserters were pardoned, and an
extra issue of rum was measured out to all. On the day following the celebration, Shirley assembled his officers in
council, to indicate to them the effect of the action at
Lake George on the course of their own expedition. The
signs were propitious. The French general had been removed from the scene and two of the four French regiments which had threatened Oswego from Fort Frontenac
were now shown to be fully committed on the Lake Champlain front. The council resolved to press forward its plans,
preparations, and boat-loadings for the attack on Fort Niagara. After dark that night, a scout of rangers set out to
watch the French at Fort Frontenac.

Ten days later the whole campaign was canceled. The
rangers had seen French vessels loading supplies and reinforcements for Fort Niagara; Indians, grown bold, had
killed and scalped a working-party within earshot of the
new Fort Ontario; and the winds and storms of autumn
were lashing up the waves on the lake. For a few days the
enthusiasm of the officers had been whetted by Johnson's
success, but that had soon been drained off from the top.
General Shirley was ready to go home, where the wheels of
events were turning rapidly. His duty, his responsibility,
and his opportunity lay at the hub, rather than at the far
outer end of a single spoke.

The battle at Lake George had been a defensive victory

on both sides. For New France, Dieskau's dashing bold stroke had been an offensive-defensive maneuver to achieve the strategic end of keeping the British well beyond the Fort St. Frédéric gate, a gate that opened onto Canada's St. Lawrence heartland. For the British colonies, the fight for life on the portage road and at the rough barricade had been a successful tactical defense, the strategic value of which was not immediately assessed.

By midsummer of 1755, Vaudreuil and Dieskau together had sensed that the border disputes, started on the Ohio and now spread to Acadia, Nova Scotia, and the sea off Louisbourg, constituted a war which challenged the very existence of New France. It was not until the end of summer that the several independent, isolated, mutually jealous British provincial governors saw in Dieskau's attack along the old traditional invasion route the threat of invasion from Canada.

But for the British, the elation after a battle won preceded the realization of a war begun. In one stroke of General William Johnson's sword, Braddock's death was avenged and the rout of the British 44th and 48th Foot was vindicated. The great French general had been taken, and the soldiers of Languedoc and of the French queen's own regiment had been humbled. Few could see behind the hero the failure of a campaign to achieve its objective. Men saw only the conqueror of "Monsieur Pouf" in a pitched battle on the shore of the newly named Lake George, a name that sang out like the war cry: "St. George for England!" William Johnson need only come back from the scene of his glory to receive his triumph and accept his crown of laurels.

But Johnson did not return at once to ride the wave of his popularity. On the specific orders of his commander in chief, General Johnson remained with his army in frustrating exile at Lake George. William Shirley's judgment was militarily sound as well as politically expedient in keeping his victorious general in the field. With a French army still at Fort St. Frédéric, a British army, still intact, must be kept confronting the enemy. Also, for the conduct of the war with Canada, the inland city of Albany must be made into a citadel, an arsenal, and a concentration point for offensive as well as defensive troops. This could be done only behind a shield—one at Oswego and another on the new ground gained by Johnson over the Hudson-Champlain land bridge. In the colonial governments there was still hope and faith that the northern army had the time and the impetus to go on, and to establish at Ticonderoga the foothold on Lake Champlain which had been one of Johnson's main objectives.

At Lake George, however, the army was digging itself in. The concord that it had achieved under the shadow of Braddock's defeat had evaporated in the afterglow of its own somewhat inglorious "do-or-die" victory. It was a disgruntled army, more likely to move back than to go forward. Not the least ready to return was its general, whose business and inclination lay back where men, red men and white, soldiers and statesmen, met in deep council. But William Johnson was a captive general, like his troops under orders to stay in the field.

Even had Johnson had the will to go on to Crown Point, to risk his victory to the chance of fiasco or disaster there, his officers would not have moved. They claimed the season too late (which it was), cited the expiration of their men's enlistment and the loss of the Mohawks, who alone could lead the army in the terrifying wilderness but all of whom had now returned to their homes. Carefully and craftily, Johnson recorded the negative votes of the council as to the advisability of the army's advance. The votes would be his answer to those who might accuse him of lacking the aggressive spirit of a soldier. The aching scar on Johnson's hip would allay any charge of cowardice, even from the scowling General Lyman.

Sitting cantwise on his camp chair to ease the pain of his wound, Johnson wrote long letters from his autumn exile. Assured and self-confident, he wrote of himself and his victory to New York, where he sought justification and help, and to London, where, if brought to the king's ear, his claim would bring a reward from the lips of the monarch. But no letter from Johnson's desk could take the place of the man himself, standing to speak at a council of chiefs in the long house of the Iroquois. Shirley's order to Johnson as a soldier kept him ineffective as an Indian agent.

At Lake George, the main body of Johnson's army had settled in. Those soldiers who would soon go home knew it, and could wait; those who would garrison the northern posts were resigned to it. Already, companies of woodsmen-rangers had been formed to replace the Mohawks as the eyes of the army. One of these rangers, Robert Rogers of New Hampshire, a towering moose of a man who stepped lightly and gaily into danger, was the first to see the French at the building of their new fort on the Ticonderoga Peninsula. Rogers had gone back to look again at the Frenchmen working where English soldiers would have been had Johnson's expedition succeeded.

When at last, on 29 November, General William Johnson left his army at Lake George, his own Fort William Henry was rising at the high-watermark of the campaign. Johnson's first military career was all but over. He resigned his commission on 1 December. He left by the portage road with scarcely a backward glance. A work-party on the northeast bastion watched the general and his aides as they entered the forest; then the corporal called the men back to their task. Slowly, laboriously, the soldiers levered and hauled a big cannon forward into its embrasure. In place at last, the black iron barrel aimed far off down the lake.

When Abijah Willard heard of General Johnson's victory at Lake George, he was carrying out the same strange, distasteful but necessary duty on which he had embarked the day that word of Braddock's defeat had reached the head of the Bay of Fundy. Captain Willard, of Lancaster in Massachusetts Colony, was burning down houses.

He had read his sealed orders, as he had been told to do, on 13 August, a day's march from Fort Cumberland, that had been Fort Beauséjour. Willard had set out with his company on what was expected to be a routine show of British strength and peaceable protective interest in the Acadians who lived beside the Minas Basin, that body of water which floods deep into the Nova Scotia Peninsula on the south shore of the Bay of Fundy. Such a trip was the kind of duty that junior officers ask for. When you march your men out of the garrison ground, all the weight of senior authority seems to jump down off your shoulders. A company officer can drop back and walk beside his men. He can talk with those he has known at home, before they enlisted as officers and privates. It had been this way on the first day's march of the Lancaster men. The day had been warm and the season dry—a big brush fire had burned out of control at Fort Cumberland—and ahead of them lay the fine timberland and rich meadows beside the lake-like Basin. The civilians there were unspoiled by the army, and soldiers could still expect to find in the farms and villages a land of milk and honey—and butter and eggs. If the Acadians there were like those who had been at Fort Beauséjour just after the siege, the price of rum to drink in one's milk would not be too rich for a soldier. And French "gorls" were pretty, even if they *did* wear clomping great boats of wood on their feet instead of shoes.

But the sealed orders which Captain Willard opened and read while the rations were stewing in the iron pot erased that picture. The Acadians, he learned to his surprise, were in fact rebellious; they lived on British land without loyalty to Britain; they had broken their oath of allegiance to King

George; they sold goods illegally to the French soldiers at
Louisbourg; they gave comfort and safe passage to war parties of French Indians; and their faith, which Britain had
tolerated, was being fomented into an explosive brew of
treason by the priests from their pulpits in the "Mass
houses." Indians and priests were kindred evils that a
Massachusetts man could understand, but could not con-
done. Willard was shocked at the orders which, as a colonial
soldier, he had to carry out: Captain Willard was to burn
all buildings of the Acadians along a prescribed route, and
return to the fort, bringing with him (tied up if necessary)
all the Acadian men he could lay hands on.

For two weeks he scourged the quiet farmland. On the
Tatamagouche River, whither his orders carried him, he set
fire to twelve houses and a church, and for proof and justification, he captured a French officer. On that river, too, he
fought and took a schooner and a sloop loaded with hogs
and sheep for the winter larder at Louisbourg. Returning to
the Minas Basin, Willard found the Acadians of the south
shore scattered and in hiding in the deep woods. British regulars would "winkle" them out, so Captain Willard returned to Fort Cumberland from his strange, disturbing,
but, as was now evident, his just duty. With him he brought
twenty-two Acadians and the arms that he had found hidden in the houses he burned.

Captain Willard's march of rapine was not unique.
Throughout Nova Scotia, that summer and autumn, British soldiers and colonial soldiers hunted out the Acadians
and eradicated their peculiar image from the land. For forty
years, ever since the Treaty of Utrecht gave Nova Scotia to
Britain, successive governors had attempted to assimilate the
Nova Scotian French. But the simple-minded, primitive
farming people fiercely maintained their foible of loyalty
to the King Louis who had forsaken them. As insignificant
little chips of humanity, the Acadians might have lain be-

neath the concern of empires but for the furious Abbé le
Loutre, who overlooked no fuel to stoke the fires of his
hatred of England. During the whole of his vicarage in
Acadia, Le Loutre and his chosen priests kept the candle of
discontent alight on the altars of his churches. By 1755, with
an outright war imminent, the soldier-governor of Nova
Scotia no longer could tolerate the menace of the perfidious
Acadians combining with the French forces from Louisbourg in an attack on the province entrusted to his protection. Governor Charles Lawrence gave the order for transportation of all the Acadians. It was a hard order for a
soldier to give his men to carry out, but the regulars accepted it as inevitable, salving the hurt where they could
with small acts of kindness and consideration. The militiamen of Massachusetts, less accustomed to discipline, spoke
out against the order, and found balm for their conscience
in the fact that their own governor long had urged that the
Papists be expunged from Nova Scotia and replaced by
worthy men from the Bay Colony.

More than 6000 Acadian men, women, and children began their hegira on British ships. Others, escaping the mass
movement, fled through the woods to seek grudging asylum
in French lands. Before Christmas in that threatening year
of 1755, all the Acadians had gone from their homes. From
their abandoned paddocks and fields, Abijah Willard gathered 500 head of cattle for the garrison home that he would
keep for the winter at Fort Cumberland. The prospects of
a colonial soldier at Chignecto were not bright, as the days
shortened and the northeast storms slanted in over the
marshes. The compassion of the regulars in command, so
patient with a wailing Acadian child, did not extend to the
colonial militia. The men were denied the comfort of dry
shelter at the forts, where redcoat sentries kept them out
when the chill winds ripped out their tent pegs. Colonel
Monckton reluctantly permitted the Massachusetts men to

replace their neat rows of tents with huts made of mud, logs, and jetsam. When the British officers forbade them to pick the cow-peas in the pastures, hungry militiamen were forced to hunt the wild herd strays in the forests. Nevertheless, haughty recruiting sergeants were sent through Colonel Winslow's regiment in an effort to entice men to join Monckton's regiments of the British line. Over the protests of the colonial officers, many of their soldiers sought immediate comfort by accepting the king's shilling for enlistment.

In late November the British sailed away from Chignecto Bay. The Massachusetts officers who were to be left behind took a glass with Monckton at the water's edge before the proud figure stepped into the waiting boat. The toast was "To Better Days!" It was repeated five days later when Colonel Winslow, too, sailed away with the 1st battalion of his Massachusetts Regiment.

Before Christmas, when Chignecto Bay froze over that year, and both Fort Cumberland and Fort Lawrence were cut off until spring, Captain Willard moved his company into the barracks of the old French fort. By New Year's Day, he was sufficiently at home among his 2nd battalion to find himself filled with drink. The great carouse and barbeque lasted until the third day of the year 1756.

To the east, at Louisbourg, the two new regiments from France kept watch from the wide walls of the great stone fortress. For the soldiers of Artois and of Burgundy there was little to see—only the evergreen hem of a strange continent and the gray sea picking at the shore. All summer the sentries had watched the white sails of the British blockade fleet on the Louisbourg horizon, but Admiral Boscawen had taken away his fifteen men-of-war before the first gale of autumn struck, howling, on the coast. Safe now were the ships and the sailors, tucked into deep harbors, leaving the lonely vigil at Louisbourg to the soldiers on the open walls.

At Oswego, Shirley's 50th and Pepperrell's 51st stood guard with Peter Schuyler's Jersey "Blues," and tried to keep the snow from blowing in under the new green doors of their bleak barrack rooms. At Fort William Henry, Captain Robert Rogers sallied on Lake George to torment the French soldiers of La Reine and Languedoc at Fort St. Frédéric and at the new fort at Ticonderoga. It was bitter cold, and a light snow had fallen while he was out on his last scout of the old year. He had returned to Fort William Henry in time for the Christmas festivities.

From the day in mid-October when Captain Charles Lewis left Winchester for Fort Cumberland, on Will's Creek, he had faced the prospect of a Christmas away from home. He had brothers in the Virginia Regiment, however, among them the major, who was a veteran of both Fort Necessity and Braddock's expedition. Perhaps they would be together. But unlike the other fronts from Louisbourg to Niagara, where regulars, French and British, and colonials, too, enjoyed a truce in the misery of winterbound and isolated forts, the French at Fort Duquesne did not acknowledge the advance of the season on the Allegheny frontier.

Shortly after Braddock's defeated army retreated over the mountains, war parties of Indians were on the sunrise slopes, following the brooks down to the streams that flowed into the Atlantic rivers. The raids, which had begun as a trickle, by autumn were a torrent. They were not without plan, and the direction of the French. Captain Dumas, who replaced the timid Contrecoeur at Fort Duquesne, had been quick to seize on the desire of the River Indians, the watchfully "neutral" Shawnees and Delawares, to demonstrate their suddenly found devotion to the French king, so victorious in battle. Even the governor general in Montreal had given his favorable notice to Dumas's aggressive war by making available the talents of the Sieur de Joncaire, whose influence—in opposition to that of William Johnson—was so successful over the western Iroquois. It was the Senecas, whose blood was an equal part of Joncaire's heritage, who stayed or loosed the "Women-Dogs" (the Delawares), and in the fall of 1755 Dumas and Joncaire had won the Senecas to France. Eager to lick or to bite whatever hand their master bade them to, the Delawares prepared for a great raid into peaceful Pennsylvania. All through October the war party of 1500 warriors gathered at the Delaware town of Kittanning. Their leader was Shingass, the son of George Washington's friend Queen Alliquippa. It was he who had once borne with pride the English name of "Captain Fairfax."

Washington's reorganized Virginia Regiment had just arrived at Fort Cumberland when Shingass struck into Pennsylvania. The Virginians had gone upcountry too late to save the Maryland-Virginia frontier from devastation, but, with his men, Washington hoped to fill the gap left by the regulars, long since gone to Philadelphia. A talkative, boastful Irishman brought the word of Indians on the Susquehanna. He told a wild tale of capture and escape, and showed two scalps wrapped in his dirty handkerchief. These, he said, were those of his captors, one of whom was an English renegade named Joseph Jack. The man stayed at the fort only long enough to sell Captain Lewis the French musket he carried. Then he went off down the Potomac with a convoy to find the friend who, he said, had escaped with him.

The Irishman's tale was true, and for the Indian dead the lives of two white captives, Charles Stuart and John Condon, were claimed. Charles Stuart stood lashed to a tree. Looking down, he could see, stuck into a log at his feet, the axe that had killed Joseph Jack. He knew it for the one, because he had been threatened with it and told that with it his fingers would be cut off, so that he could eat them one by one. Stuart could see little else, for in front of him a big fire was burning. It warmed the bound man with a chilling glow. From it, he knew, would come the brands of torture and the match which finally would ignite the fuel piled around his feet. On either side of the fire, Stuart could see some of his captors, painted for war, sinister in ridiculous plundered finery, in solemn conclave to decide his fate. He knew that beyond the circle of firelight and Indians, perhaps under the big pine branch reflecting the flames, stood his wife with six-year-old Mary and her little brother Will.

Saturday morning he had done his barn chores and harnessed the plow horse before breakfast. The two men he had to help him were still in the barn when he returned to the cabin for his morning meal. There was no shout or scuffle to warn him before the Indians, coming from nowhere, burst into the cabin. They took Stuart and his family as they sat around the rough pine table. There had been no time to resist. The hired men had been killed. As the Stuarts were hurriedly driven up the valley toward the Martin farm, they saw the men's bodies, red with blood and splashed white with milk from the overturned pails in the cowshed.

Stuart and his family were kept at the Martin place by their captors that night and all day Sunday. Throughout the day, parties of Indians had come in bringing prisoners, for the most part women and children. From the new prisoners, Stuart learned the fate of other neighbors: Will Berryhill was dead, Scotch David McClelland, too; and at the new camp to which they were moved Sunday night, a young buck had shown them the gray scalp of old Mrs. Galloway. Contemptuously, the boy had tossed the thing into the fire.

The following day Charles Stuart met John Condon, whose fate was to be like his own. He could now hear the Irishman praying aloud to the Mother of God, but he could not see him, tied as he was on the other side of the tree.

By Tuesday, Stuart had come to realize the size and scope of the Indian raid in which he and his family had been caught up. King Shingass's party of more than ninety warriors had taken Stuart and his neighbors; at Raystown, other parties had come in. The Indian "Captain John Peter," who spoke fluent English and was not unkindly, described the raid, pointing out the other captains as Delawares, Shawnees, Mingos, and some big warriors in buffalo-skin caps, who, he said, were brothers from beyond the westernmost lakes.

It was at a place called "Shawnee Cabins" that the now considerable company of Indians and their prisoners learned of the death of the renegade Jack and his companion. It was after dark when the Indian guards strode in among the captives, and Stuart and Condon were pulled roughly to their feet and rushed to the tree to which they were now tied. Helpless and hopeless, they had stood for what seemed like hours. Condon was sustained by prayer, but Stuart could only dread what his wife and children would have to watch. When at last he saw the torturers coming toward him from around the fire, he braced himself for the first unimaginable stroke of pain. Instead, the knife stroke fell on the bonds that held him. Free, Stuart took one step before his knees gave way from relief, or fear, or from the long binding, and he stumbled forward. The hands that caught him were friendly and helpful as they guided his uncertain steps in the direction of Shingass, who sat on his blanket with the other chiefs and war captains nearby.

The Delaware king had won a reprieve for the two men, to whom he now addressed his lengthy and detailed apologia. It was Braddock who had dismissed the friendly Delawares as dogs, and sent them to the French who welcomed them as men. It was true that the English inhabited and inherited the land, so changing its face that the Indian no longer recognized it as home. The French, on the other hand, came only to trade and kept the Indian way in the Indian lands. But the French trade goods were inferior to those manufactured in England, although French brandy was as intoxicating as English rum. Now, if the English brothers would send to their brothers, the Delawares, men to teach them to mine lead, mend rifles, make cloth in the English way, then could the Delaware Nation be equal with their brothers. . . .

But no overture by the Delaware king could save Stuart from a long captivity. When "Captain Jacobs" and his monstrous son, who stood "seven feet tall and as high as fury," joined Shingass at the rendezvous after raiding Bedford, the great war party scattered. The Delawares and Mingos went to the northeast, "Captain John Peter" and his Shawnees set off toward Fort Duquesne. With the latter went little Mary and Will Stuart. The parents ended their captivity in a Wyandot town near Detroit, where they were bought by two French priests. It took the Stuarts nine months of hard work to pay off the Fathers and regain the freedom snatched from them so suddenly that Saturday morning in November 1755.

VIII

The Governors Turn Soldiers

The autumn winds of a rising war swept away many leaves in 1755. The houses of the Acadians were empty, stark ruins. From northern New Jersey to western Virginia the log cabins of frontier colonists were charred squares of ashes surrounded by stumpy fields. In their rubble lay a few forsaken bodies, which the occasional patrols of militiamen found, buried, and tried to forget as they toasted the New Year in the few scattered forts to which they returned. As Abijah Willard dined in *his* Fort Cumberland and Robert Rogers celebrated at Fort William Henry, so, in Fort Cumberland, Virginia, Charles Lewis drank the royal toasts while a tipsy drummer beat out the long roll. Drums beat in the French fort, too, where the representatives of Louis XV accepted the homage due to His Most Christian Majesty in the New Year.

In all North America, no one stepped into the bright new year of 1756 with such confidence as did the Marquis de Vaudreuil, governor general of New France. Never humble, with modesty no part of his high office, the Canadian marquis accounted to himself every success during the short tenure of his governorship. The failures he attributed to his predecessor or his appointees. In these rationalizations

93

Vaudreuil was aided by his court of sychophants, who preened the governor's vanity. To ease the governor of his administrative burden, and thus give him full scope to glitter in his vice-regal majesty, was the intendant, François Bigot, whose office managed the affairs of the colony. So all-embracing were the duties and powers of the intendant that he did not have to answer to the governor, but had only to flatter him and, if necessary, to include him in the profits. With Governor de Vaudreuil, François Bigot worked in harmonious accord; the former strove innocently for a great French Canada and the latter worked industriously for a New France sufficiently prosperous to afford his services. So great were the opportunities of his office that Bigot had no need to be greedy. He could easily afford to give away great slices of his perquisites to subordinates who were thus bought and paid for, and who were meaner than he only because their opportunity for iniquity was less. Bigot did not tamper with the military establishment in Canada, though by purchases he furnished it. It was for the governor that the guns boomed in salute and the soldiers turned out in parade as though for a marshal of France. That Bigot received the honors usually accorded only to a lieutenant general was because the governor granted them to him, and not because the intendant associated himself with the security and defense of New France. That was solely the province of Vaudreuil, who assumed the increasingly apparent risks and on whom would fall all the blame in case of failure.

Because he was a Canadian, the Marquis de Vaudreuil favored the Marine, which was basically colonial. Dieskau's capture left the army under the command of a regimental colonel, a rank beneath the consideration of a governor general, so Vaudreuil was unhampered by professional advice in planning his campaign for 1756. The autumn successes of the Indian raids over the Alleghenies needed no improvement; weather permitting, they would continue through the winter and into the spring. Dieskau's impetuous action in September had given Vaudreuil time to build the new fort at Ticonderoga which, in theory, would hold the British at bay on Lake Champlain. Offensive action for 1756 was directed toward Fort Oswego. Already, the governor had arrayed some of his forces at Fort Niagara and Fort Frontenac. In the spring he planned to amass seven thousand men of the Marine, the militia, Indians, and regulars for a descent on the British post on Lake Ontario. Sleighbells could be heard in the streets of Montreal while the governor and Lieutenant Chaussegros de Léry were discussing the opening stroke of this campaign,

In his planning for 1756, Vaudreuil gave little heed to the Maritime Provinces of New France. Louisbourg was secure in its own might of walls and guns. It was so remote from Montreal that the governor scarcely considered it a part of Canada, and in fact Louisbourg was tended by the French Navy, directly from France. Only in Acadia had Vaudreuil's efforts foundered. But that, too, was a remote land. The governor had hoped to duplicate in Nova Scotia the savage Indian raids with which Dumas at Fort Duquesne had been so successful. But the Micmacs, who would have been his instrument of terror, were immobilized by an epidemic of smallpox, and Boishébert, in command in Acadia, was inert by nature. Since burning his fort on the St. John's River, on the north shore of Fundy, early in the season, Boishébert had contrived one feeble raid in succor of the Acadians. Then he sat in the woods and did nothing.

Vaudreuil, therefore, planned his campaign to Oswego with little concern for distant Acadia, with full confidence in himself, and without regard for the army. But in Commissary Doreil, who had come out to New France with Baron Dieskau and the four regiments, the army had a man whose quiet manner belied his capacities. As commissary of the army, Doreil sat where he could observe Bigot and the working of the government, which in fact was the purpose for which he had been sent out to Canada. Vaudreuil suspected Doreil of reporting directly to someone in France, but he was sufficiently self-confident not to be disturbed by this fact. Perhaps he knew the Court at Versailles well enough to know that it was indifferent. But Doreil's reports to the minister of war gave Count d'Argenson a true picture of the grave dangers, from within and from without, which encompassed New France. The Count had Doreil's report in hand, with all its recommendations, when the tall, painted doors of his private bureau opened and the man whom he hoped to persuade to be the savior of Canada was shown into the room. Count d'Argenson rose quickly to greet, with the courtesy of friendship, the Marquis de Montcalm.

In November 1755, William Shirley received from London his confirmation in the office of commander in chief in North America, a position he had assumed on the death of General Braddock. Like the governor of New France, the American general and governor of Massachusetts focused his attention on the military aspect of his titles, and addressed himself to his duties as a strategist and campaigner with the same portentious confidence as did the Canadian politician.

Shirley established his supreme headquarters in New York City, which was centrally located to the colonial governments and to the probable fighting fronts. It was there, on the Turkey carpet in front of his writing table, that Major General William Shirley brought on the confrontation with his political rival, William Johnson. Though summoned out of the field at Lake George, Johnson did not hurry to the appointment. Kept too long from his Indians, he hastened instead to the central council of the Iroquois at the Onondaga Castle, in an effort to stem the bolt of the western

Iroquois to the French, and to restrain the Ohio Nations from raiding the Pennsylvania-Maryland-Virginia frontier. At the same time, Johnson was carefully divesting himself of all the military rank bestowed upon him by the several colonial governors whose troops he had commanded, so that when he finally presented himself to the commander in chief his rank as colonel would be not colonial but British, a rank which went with his appointment as agent to the northern Indians. Then, too, Johnson delayed his departure for New York so that his political friends in that city could make their preparations to receive him at the maximum discomfort and disadvantage to his rival.

The victor of Lake George and the conqueror of Dieskau entered New York on 30 December to the sound of the city's rejoicing, while Shirley watched through the frosted panes of his office window. Later, in a carefully contrived private interview General Shirley tried to humble Johnson, but found a hawk where he had expected a sparrow. When Shirley, in his capacity as commander in chief, canceled Johnson's appointment as Indian agent, the hero of Lake George politely refused to acknowledge the Massachusetts governor's authority to do so. The "contemptible little farmer" had become a great country squire, and the dispute had now to be referred to London.

Politically, William Johnson was ready. At a quiet dinner, when the port was on the table, the Johnson faction propounded their scheme. Thomas Pownall, who had come out to New York as private secretary to the now-deceased Governor Osborn, was returning to London, where his brother was Secretary to the Lords of Trade and Plantations. Pownall was one of the clique, and his winter crossing of the Atlantic was on mutually advantageous business. Johnson's "only victory of the year" was to be played up. Shirley was to be destroyed through his meddling with Indian affairs and his military bungling on the Niagara expedition. Pownall hoped to be governor of Massachusetts. Privately, he was to represent to the emergent statesman, William Pitt, the considered plan of the group of Americans around Johnson for the conquest of Canada by a direct attack on Quebec. It was the old plan of choking the mouth with a cannon ball rather than tickling the whole swollen body with grouse shot.

Pownall sailed away down the Narrows, and Shirley left New York by way of Lond Island Sound, to gather his strength from the cheers of his hero's welcome in his own town of Boston.

The commander in chief for North America cautiously laid out his plan of campaign for 1756 on the old timbers of the plan that Braddock had brought out with him, ready made, from the War Office in London. But Shirley, still holding to the policy of a border dispute with New France rather than a war, shifted the emphasis and weight of his attacks to the water routes out of Albany: one to Niagara out of Oswego, the other to Crown Point from Fort William Henry. Shirley himself would again lead the Niagara attack with his own 50th Foot, and the 51st, augmented by Braddock's two regiments, the 44th and 48th, and, of course, the Jersey "Blues." "General" John Winslow, who, with Monckton, had stormed Fort Beauséjour in that forgotten victory of 1755, would assume leadership of 9000 provincials to finish the work left undone by Johnson on Lake George.

Down the east wind from Boston, Shirley planned a bold endeavor. Two thousand Massachusetts men from Maine were to ascend the tortuous Kennebec River, cross over the mountains, and go raiding down the Chaudière River, which enters the St. Lawrence only a short distance above Quebec. With colonial rangers terrorizing the fertile farmlands and seigneuries so close to the capital of New France, the *habitants* would scream for French soldiers to come from the other forts to protect them from the savage *"Bostonais."* But, lacking leadership sufficiently determined to make the difficult overland journey, and with the Maine men unwilling to leave their homes defenseless against Micmac attack from Acadia, the expedition foundered at Fort Halifax, scarcely above tide-flow on the Kennebec.

General Shirley's concept of 3000 Pennsylvanians, Marylanders, and Virginians taking the twice-traveled invasion road to the forks of the Ohio River never materialized. The contentedly retired old soldier, Governor Stark, who was the designated leader, could dredge up no enthusiasm for the campaign, either in himself or in his brothers in the neighboring government houses. At the palace in Williamsburg, Dinwiddie, who like Shirley had been imbued with his own martial importance, was directing his field commander, George Washington, from a distance. The military policy that the drab little thistle of a bureaucrat had entered upon was one of a 300-mile line of frontier forts to stem the flood of Indians from over the Appalachians. Washington, who carried out the governor's plan, saw the forts as stones in a mountain river, easily passed by and, when the storm clouds broke on the mountains, submerged in a freshet. Yet the young Virginian, whose own plan of defense lay in counterattacks from strong points, built the forts and sent out his contact patrols. Once during the winter Washington left his command to go to Boston to see Shirley. The seniority of his colonial commission was still being disputed. While he was away Major Andrew Lewis, with a force that included Cherokee Indians from South Carolina, had set out for the Shawnee towns downriver from Fort Duquesne. On Washington's return by way of New York and Philadelphia, he found Lewis still out. After six weeks in the dreadful mountains of winter, at last Major Lewis appeared, tattered, gaunt, haggard, starved, and unsuccessful.

Some of the other patrols did not return. Among them

was that led by Captain John Mercer of the Virginia Regiment. Nor did the very young Cadet Ensign Alexandre d'Agneau Douville return, though Captain Dumas waited long for his youthful officer. Douville's dried scalp lay in the patch of April sunshine on Washington's work-table. Governor Dinwiddie, his burgesses, and his soldiers were much too busy on their own border to help in implementing General Shirley's plan to attack Fort Duquesne in the summer of 1756.

Governor Robert Hunter Morris of Pennsylvania was likewise building forts from the upper Delaware River down to the Maryland line. With all the frontier settlements pushed back along every river in the colony, the war party in Pennsylvania at last had prevailed over the quiet Quakers and the apathetic merchants. Money became available for building forts, militia companies were melding into two good regiments, and military districts of responsibility were being set up. Even that philosophic guide of destiny, Benjamin Franklin, assumed briefly a colonel's rank. In 1756 the government and the men of Pennsylvania were too busy bracing their own back door to go elsewhere at the behest of the governor of Massachusetts.

Captain Dumas, with a few cadets and some officers of the Marine to direct the raiding parties of French Indians, had succeeded in pinning down the manpower of all the British Appalachian colonies. Except for Peter Schuyler's Jersey Regiment and a token force of 200 North Carolinians (twenty-five of whom deserted immediately on arriving at Albany), no soldiers from those colonies south of New York joined Shirley or Winslow for the main British campaigns of 1756. Vaudreuil's Canadians and Indians in the west were sending back valuable dividends for the governor general's army to spend on the Oswego campaign. In the second week of March, the Marquis de Vaudreuil had his first victory at the English forts toward Lake Ontario.

Since going west in 1754, Chaussegros de Léry had met with considerable success. He had been sent to Detroit, as ordered, and as he wished, had inspected, criticized, and planned improvements at Fort Duquesne. At the end of the 1755 campaign season he had returned to his wife in Quebec. But, being a restless man, devoted to the great land of his birth, he was ready to be off again on Canadian duty at the first sign of spring.

The winter had been an unusually open one that year, with only light snow, so that by 27 March Lieutenant de Léry was two weeks on his way from Montreal. From the two English prisoners he had taken, he knew that the portage road between the Mohawk River and Oneida Lake—the British supply line for the Oswego forts—was nearby. Léry knew, too, that a third Englishman (a Negro) had escaped, and that the British in their guard forts would be warned of the French approach. But now, as he stepped out of the marching file to stand against a big beech tree, his principal concern was for the men of his command. They had eaten no food for two days, and already they had been marching more than twelve hours.

The men passed by, hunched in their big outer coats, the skirts hooked back to free the plodding knees, moving in the rhythm of the long march. The set and expressionless faces of the Canadians were the brown, smoked color of the meat that they hung from the rafters of their thick-walled houses. Though their natural gaiety had been dampened during the hours of march, it would be rekindled with the evening meal, consisting of a pipe of strong tobacco and a drink from the brook. Léry studied even more searchingly the faces of the regulars as they came by him. Forty-nine men and seventeen officers of La Reine, Guyenne, and Béarn had come along with the expedition in order to learn the strange ways of fighting in the Canadian woods. They had stood the march well, adapted their dress, their pace, and their habits

to the forest. Now they appeared lean and alert in spite of
their hunger and their fatigue. Satisfied, Léry fell in beside the officer of the Marine bringing up the end of the
column and walked along with him. Up front, the Indians
would stop the march short of the portage road. He would
then go forward to reconnoiter and set the ambush.

At ten o'clock the next morning the French sprang their
trap, and caught the English, whose sleighs were loaded
with butchered meat. It was a feast for the starving Frenchmen, though the hunks of meat were only half cooked over
the small toasting fires and smelled of singed hair. Con-
tented with the ambush and the meal, the Indians declared
their intention of going home, and though he pleaded and
promised rewards, Léry could not persuade them to go
on to Fort Bull with their French comrades. Eventually,
they consented to keep the ambush on the road in case the
British sortied from Fort William at the east end of the
portage. As the Canadians and the French stood ready to
march, twenty of the Indians joined Léry, and asked if
there would be brandy at Fort Bull. They thought it worth
the chance.

From the edge of the fort clearing, Lieutenant de Léry
saw the gates of Fort Bull standing wide open, as though to
welcome him. He decided to accept the welcome and to
march into the fort, counting on the ragged look of his men
to cover their national identification. It would be simple,
easy, and quick. But as he turned to go back to his men, the
rum-thirsty Indians rushed past him with whoops and horrible shrieks, making their own attack. Shouting to his own
men, Léry dashed forward. As he ran down the road,
hatless and yelling, British soldiers were tugging and pushing at the heavy logs of the gate. The gate swung closed as
the Frenchman threw himself against it. He heard the bar
fall into its brackets on the other side of the logs. On either
side of the lieutenant, a French soldier crashed into the tim-

bers. Hopelessly, he turned to see the 260-odd men of his force running toward the gate. Shouting to them, he was able to turn the mob, some right, some left, so that in the split-seconds of the English panic, the French, close in under the wall, won the loopholes and turned them to their own use.

It took the Canadian axemen an hour to hack their way through the gate. The fury of battle was still on the French as they burst into Fort Bull, and they spared few of the English inside: a woman, weeping beside a dead man, and thirty men, found in hiding after French tempers had cooled.

The Frenchmen worked hard and quickly to destroy the stores of powder and ball and the food and good warm clothing, in transit in the fort. Momentarily, they expected a force to come from the companion British fort, for Léry had heard musket fire, and an Indian runner had told him that the ambush left on the portage road had driven back the advance scout from Fort William Henry. Before the British could come in relief, the French had gone, leaving Fort Bull only charred and blown-up ruins, a charnelhouse of men and horses. Léry had made sure that his men would not go hungry on the long march home.

September 1755 the Abbé Picquet, of the Indian village of La Présentation on Lake St. Francis, had sent his warriors to Fort Oswego. They had taken their scalps and their prisoners and had brought back encouraging news of the British garrison. At that time the two regiments rated as British regulars—but in fact poor-quality men from New England tricked out in British uniforms—were 600 under strength. Sickness, punishment, and desertion, resulting from disorganization, disgruntlement, and dispirit, had wasted the regiments. Now, after a lonely winter locked in a prison which was clearly defined by the path where the French Indians crept, the morale of Colonel Mercer's troops was as low as the mud under a Boston wharf. Spring brought no relief, only word that Fort Bull had fallen, and with it had gone all the new clothes the men so badly needed.

Even on the lake, the men holding the mouth of the Oswego River for Britain found little cause for cheer. Only the sloop's speed in getting away had saved some of the Jersey men, who had gone in boats to reconnoiter Fort Frontenac. They reported that French boats had attacked them from behind Au Galot Island and that the enemy were led by yet another brother of Jumonville killed in the glade two years before. Villiers was in command in Famine Bay, where the French and their Indians had made a base to keep the Oswego forts in a constant state of alarm, and made of the British supply line a gauntlet of attack.

After Léry's raid, Captain John Bradstreet of the 51st Foot succeeded in getting ten bateaux through to relieve the distress of the troops at Oswego. Transportation was a specialty of the veteran captain. He was in charge of the 2000 bateaumen, Dutch and French for the most part, who were recruiting into a "regiment" to travel the supply line from Albany westward to Oswego and beyond, when the attack on Niagara was launched. The new organization had failed its captain after Fort Bull was leveled, but by summer it was moving to and fro over the portage at Oswego Lake in big, secure convoys. In late July, Villiers struck a convoy returning to Albany, scattered its men for the Indians to kill in the woods, and left the bateaux, stove-in wrecks on the river bank, to warn others who dared to use the road. After that, Bradstreet's bateaumen hung back from the dangerous journey, while the soldiers at the Oswego forts waited for supplies, and for the regiment which was due to join them on the campaign to Niagara.

IX

The Captains Gather

In the army of the French king they called him "Fan-Fan la Tulipe"; the Americans referred to his British counterpart as "Lobster," while he, in turn, called the colonials "Pumpkins," or used the new name "Yankee Doodle," or plain "Yankee." Whatever the derisive nickname, whatever his allegiance, he was the soldier in the ranks, with a heavy pack on his shoulders and a sergeant on his neck.

In the spring of 1756, the rulers of the European world set him to marching once again. The Hohenzollern King of Prussia, Frederick, called "the Great," first gave the order "Forwatz!" to the tall grenadiers of Potsdam. The Hapsburg Maria Theresa of Austria, the "Mother Monarch," sent her white-coated children in their thousands down the roads of her kingdoms. The Empress Elisabeth of all the Russias sent her wild horsemen from the eastern steppes to march with her pampered guard. The lesser kings of Sweden and Denmark and Germany, too, lined up their true men and sent them off in the wake of a great world war.

During the winter of 1755-56, the final pieces of a great coalition were assembled. Maria Theresa stitched together its strange patchwork to smother the King of Prussia. For her province of Silesia, stolen by the Hohenzollern, the prim

Austrian Empress joined her chastity-commission morality in a sisterly pact with the lascivious amorality of Elisabeth of Russia. Then Maria Theresa, regally above pride, for her ancestral House of Hapsburg, put out her other hand to the immoral seamstress to the Bourbons, and called the Marquise de Pompadour "Cousin." Such a greeting and invitation Jeanne Poisson could not resist, nor would Louis XV, Bourbon King of France, deny his faithful, understanding, official mistress even so unlikely a family compact—this one in particular, as the Prussian king composed scurrilous verses about the Pompadour.

So the three strangely matched women of Europe sat down together to sew a shroud for Prussia, and half a million soldiers marched against 200,000 to provide the corpse. But the Protestant King Frederick was not alone against the women. George, King of Hanover and King of Great Britain, joined the Prussian ruler in a masculine alliance to bring to the game of soldiers ships-of-war, with sailors in the rigging and behind the 'tween-deck batteries.

For the king in London, the war that began in June 1756 was but a new phase of a second Hundred Years' War with France. From time to time the formalities of a treaty were gone through with to give a pretense of peace, but at sea and in distant lands antagonism and hostilities continued. For two years before the new war started, Canadians and Indians and colonists, "Fan-Fans" and "Lobsterbacks" had fought each other in the vastness of the North American continent, and the bodies of soldiers who had not waited for a declaration of war lay forsaken in the forests. Many months of voyaging-time away from Europe, India seemed to hang suspended in an unrelated epoch of its own. There, too, Europeans, regardless of the confusing echo of peace or war at home, jostled each other for the fragments of the rich empires of the Moguls. Joseph François Dupleix and Admiral Count de la Bourdonnais were fighting Charles

Saunders, Stringer Lawrence, and Admiral Boscawen on the Coromandel Coast when William Shirley sent Pepperrell with Admiral Warren to take Louisbourg. The fickle painted savages in North America were one with the bejeweled nawabs of the Indian sub-continent, watching their own advantage as the weighing-bar of the old war tilted first toward England, then toward France. Before the new war started in Europe it appeared to the subahdar in Bengal, as it did to Shingass, the Delaware, that the French raj had won. With a host of 40,000 Siraj-ud-daula took Calcutta, drove out the British governor, and on 20 June 1756 made prisoners of the soldiers and white men who had garrisoned Fort William. Most of the prisoners died that night in the guardroom of their fort—the "Black Hole of Calcutta."

The admirals and captains of the British navy were eager to put to sea early in 1756. In the previous sailing year, when they had not been at war, they had taken many French prizes in the waters off Brest, in the Mediterranean, at the mouth of the St. Lawrence, even rich East Indiamen homeward bound around Africa. The ships of the line *did* sail early, but they did not set sail as gaily this year, for there was far-flung and scattered work to be done. The merchants of London were demanding convoy guards to bring their cargoes home, while, on the French side of the English Channel, an invasion was mounting. Flatboats and 50,000 soldiers waited for the French fleet from Brest and Rochefort to keep the Channel open for their crossing. Under pressure from a weak and fretful government, Anson, at the Admiralty, brought his ships home to the anti-invasion ports of Plymouth and Portsmouth.

But the French fleet never came out to meet Boscawen and Hawke in the narrow sea. The French Atlantic fleet was stopped deep in the harbor of Brest, and there, one night in May, young Captain Cockburne had himself rowed in to count the ships. Around he went from French ship to silent French ship, then cut himself out a scow and sailed her out, all loaded with wine, to treat the blockading fleet. But if the French fleet at Brest and Rochefort lay at anchor, the Mediterranean squadrons of La Galissonière at Toulon were readying to invade the British fort and station on the island of Minorca. To strengthen the defenses Rear Admiral Byng had sailed in April with only ten ships of the line. That same month Admiral Holburne had sailed for New York with General Abercromby, two regiments of foot, and the officers of four battalions for the new Royal American Regiment to be recruited in the colonies.

Commodore Charles Holmes himself took his turn on blockade station off Louisbourg. Although his squadron of six ships of the line and frigates based and victualed at Halifax and cruised Newfoundland and the Gulf of St. Lawrence, the commodore's main responsibility was the blockade of the French in Louisbourg. Two big ships and their tending frigates kept constant watch on the entrance to Louisbourg Harbor. Since the sailing season for 1756 had begun in those waters, the British had closed the port to incoming supply ships, and had taken several prizes. One of the British captures was *L'Arc-en-Ciel*, a French warship of fifty-two guns which had, indeed, given up a pot of gold. She carried a full pay-chest for the garrison, and, even more valuable, 150 recruits for the two French regiments in the fortress.

On 26 July, Commodore Holmes in *Grafton* (seventy guns), with *Nottingham* (sixty guns), had dropped south by east off station to cover the frigate *Hornet*, gone into a bay where she had driven a large Frenchman ashore. At eight o'clock that morning, *Grafton*'s man at the masthead had sung out that there were four sail to windward, standing in for Louisbourg. Holmes ran up the signal to "Chase!" but, though the Englishman was pleased with his ship's maneuvering into the wind, the French commodore had made good his weather advantage, and at half-past one Holmes could see the bare spars of the French squadron in the anchorage beyond the roofs of the fort and the town. Calling up the frigate from her stranded quarry, the British commodore set a close watch on the harbor mouth. His tactics were to bring his four vessels into position for a French sortie at each good tide and wind. The next time for the French to come out would be early the following morning.

Commodore Beaussier de L'isle had not beggared a fight with Holmes by going into Louisbourg Harbor. He was not that kind of French naval officer. Born of the sea, his life spent at sea, Beaussier was, above all, a sailor. In the Royal Navy of France, he was an *"officier bleu,"* that is to say that he wore an all-blue uniform that differed markedly from the blue and red worn by the nobility who secured most of the appointments to command on Louis's ships. Because he was a *"bleu,"* the nobles were casually insolent and personally safe in their insubordination to Beaussier, who further differed from their magnificence in that he would fight.

Beaussier would have engaged on 26 July had it not been that he carried a chest of treasure, his decks were cluttered with cargo, most of his guns were dismounted, and he was short-handed aloft and at the batteries. Also, it seemed well for the commodore to reassure himself as to the co-operation of the aristocratic Captain Montalais of his other capital ship, 64-gun *Illustre*. So the commodore brought his squadron through the bight, and before the anchor struck bottom his boat was in the water, the treasure was being swung outboard, and his mate was bawling at the port for lighters to come and clear the decks of hamper. Within an hour of the commodore's arrival at the foot of the Rue Toulouse, the muster drums were in the streets calling out the volunteers to go and fight the enemy, pacing without the gate. In a surge of eagerness that burst the bonds of boredom, the whole garrison and town of Louisbourg clamored to be chosen for the cruise against the British ships. Beaussier, however, picked only 200 men, beached seamen who knew their trade and gunners who were devotees of their patroness, St. Barbara.

All afternoon and all that night they worked to ready the vessels for action. At dawn, the commodore would wait no longer. Though of the seventy-four guns on *Le Héros* only forty-six were mounted, the flagship sailed with its squadron. From his own cleared quarter-deck, in the face of a rising sun, Beaussier gave a sweeping bow to Governor Drucour's lady, standing beside her husband in the cheering crowd on the quayside. By the time the bow of *Le Héros* dipped to the Atlantic swell at the island battery, the commodore's white pennant was snapping to a good offshore breeze, and the whole squadron was under way. A seemingly chastened and obedient Montalais was riding close—too close for good seamanship—on the flagship's counter; astern him was steady Brugnon in the 36-gun frigate. Just getting under way, her anchor still unsecured, was 30-gun *La Licorne*, whose captain was the nobleman Larrigaudière. The British squadron, now two ships and a frigate, was out to sea on a tack that stood in for the land. As Beaussier watched Holmes through his long glass, the Britisher turned downwind in a move to draw the French out into sea room. Beaussier snapped his glass shut, ordered the signal "Chase!" to be flown, and went down for his chocolate and the treat of fresh brioche, sent aboard at the very moment of sailing by the thoughtful Madame Drucour.

Brugnon, in *La Sirène*, began the action about half-past one in the afternoon. A little sloop, tending the British frigate, came within range and was driven in on *Nottingham*, man-of-war. Watching this first encounter, Beaussier noted that the British frigate was standing off to the southwest, so he called for signals which sent his two frigates in a chase to separate her from the two big British ships which, he now saw, were outweighed in guns by his own ships.

Both *Nottingham* and *Grafton* were firing on *Le Héros* with their stern chasers, and *Grafton*'s shot was reaching. Beaussier ordered the long cannon at his bows to open, and when the smoke cleared, he could see that the twinkle had gone from the window light in *Grafton*'s transom—the British commodore would dine in a drafty cabin, if he dined at all that night. But the sting in his tail had angered the British commodore, who hauled up his courses, bunted his mainsail, and bore down on *Le Héros*.

Each on his own quarter-deck, the commodores stood braced for the shock of recoil from the broadside they would order and receive. On *Grafton*, the gun captains of the starboard battery blew on their matches until they glowed red as a ruby in the crown. At the quarter-deck railing, Beaussier watched his gun captain lash down the last big gun, rolled across the deck to fill the larboard battery. Under the overhang of the quarter-deck, the ship carpenter's damage party of axemen and sawmen chattered excitedly. Beaussier leaned far out over the rail and called down to the men to be quiet. The distance was rapidly closing.

With a quarter of a mile of water between the two flagships, the wind suddenly dropped. For the single moment before the two big vessels lost all headway and lay dead as chips on the sea, the captains strove to bring their bows around in order to bring all their guns to bear. Seamen both, gunners all, the first broadsides crashed out together.

Becalmed, the two flagships entered a long, bloody, damaging slugging match. They had no help, for *Nottingham*'s guns were masked by *Grafton*, and Montalais had dallied astern of his *"bleu"* commodore, showing little inclination to brawl along with him. On *Le Héros*, the damage-control party had gone from under the break of the quarter-deck.

Some were aloft, clearing the shambles in the cordage and spars, but most were below, where, under the rumble of the carriage wheels over their heads, they strove with canvas and planks and balks and wedges to shore up the cracked and splintered sheeting of the ship's frame along the water line. Holmes, the "lion of the sea," was fighting savagely to sink his enemy. Beaussier, the soaring "sea-eagle," was aiming his guns for *Grafton*'s masts and spars and stanchions, in which lay his enemy's ability to maneuver—and to escape.

As the afternoon wore on, the French commodore could feel, in his feet and on his quarter-deck, the shift of angle and the heaviness of the water trickling into his bilges below, where the carpenter and his men worked in the cramped space. There was damage aloft, too, where his signal flags recalling the frigates flapped lazing in only a stirring of air that was not a wind. At one point in the battle a cry of anguish from the cockpit told him that his steering had been hit. Calmly, he waited for the report to come to him. A hatless junior, gingerly holding his broken hand, came to tell him that the rudder had been hit but the wheel still answered; the damage was slight. There was blood on the sanded deck where the dead had lain before being found and pitched overboard, but Beaussier could not watch in detail the scene around him, which moved inexorably in the groove of battle-training. On his quarter-deck, the commodore had to be aware of, to ponder, and to judge quickly the turn and course of the advantages and disadvantages presented by each moment of the battle, every nuance of changing weather. A light wind was coming up. The sails, in need of trimming, were flapping idly on the strained masts. The wind was enough to bring Montalais, in 64-gun *Illustre*, to his aid. Looking over the torn and scarred counter of *Le Héros*, Beaussier could see the aristocrat's tall ship, out of the fight, proudly waiting for nothing. A mile to the west, with the wind at last, Brugnon was slowly making steerage way toward him. *Le Héros's* sails were filling now, and Beaussier moved his ship toward his supporting frigates, leaving the crippled but fighting *Grafton* before the telling weight of *Nottingham* could join Holmes in the bombardment of leaking *Le Héros*.

By morning Beaussier knew the extent of damage to his hull and knew, too, the gunnery of the British, whose accuracy Brugnon likened to musket fire. The French squadron bore home for Louisbourg. Tentatively, with braced mast, Holmes followed for awhile, then turned to run down the coast to Halifax and repairs.

Commodore Beaussier rested a fortnight in Louisbourg Harbor, effecting repairs to *Le Héros* and seeking (but not getting) satisfaction from the peers of the hesitant Captain Montalais, charged with cowardice. On 13 August, the four French vessels of war resumed their interrupted voyage to France. They were not seen leaving port by *Nottingham*, alone on blockade since *Grafton* was still at the work of repairing her cracked and broken masts. Beaussier's luck and seamanship held good throughout the voyage home. He missed the British fleet that was blockading Brest and sailed proudly up the Goulet, all in line, to drop anchor in the roads where the bottled-up navy of France lay rotting in inaction.

Early in April, Beaussier had begun his 1756 cruise by eluding the British frigates watching Brest. He had on board *Le Héros* the regiment La Sarre, for safe delivery to Quebec. Sailing with him for company was the fast frigate *La Licorne*. Together, they made up the first of three ship-and-frigate convoys carrying troops to the two-year-old war in North America.

As passenger in the after-cabin of *La Licorne*, saying his farewell to the France he had always served so faithfully, was Major General the Marquis de Montcalm, the new commander of the French army in Canada. Louis Joseph, Seigneur de Saint-Veran, Candiac, Tornemire, Vestric, Saint-Julien, d'Arpam, Baron de Gabriac, Marquis de Mont-calm-Gozon, was at forty-four years of age a veteran of thirty years of service. He wore the grace mark of a saber slash on his forehead, and when he was stripped of wig and shirt to shave his heavy blue beard, four additional white scars marked his dark, southern skin. It had almost been his destiny, despite the tradition in his ancient family, to end his life in peace on his loved estate at Candiac with his wife and children. But a chance visit of courtesy to the minister of war about the time that word of Dieskau's loss reached Versailles reminded the Count d'Argenson of him, and in January 1756 he was given the German baron's former com-mand, augmented by two additional regiments of infantry. The brief days of retirement at the château of Candiac were over for Louis Joseph.

Commissary Doreil's confidential report had prepared the dedicated new major general for a vainglorious governor general of New France and for a murky colonial adminis-tration. Thus, he was prepared for, but not deceived by, the magnificence of the reception tendered him on his arrival at Quebec on 13 May. In the absence in Montreal of the Mar-quis de Vaudreuil, Bigot made Montcalm and his suite wel-come to Canada at a reception and banquet at the intend-ant's own palace. François Bigot received his soldier-guest with his own dazzling mistress glittering at his side, and in a tawdry mirror that mocked both Montcalm's king and Bigot's patroness, La Pompadour, presented M. Péan, the lady's husband, among the close circle of the intendant's intimate friends. Montcalm sat, fingering the rich service and plate throughout the long parade of elaborate dishes, until he could make his exit before there was thrust at him a choice of the ladies at the dance or the easy win at the gaming table.

But for a soldier there was hope in the clear air of a Canadian spring, with the stars bright above the bastion-like palisades, no matter how low the smoky candles guttered in the privy chambers of the palace. The City of Quebec was defensible; impregnable, too, as the general from France viewed it in reconnaissance against the eventuality of a day.

When the last convoy was reported downriver, waiting only a favorable wind to make the difficult approach to the city, Montcalm was off for Montreal. There the marquis general met the marquis governor, and the Canadian talked kindly and paternally with the Frenchman, telling the general what he should do. Blandly, the governor offered to put his own brother, Louis Philippe Rigaud de Vaudreuil, in comand of all the Canadians and Indians at the threatened Lake Champlain forts. The new fort, Carillon, the governor now fancied as Fort Vaudreuil.

Without lingering at Montreal, Montcalm hurried on to see the southern frontier for himself. He found the new Fort Carillon poorly sited on its peninsula. As he had been led to expect, work was going forward slowly, with the laborers crowding the tavern run as a concession by a friend of Monsieur Bigot.

From Carillon, Montcalm poked his inquiring finger south, from which direction the English would come in their might, and where he would have to go if he chose to attack. With Montreuil, who had traveled the route with Dieskau and was now adjutant general of the marquis's army, he saw the marshland teeming with water fowl, and the bay at the nether end of Lake Champlain. On another reconnaissance, Montcalm took a canoe from the French post at the northern end of Lake George, and keeping to the east shore, ventured up the lake until he could see in the distance the green blot of islands where the lake is narrowed at its waist by high-rearing mountains. Ten miles beyond the islands, Montreuil told him, the British General

Winslow, with an army of 10,000 colonials, was gathering boats at Fort William Henry, which now stood where Dieskau and the grenadiers had fallen.

The French Indians and their Canadian officers and cadets who went with the Marquis de Montcalm on his little tours of observation took this duty grudgingly. They had better work to do, with British scalps at French £60 each and a live prisoner fetching fifty crowns. Business had been brisk around the English forts and down the Hudson River supply line toward Albany. It was the buckskinned Sieur de Pécaudy who had shown Montcalm his first raw scalp, while other durable men with singing names like La Colombière, Langy, Marin, La Perrière, and Florimond spoke to the officers from France of the "little war" of the silent forest.

At night, on the bench outside his headquarters in the raw clearing of the new fort, Montcalm heard of the British rangers and their tall leader, Captain Rogers, whom the Indians were beginning to call "the white devil." He listened while his own ranger leaders plotted to take this most prized of all British scalps, still worn in health by the burner of the village at Fort St. Frédéric, who ate only the tender tongues of the French cattle that he killed in their pens, and who, though mortal, had but to cast his great, awful shadow over the night fires in the guardroom, and the next guard shivered in their blankets.

The menace of Rogers's whaleboats to the French overwater supply line—he had sunk two provision boats and had only just missed taking the one large scooner on Lake Champlain—was a tangible military fact which the French general could counteract. This he did, with a strict convoy system, and a heavy guard that turned the schooner into a war vessel. Later, a navy must be built.

Meanwhile, the governor general of New France was showing signs of decision in regard to his planned attack on Oswego, to be led by Montcalm. The marquis general hurried back to Montreal. At Carillon he left, with Indians and Canadians, the regiments La Reine, Languedoc, and the newly arrived Royal Roussillon, to learn from the others the ways of staying alive in this outlandish place. Le Chevalier de Lévis walked with Montcalm down the hill, through the workmen's village and past the closed tavern door to the landing stage on the morning of the marquis's departure for Montreal and Oswego. Lévis was the general's exuberant brigadier, a brilliant soldier of thirty-six years, capable of obeying and of commanding. Without Montcalm's full responsibility, he could be gay. He had already chosen, but not yet achieved, as his mistress for his long stay in Canada, the friend of Bigot's cuckold, Péan. His own military career was firmly rooted in his men's love for him, for his dash, his tenacity, and his acumen. With his general, he could be frank, understanding, and a friend, for the Lévis were secure in their antiquity, claiming, through a crusading ancestor, direct and natural descent from the family of the Virgin Mary.

Though Winslow, with 10,000 heretics, threatened 3000 Frenchmen digging in at the Most Christian King's peninsula of Ticonderoga, Montcalm left Carillon with a confident and easy mind. Lévis and the troops were staunch, and the country favored the defense, even against the problematic odds.

The Massachusetts general Winslow and his army of New Englanders and Yorkers did not go against Lévis that summer. During the third week of August, the decision to call off the expedition to Crown Point reached General Phineas Lyman, for the second year the second-in-command at the Fort Edward-Fort William Henry cutting edge of of the colonial army. It was at the hilt of the sword in Albany, however, that the thrust north was stayed. Since June,

no one had had the authority or the determination to lunge
forward. Colonel Daniel Webb of the regular army was the
first of a cautious trio of British officers to stay the campaign of 1756.

Colonel Webb had been hurriedly commissioned and sent
from London to relieve General Shirley from the supreme
command in North America. Webb was the new colonel
of the 48th Foot, and would be a major general in America
when the Earl of Loudoun arrived to replace the super-
seded Massachusetts governor and general. Daniel Webb
was not one to risk his position or prospects by action. He
came to America as a running footman for his superiors, and
having made the way, he subsided into what comfort an
English gentleman could find in the colonies.

Webb preceded Major General James Abercromby into
New York Harbor by only eleven June days. As the colonel
was the flunky, Abercromby was the coachman, driving the
fine military equipage in which the commander in chief
would make his entry on the North American scene. Like
all coachmen to the nobility, James Abercromby was a snob
as well as a good coachman. He tended well to his teams,
seeing them fed, watching their health, constantly testing
and polishing their harness, and, in a well-greased coach,
driving about smartly where he was told to go. He was
above advice, secure in his cloak of a major general,
achieved after thirty-one pedestrian years as a soldier.

To the British regiments stationed in pairs at Oswego,
Albany, and in Nova Scotia, General Abercromby brought
two more. These landed from transports at New York, to
the delight of the citizens there. The skirling of bagpipes
brought them running to the docks to see the Highlanders
come ashore, and there were many in the crowd who had
left their hearts and their kilts in the Highlands at the putting down of the rebellion ten years before in "the '45."
The other regiment that came with the Black Watch was a

Sassenach regiment, Otway's 35th Foot. Hardly noticed at the landing was the group of officers dressed in red coats with plain blue facings on which were neither button-loops nor edging. These men were Swiss and Germans, commissioned by the Crown to officer a new corps of four battalions of 1000 men each, to be forever identified with the colonies as the Royal American Regiment. Quietly and quickly going about their business and their profession, and in spite of jealousies because they were not American, the foreign officers mustered their men into the battalions of the new corps. It took three months for Henry Bouquet, born on the shores of Lake Geneva and hired out of the Dutch Service, to have his 1st battalion, 62nd regiment, Royal Americans at Saratoga, on the line above Albany to the northern forts.

With all Britain's armies in North America marking time until his arrival, their new commander in chief delayed his departure from England. The Earl of Loudoun finally made his entrance into the affairs of North America at New York, at four o'clock in the morning on 3 July 1756. Those who attended his levee at noon that day were affably received by a short, sandy Scot, of good humor, with an open face, first construed as candid, though later deemed vacant. For three days he did business and received petitioners, while his considerable retinue (including his mistress, whom he had cautiously imported rather than chancing a colonial) was transferred from the man-of-war to the vessel that was to take the party up the Hudson to Albany.

And so the noble earl arrived at the headquarters of his command, eagerly anticipated for the things that he would do, and weighted down with his baggage and importance. From where the units of the army marked time on the two tentative lines of advance to the north and to the west of Albany, the colonels and the generals came to wait upon their commander in chief. They waited while he listened to reports, and they waited while he made up his mind. They waited.

To the colonials, who hunted the wild duck in their home marshes, the Earl of Loudoun, particularly in his native Highland dress, resembled a foolish bittern, standing on one knobbly leg in the shallows. The bittern stands with a homely dignity and grace, presumably waiting for a fish that it thinks it can catch to swim slowly by. Few hunters have ever seen the bird strike, though many have seen it stalk ponderously away from uncertainty and danger.

X

Oswego 1756

West from Albany the road to the Oswego forts lay overland to the old town of Schenectady. There it took to the
water, and the supplies and soldiers went on board the
bateaux for the trip up the Mohawk River. About twenty
miles upstream, the convoys passed by the houses and barns
of Fort Johnson, where sheep grazed in the river meadow
and a flock of tame pigeons wheeled over the boats as the
birds slanted into their tower. From the passing bateaux the
men at the oars sometimes saw the hero of Lake George,
Sir William Johnson, now an even richer man with a Crown
gift of £5000 for his victory, welcoming or bidding farewell to the Indians in their canoes, come to confer with
their friend in the council house that he kept under the high
hill. Beyond Johnson's big stone fort-house, except for a
few settlements of Dutch and Germans, all was Indian land,
its people, in 1756, less friendly with each day's journey
west. From the burned-out ruins and slab headboards on
the graves at Fort Bull, over the portage road to Lake
Oneida, across the lake and down the Oswego River to the
forts at its mouth, the Indians were hostile. At many places
along that stretch of the road the bateaumen could point out

to the green recruits places of former ambushes. There was no need for words when the convoy saw on the river bank a severed English head, stuck on a stake as a jeering warning. An officer ordered a boat ashore, and the thing was taken down and given hasty burial in the earth.

Captain John Bradstreet was the roadmaster, taxed with the problem of getting through to the forts on Lake Ontario. Somehow or other this regular officer, who had acquired the knack of the forest and its streams, got his supplies through in spite of the near-mutiny of his bateaumen and the raids of the French Indians. Johnson accused him of freighting, for his own account, rum which was distributed to the Indians by the old settler Herkimer and the commander of the staging fort at the Oneida portage. If so, the pleasure in the bottle kept the local Indians occupied while men and stores went through. At Oswego, Lieutenant Colonel James Mercer welcomed even the most callow recruits into his two sad, sick regiments, which were rated as regulars. More and more welcome were the South Carolinians, sifted down by the desertions at Albany to a hardy core of back-country men, with a smattering of non-commissioned officers who had traveled Washington's road to Fort Necessity with Mackay. The guns that came up were needed at the embrasures and on the new vessels building in the harbor at the mouth of the river.

Later in the summer, when the long-awaited Loudoun came from England, Colonel Mercer could expect regulars from the old country. They would come in numbers that would discourage the swarms of French Indians who made a prison compound of the three-fort complex that was Mercer's charge. Then the 1500 men could roam free, even as far as Fort Niagara, which was still the long-delayed dream of the officers penned up in the isolated forts. It was Major General Daniel Webb whom Loudoun sent to Oswego with the 44th Foot and other troops. By the middle of August,

Captain Bradstreet was getting the men and their mounds of baggage over the Oneida Carrying Place.

The French regulars were the first to arrive at Fort Oswego. After a quick passage down Lake Champlain, Montcalm paused at Montreal only long enough to be convinced of Vaudreuil's hesitant decision to allow him to attack the British post on Lake Ontario as a diversion to draw the British from Montcalm's southern front. Colonel Bourlamaque, the third-in-command, had been sent ahead to Fort Frontenac with the regiment La Sarre and the siege guns. There were already two regiments, La Guyenne at Frontenac and Béarn at Niagara, guarding the Lake Ontario front. The stolid, workmanlike dragoon, now a colonel of infantry, had the boats ready, and all the French troops around the lake had been alerted for the arrival of the general. The regulars, with militia companies which Montcalm had brought with him from Montreal, left Fort Frontenac on 4 August. Two days later they picked up Villiers's Indian and Canadian raiders at their camp in Famine Bay, and moving by night and hiding by day, made their landing at midnight on the right bank of the Oswego River, half an hour's march from Fort Ontario.

The summer night was oddly quiet and very calm, as though it grew, apart from eternity, in a brittle bell of clear blue glass. Voices were subdued at the water's edge, where the shadowy French soldiers were carrying ashore all manner of things. A heavy, bronze gun barrel knocked with a hollow sound against the gunwales of the bateau from which it was being lifted. The sudden noise was challenged only by the bombardier's quick laugh as his men took a shorter grip on the lifting slings.

The night air over the meadowland around Fort Ontario was filled with the fragile sound of the summer chorus of insects. The two Frenchmen, Montcalm's engineer officers,

crouching together at the edge of the clearing, heard the
kettledrum bass of a bullfrog down on the river bank. They
could see the silhouette of the English fort, straight lines of
darkness against the dark sky. It was silent, brimming over
with sleep. The engineers had come from the landing place
on Montcalm's orders, walking the forest behind their Canadian guides, finding the way of the road for the guns to
be brought up. Behind the officers came their escort of
grenadiers. Keeping the pace, unseen, unheard, were the
Indian flankers. At the edge of the wood, the two specialists
did their work together in whispers, selecting the positions
for the guns and tracing in their agreement the course for
trenches, saps, and traverses to bring the assault troops
safely under the walls of Fort Ontario.

A guide tapped one of the engineers gently on the shoulder and pointed toward the lightening sky over Lake Ontario. It was time to go. In the woods the two men separated, a precaution to preserve from an English ambush the
plans and knowledge each held in his own mind.

The Sieur de Combles, walking with a Canadian officer
before and behind him, took no notice of a friendly Indian
staring at him from a little distance in the woods. The senior
engineer was deep in thought as he walked, his blue coat
over his arm, his red waistcoat and breeches bright as an
English uniform in the first morning light. Seeing, as he
thought, an enemy prisoner and a British scalp, the Indian
quickly raised his musket and fired. The Sieur de Combles
pitched against the white coat in front of him, stumbled a
step further, and fell to the ground. In that accident the
Marquis de Montcalm lost an engineer officer whom he had
brought all the way from Old France, one whom he badly
needed in the New.

A gun from Fort Ontario answered the single shot heard
from the woods. Still, the English did not realize that the
French had come. A canoe found the French bateaux pulled

up along the shore, a mile and a half from the mouth of the Oswego River, and the British war vessels put out to destroy them. But the French guns, emplaced on the shore, drove them away while the French soldiers hacked an artillery road through the woods to Fort Ontario. Other Frenchmen, with the Canadians, made gabions of brush in preparation for the siege-works and the battery positions.

On the following day, 12 August, the regiment of Béarn arrived from Fort Niagara and the siege guns from Famine Bay, while the British ships cruised at a distance, unable to come within range. That night the soldiers, working turn and turn-about in groups of fifty, began their trench from the edge of the woods. By dawn they had gone 600 feet into the clearing, hacking through the old roots that made the task a hard one. The end of the trench was in the abatis of tangled dry branches, only 160 yards from the log walls of Fort Ontario. All day the English guns fired on the trenches, where two companies of grenadiers sheltered. Back at the edge of the woods, the English cannon battered at the gabions of the French gun emplacements—the guns were coming up the road from the landing place.

At four o'clock in the afternoon, Colonel Bourlamaque, in charge of the siege, called Montcalm up to judge the meaning of the slackening fire from the fort. Together, the two men stared across the trench-scarred field, dredging deep into experience for the insight to ascertain what was inside the angles of the brown walls. Before six o'clock the general had made his decision, sending the grenadiers out of the trench into a probing assault. Almost gratefully, the white-coated infantry stood up, filed through the remaining abatis, and deployed toward the fort. The soldiers disappeared into the ditch without drawing any fire. They reappeared under the wall, where they could be seen, some making pyramids like acrobats, others climbing up their comrades' backs to enter into the fort through the gun embrasures. Soon the troops, watching from the woods and in the trenches, saw the crossed British flag come down. Leaning on their shovels the men snatched off their hats and cheered.

But their digging was not done. They continued their trenches past Fort Ontario to the high ground overlooking the other fort, Oswego, and the fortified British camp across the river. During the night they built twenty open barbet batteries and, sweating under their burdens, carried up the guns and the ammunition.

Four miles upstream the Indians and Canadian militia, under the command of Rigaud de Vaudreuil, were making a wet crossing, their muskets and powder horns held high over their heads. Montcalm had sent them to harass with fire the landward British position while the guns, his own and those taken with Fort Ontario, pummeled the British from the right bank of the river. At dawn, the regiment Béarn was taken off the supply line to ready itself for an expedition. With three small guns, Montcalm explained to the assembly of officers, the regiment was to make a crossing of the river, pass behind Rigaud de Vaudreuil's firing line, and invest Fort George, the most distant, the smallest, and the newest of the Oswego forts.

As the officers of Béarn left the order group to return to their commands, a Nippissing Indian was brought up to Montcalm. The man was one of those Indians set in depth along the way to Albany to intercept any British messenger. He had a fresh scalp at his belt and a bundle of letters in his hand. Written at four o'clock that morning by Colonel Mercer, the letters urgently called for help from Sir William Johnson and the British general. The latter was Daniel Webb, whom the commander at Oswego did not know to be then at Oneida Lake, a day's forced march away. As the letters were read to Montcalm, the French guns on the high ground came into action, one after the other, as each was set up in its battery. Montcalm did not then know that the writer of the desperate letters was dead, cut in two by one of the opening guns of the bombardment, or that the siege was ending. An hour later, at ten o'clock in the morning of 14 August, a white sheet was run up over Fort Oswego.

To Colonel Bourlamaque, who had received a bloody but slight head wound, Montcalm gave the honor of occupying the forts and accepting the surrender sword. There was a rich haul of booty in the forts and camp: eighty officers, 1700 men and women, five proud flags, a chest of gold, over seventy cannon, with munitions in plenty, and vast stores of supplies. In the river-mouth harbor lay four vessels armed with cannon and naval officers to fight and sail them. Two hundred transport bateaux lined the shore. Together, men, matériel, and transport represented, unused but ready to hand, Britain's hammer to batter down the French forts Niagara and Frontenac, a wedge to split away the Indians' loyalty to King Louis, and the tongs to snatch the northwest trade from New France.

For six days Bourlamaque culled and loaded on the captured bateaux the treasures of Oswego. As the contents of each warehouse was sorted, each barrack and warehouse stripped, it was burned. For six days the clouds of smoke rose into the August air, drifting out over the French lake on a land breeze, rolling back over the Iroquois forest when the whitecaps lapped the shore.

For a week the Marquis de Montcalm, anxious now for the Lake Champlain front, waited while the work at Oswego was done. With a firm hand that rankled Rigaud de Vaudreuil, Montcalm kept the Canadian militia in their ranks. Even though Webb threatened, the *habitants* wanted to go home to the harvest. Despite his own abhorrence, the Marquis placated his Indians with rations of plunder, and paid out the bounty money on the pathetic bits of English hair that were brought to him.

On the morning of the French departure from Oswego, the Abbé Picquet raised a great wooden cross on a blackened mound of ruins. An inscription read *"In hoc signo vincunt."* Beside it Montcalm raised a strong post placarded with the golden lilies of the French coat of arms. Written beneath the shield was the nicely turned phrase, *"ex manibus date lilia plenis."*

During the hot days of August at the Oneida Carrying Place, Major General Daniel Webb pondered the great silence from the direction of Oswego. True, there was gossip among the colonials, and Sir William Johnson's man who led the savage Mohawks at the carrying place had had Indian word that the French were coming, were attacking, and had already captured the British forts to which Major General Webb was going. There was no word that, as a British major general and gentleman, Webb could quite accept, but the rumors were enough to put an officer, without imagination or initiative, on his guard, and mindful of the care and safety he owed himself and his men.

Loudoun, ever moving with the dignity of disdain, turned round from the collapsed structure of Britain's Lake Ontario campaign to face the scaffolding built at Fort William Henry and Fort Edward for the invasion of Lake Champlain. He continued unhurried in his movements, though the lost army of France that menaced Webb at German Flats was even more of a threat to pivotal Fort Edward. It was not until late in September, when there is a crispness in the wind, that Loudoun sent his second-in-command to the Great Carrying Place. Major General Abercromby came into Fort Edward with 100 Highlanders marching behind their pipers, and the colonials, who had been there a year, rested on their tools to watch the fine sight. The Earl of Loudoun himself arrived on 6 October, with an escort of the 44th and forty-two painted savages. Again, the colonials stopped to look. They had seen Indians—as had the 44th with Braddock—they had never seen an earl.

A great British army was assembled at the launching stages for the invasion of Crown Point and the new fort at Ticonderoga. There were 4500 colonials at the two forts; 2400 British and Scottish regulars, in three regiments, had come up with the generals. Behind them at Saratoga, Colonel Bouquet had 1000 men of the 1st battalion, 62nd regiment, still drilling, but ready in the second line of battle. Lieutenant Colonel George Munro waited at Albany to come north with the 35th of foot.

The days of October passed with the dead leaves of summer. The provincials grew accustomed to the sight of kilted men. Even the strange figure of Captain Joshua Loring of the Royal Navy, come to command a fleet that they would build, became familiar. The men talked of the forays of Rogers's rangers and the heads of the rangers, found by a party going up to Lake George, stuck on stakes in the middle of the portage road. One morning the news spread through the camps that a packet of letters was found hanging from a branch beside the road. They were from the officers taken at Oswego, telling their friends that they lived.

On 1 November the Earl of Loudoun, with a suitable retinue, went back to Albany on his way to even more congenial winter quarters in the coastal cities. General Abercromby would have followed him on 25 November, but the first snowstorm, presaging a hard winter, held him over at Fort Edward. The delay gave to the general's nephew, aide, and namesake the opportunity for yet another evening spent in drinking and talking with Captain Robert Rogers in the latter's log hut on the island in the Hudson. Captain Abercromby had been out on a scout with the ranger leader, and in common with other ambitious, adventurous, and keen young British officers found an interest, a release, and a thrill in the work of a ranger.

William Johnson's Indian scout had been wrong: no French force of consequence had left Ticonderoga. Rather, since the fall of Oswego, the French had built up their manpower at Carillon and Fort St. Frédéric. Montcalm himself had hurried the Oswego battalions all the long way down the St. Lawrence and up Lake Champlain to block the expected British advance from the Hudson and Lake George. Without delay the spoilers of one fort were put to work a-building another. Along with the regulars, militia, and Marine at Carillon, the new arrivals took shovel and pick, axe and wedge, drill and hammer to complete the great stone fortress at Ticonderoga, southern bastion of New France. Montcalm regretted the loss of his first engineer, the Sieur de Combles, for he and the army scorned the work of the Canadian engineer, Lotbinière, as a governor's man. But before General Abercromby had quit Fort Edward, Fort Carillon was strong in defense and the Chevalier de Lévis had gone to join Montcalm in winter quarters at Montreal.

The French commander himself had not even waited for his enemy, the Earl of Loudoun, to leave the array of his troops before he himself returned to Montreal. French rangers, spies, and scouts of Indians had kept close watch on the British build-up at Fort Edward. Montcalm knew their numbers and the numbers of their boats and the temper of their men, even as Loudoun knew Montcalm's, and he too saw the high, honking wedges of the wild geese flying south. When the puddle ice bore the tread of the squads marching to work along the quarry road, the threat of invasion at Carillon was over for that campaign season. For the commander of the French army in Canada, work on next year's campaign was beginning at army headquarters and at the governor general's court in Montreal.

Before the last fleet left the St. Lawrence ahead of the big freeze, the Marquis de Montcalm must write his reports and recommendations to the minister of war. Before the couriers should sail, Montcalm had to reach some accord with Vaudreuil on policy and the details of reinforcement, supply, and co-operation for 1757. But already in the few short, busy months that he had been in Canada, Montcalm had found profound difficulties in his relations with the governor general, difficulties that demanded patience, tact, and tenacity to the limit of his endurance.

Time and again, the general from France had flattered the governor's Canadianism; an instance was at the Te Deum Mass for the army's victory at Oswego, where the captured British colors had been given to the Indians to carry in the procession to the church. To uphold the army's dignity in New France, Montcalm had ordered the old regimental officer, Colonel Bourlamaque, to accept honors and salutes which he neither wanted nor merited. It was Vaudreuil's elaborate fancy to render these compliments also to sailors of comparable rank. Due in part to the governor's interference in Montcalm's billeting orders, the colonel was sent to winter in Quebec. There an old soldier, unaccustomed to the frippery even of a shadow court, could pull off his boots and drink a stoop of rough cognac beside his own hearth. The rearrangement of billets brought the Chevalier de Lévis to Montreal in Bourlamaque's stead, a shift which provided a measure of comfort and companionship to Montcalm in his isolated position of command. As a soldier, the lighthearted young brigadier was extremely capable and he was readily adaptable. Already he had captured a fine mistress from Bigot's own inner circle and, without need for ambition, he remained untainted. Montcalm's brigadier was closely related to the Duc de Lévis at the court of Louis XV, which connection was useful not only to the young scion of the family in Canada, but also to his superior.

In the Count d'Argenson and in his son the Marquis de Paulmy, soon to succeed his father as minister of war, Montcalm had staunch friends and powerful patrons. To them the general could write openly of his trials with the governor and his hopes for the coming campaign. On 2 October 1756 Montcalm wrote to his friends at the ministry of the precautions to be taken against a British attempt to return to Oswego. He said that the main point of danger to New France was, in his opinion, by way of Lake Champlain, and that in 1757 he wished to recapture Acadia, before the British there could seize the Gaspé Peninsula and close the mouth of the St. Lawrence.

In the same letter, he wrote on behalf of his aide-de-camp who wished to have the post, then open, of geometrician to the Court. The twenty-seven-year-old aide's ample qualification for the scientific position was the least remarkable of Louis Antoine de Bougainville's varied accomplishments. A drab young law student, Louis Antoine had been fortunate in the patronage of Madame de Pompadour, who, as Jeanne Poisson, had lived on the same mean little Paris street as did Bougainville's uncle. As an aspiring diplomat in London, the young man had become an expert on the French-British border claims in North America. It was incidental and unusual that the British had admitted him to membership in their Royal Academy of Science. A restless step turned Bougainville into a soldier, and by the time Montcalm took him as his aide-de-camp, he was a captain of dragoons, brave, brilliant, and by his own personality and accomplishments borne far beyond the obscurity of his beginnings. Montcalm liked the younger man, and throughout a long life of many and varied experiences, Louis Antoine de Bougainville never ceased to venerate his general.

By the post that carried his letter seeking preferment for his young aide, in a special traveling box Montcalm also dispatched a beaver cub as a pet for D'Argenson. By the same convoy, the British regulars taken at Oswego sailed away to a captivity in Europe, a land as strange to the soldiers of the 50th and 51st Foot as it was to the little brown animal taken alive out of a Canadian pond.

September is the month of the harvest moon, when men who live by the plow and the scythe count their year's work by the fullness of their barns. At the end of the summer of 1756, the farmers on the seigneuries, who tended the long strips of land ribboning back from the St. Lawrence, made a poor tally of their year's labor. For the second consecutive year their crops had failed. Too many farmers had been away too long with the militia at Oswego and Carillon to nurse the young plantings through an unfavorable season. The weather had been better on the New England coast, but there, too, the men had been away on militia work on the roads and forts strung out from Albany to Lake George. On the back-country farms in the colonies of Virginia and Pennsylvania, there was no crop at all to be gathered in the harvest moon of 1756. For a whole year's cycle, since the Indians had come raiding up out of the Ohio Valley, the untended fields on the east slopes of the Allegheny Mountains had been putting up brush. Fireweed grew tall in the ashes of burned-out cabins and barns, paddocks and folds.

Only in the settlements of the marauding Shawnees and Delawares was there occasion to feast the harvest moon that year. The Indian women had tilled and gathered their patches of squash and beans and corn. The men had traveled far to reap their crop of British scalps, drying now on poles set in the Dancing Ground.

At Kittanning, in the huts of "Captain" Jacobs on the left

bank of the Allegheny River, the Delawares were celebrating under a waxing moon. It was a triple celebration that they were dancing on the night of 7 September. The harvest was in. Jacobs and his men had but recently returned from capturing the Pennsylvania Fort Granville. Jacobs himself had set the torch to the place. As the Delawares danced the victory dance, they danced a war dance too. Expected next day were Indians from the west, with French officers from Fort Duquesne, to go with the Delawares to Fort Shirley as they had gone to Fort Granville with Coulon de Villiers. There was much reason for Captain Jacobs and his warriors to dance. The French cadets danced with them, and in the shadow of a scalp-pole cast by the blazing fire, hidden under a Frenchman's coat, there lay an earthen jug of cognac.

Well out of the fire glow, beyond where an Indian or a Frenchman might wander with a girl, but with a view into the dance ground, Lieutenant Colonel John Armstrong watched and waited for the moon to go down and the orgy to end. Behind him, lying on their weapons, were most of his force of 300 men of Armstrong's 2nd Pennsylvania Battalion. A small detachment had been left to watch a party of Indians found lying up in the bush that afternoon, and to make an attack the following morning. The Kittanning raid had been planned before Jacobs had burned Fort Granville, but it had now taken on the gleam of reprisal. The scalp dangling over the now-silent drum was that of Colonel Armstrong's brother Edward.

When the dance was over, the Indians wandered off to their huts or lay in heavy sleep on the ground. A French cadet carefully picked up his white coat, took a few unsteady steps, and returned to pick up the jug. He then continued his way toward one of the huts. The unattended fire blazed on, then sank to ashes. When the moon dropped below the leaves of the treetops, Colonel Armstrong and his men moved to the bushes that edged the forest and the clearing. One party circled wide through dark, unfamiliar woods to bar the road at the far upstream end of Jacobs's sprawling village.

Armstrong gave the first dawn light a few minutes to strengthen and give substance to the view of the sleeping town. Then he stood up, and heard the scrambling in the dry leaves around him, as his soldiers got to their feet. The village of Kittanning slept on as the Pennsylvania men, with muskets held high, walked toward the huts. From out of the woods behind the advancing battle line, other Pennsylvanians came running with flaming pine torches, kindled at hidden fires. These last, with the musketmen now running with them, burst in among the houses.

First roused, first killed, first to flee yelling before the onrush of shouting Pennsylvanians were the drunken sleepers at the dance ground. Naked, bewildered, sleep-silly Indians appeared, crowding in the blackness of low doorways, to burst out into the open as those behind them shoved to get out. They, too, ran. They ran in every direction, where each thought safety lay. In the midst of the panic the Pennsylvanians stood, whooping, jabbing with their bayonets, while on each dry bark roof lay a torch, kindling fire and black smoke. Muskets began to fire as the soldiers loosed their one precious shot in close defense, or at the broad back of a warrior breaking away into the open. There seemed to be time now to reload, and safe room around them. Armstrong shouted to the men to move on, move on through the village. Soon the panicked Indians had disappeared. No women or children were to be seen, and in the distance the shadows of Indians warriors raced through the smoke to snatch a weapon out of a burning house. At the far edge of the village, where Armstrong's cut-off party should have been, a fire fight was developing. There the five French cadets had made a stand to cover the fleeing women and children and to rally the warriors, once their families were safe.

With their backs to the swirling smoke, the Pennsylvanians fought. They took casualties as they moved in on the five Frenchmen and those Indians who had found arms with which to fight. Colonel Armstrong was grazed and one of his captains, Hugh Mercer, was hard hit and down. Mercer, a doctor turned soldier, knew the ring of battle and the throb of defeat from a far-off day in Scotland, where he had stood with the young Pretender on Culloden Moor. Dazed, he heard the sound of firing change as, with the astonishment of slow realization, the Pennsylvanians found they were no longer firing *at* anyone. The French and the Indians had drifted away into the forest.

The thirty houses of Kittanning were burning fiercely, and all about lay the dead bodies of some forty Indians. There was one body that all the Pennsylvanians came to see; it was that of "Captain" Jacobs's giant son, who lay stretched over seven feet of the black charred earth. Elsewhere they came upon the naked corpse of Jacobs himself, and recognizing it, pulled it from the doorway of the burning house in which it lay crumpled. The men walked away, recalling grim pictures of other charred remains in doorways at home, now avenged.

Though Armstrong had expected to liberate many more, only seven colonists, prisoners of the Delawares, crowded around the colonel, thanking him and blessing him for their deliverance. They warned him, too, of the French and Indians from Fort Duquesne, expected at Kittanning that very day, and they told him of the war party making up to attack Fort Shirley on Aughwick Creek. While they talked, Armstrong's officers came up with their reports, which were not good. Seventeen Pennsylvanians were dead and thirteen had turned up wounded. The attack on the Indians discovered in the bush had failed. Across the Allegheny, the

Indians in Chief Shingass's village had been strangely, ominously silent during the whole attack. Armstrong could stay to gloat no longer. He had raided deep into Delaware-Shawnee country and had destroyed Jacobs's town. Now he must go, before the Indians and French, hiding in the forest all about him, could gather to attack. And he must get back to defend Fort Shirley, which lay in that part of Pennsylvania west of the Susquehanna which was the responsibility of Armstrong's 2nd battalion.

At noon of the same day on which they had come, the colonial troops left Kittanning on their own back-track. Moving fast they did not pause till dusk, when a head count showed nineteen men unaccounted for. It was too late to wait, too dark to look for the missing stragglers, and Armstrong marched on through the moonlit night.

Far behind the main body, the wounded Captain Mercer had turned at right angles to the line of retreat to avoid being caught up in the almost certain pursuit. He walked in pain, fighting off the irrationality of fever, struggling to keep in command of the seven men with him. They were his own men, sustaining and guiding their captain, who led them, on a long two weeks' journey, back over the ridges to safety.

Across the Allegheny from the burning town of Jacobs's Kittanning, Chief Shingass watched as the fires died down. Once when his mother Queen Alliquippa had been George Washington's friend, he had been proud to be called by his English name of "Captain Fairfax." Now for over a year, since Braddock had shown his weakness, Shingass had carried the red hatchet of war to the English. A cold September wind made the Delaware chief's small frame shiver as he looked out on the desolation left by the English. The next morning, Shingass gave the order to move his town downriver, nearer to the protective French in the reassuring big fort.

XI

The Hard Winter

A chill wind of discontent blew up the valley of the
Thames at the end of the old year of 1756. It was cold and
growing colder in the prison room at Greenwich, where
the Admiral John Byng looked across the wide lawn to the
curving river and the Isle of Dogs beyond. In the city, the
wind grew strong in the 'changes, blowing hard up the
reaches to Whitehall, where the Pelham-Newcastle government swayed and creaked like a dungeon door. There was
no warm breath of victory to comfort the old king in his
great stone house at Windsor, where the Thames twists like
a stream by castle, town, and field.

"To the block with Newcastle, to the yardarm with
Byng!" sang the gay songs of satire in the London streets.
There was no Sir William Johnson for the king to give as
hero to his people, that autumn of defeats. Thirty Red Indian hovels burning at Kittanning hardly made a pyre to
scourge the loss of the Mediterranean shipyard on Minorca
by Admiral Byng. A fort near Bombay, taken by Sir Hyde
Parker months before, could not make up for the loss of a
good general at Fort Mahon because Byng would not sail
in. News of Calcutta and the tortured night in the Black
Hole of the guardroom had not yet come to London. But

the people did know of Oswego's feeble defenses and the fall of their forts to France, and, though Shirley was counted suspect, they mourned for Minorca, and the cry to Government was "Shoot Byng and take care of your king."

Since 1710, the Balearic island of Minorca had been that star in the British Crown by which the Levant traders steered, fat with rich cargoes for the merchants of London. "June, July, August, and Port Mahon are the best harbors in the Mediterranean" according to a Spanish jingle, and from that Minorcan port, British warships controlled the inland sea the whole year round. In 1756, France tried on the British there, with Marshal Richelieu besieging General Lord William Blakeney, and Admiral de la Galissonière blockading Minorca at sea. Admiral John Byng was sent out from England with troops to succor Blakeney and ten ships of the line to trounce La Galissonière. On 21 May, Byng met the French fleet, equal in size to his own, with the weather gage in his favor but with the ancient rule-book at the end of his nose, where his initiative also came to an end. Because the exact situation was not so described, Byng dared not improve on his initial advantage, and because his bravery was without the courage to flaunt the printed word, he sailed back to Gibraltar, taking with him the troops intended for Blakeney. Unrelieved and unsupported, Minorca, with its garrison and its shipyard, fell to the French after a siege of seventy days.

A new paragraph had been added to the ancient time-honored articles of war, demanding death for the commander who did not do his utmost to engage the enemy. Kneeling on the quarter-deck of *HMS Monarch* in Portsmouth harbor with a handkerchief held high in his hand, John Byng read the new paragraph to its end. Then he let the handkerchief drop, in a signal to the marines of his firing squad.

Thus the book was closed on the long, inglorious government of the Pelhams during that blustery autumn of 1756, when every wind blew ill for British endeavor. In the Parliament on the Thamesside, the old leaders struggled to keep their positions of power. Briefly they were swept from office by the gale of national discontent. Before the Pelhams could regain their control, William Pitt was three months in power. In that short space of time the first flicker of England's great flame of empire was kindled by the fresh draft of Pitt's vision.

The dray horse's cleated shoes rang and re-echoed on the stones of the narrow, low tunnel of the covered way. Out again onto the parade ground, the rider had but time to straighten, draw in, and before the steaming animal could come to a halt, kick off the bare back. Men were filling the parade square of Fort Carillon even as the messenger ran over the wet, trodden snow toward the steps leading up to the commandant's door. Running, the soldiers from without the walls burst out of the covered way. By every interior door, men, coatless and hatless in the cold January drizzle, crowded out of the warm barrack rooms to hear the news coming in such haste from the north. Most recognized the man and the harnessed horse as of the convoy that had set out for Fort St. Frédéric two hours before. The sentries had marked the rider and his horse pounding up the ice road, and had taken up his cry, "To arms!" as the tiring beast slowed his pace in the sled track off the lake, where it climbed up under the new, unfinished walls of the northeast bastion. Monsieur de Lusignan stood before his open headquarters door, tying a colored woolen scarf around his neck. Behind him, still holding the order book, the clerk stood staring at the wild rider climbing the stairs.

The soldiers in the square caught the words "attack," "rangers," and, in awe, "Rogers" before the Commandant de Lusignan shoved the messenger into the office room and slammed the door shut. Shortly after, the door opened and a drummer of Languedoc stepped onto the landing to beat the officers' call.

Five or six miles down the lake, one of the sleds of the early morning convoy had carelessly pulled far ahead of the others and prematurely had sprung a trap set by Rogers and his rangers. Warned, the ten other sleds had turned back. The rangers had given chase, overtaking two more sleds.

Lusignan explained this to the officers, with the fact, extracted from the excited messenger, that instead of "hundreds" Rogers probably had 120 rangers with him. With a counter-ambush in mind, Lusignan looked over the officers crowding the small room, filling it with their eagerness to be chosen. At Carillon that morning, 21 January 1757, there was but one Canadian ranger. Lusignan quickly selected him: Charles de Langlade, fur trader from the distant crossroads of Lakes Huron, Michigan, and Superior, who with his western Indians had killed from ambush many times, and would do so again and again and again. The rest of the officers were gentlemen of France. Many of these, however, had taken to the strange woods warfare of the Canadian wilderness. The young officers from France and many of their soldiers had mastered the difficult art of walking with snowshoes, had learned the way to lie in ambush, and had survived in the muffled stillness of the winter-white forest. Captains de Basserode and La Granville, together with a lieutenant, were chosen to go with Langlade and 100 picked men.

About two miles west of Fort Carillon, Langlade and his Frenchmen came upon the outbound trail of Rogers and his men. They followed it north to a place where the tracks dipped down into a narrow valley, perhaps 100 yards across, to another rise. Here, with plenty of evergreen and dead ground, the French had their killing ground, which, in their classic pattern, they fixed between the horns of their advance.

From where he crouched in the cold slush of the old track, the French captain could hear the British singing as they came down the far rise. Listening rather than looking, he was caught unawares by the first green-clad ranger to break over the crest of ground scarcely five yards in front of him. Firing as he rose, the captain saw the leading Englishman take his bullet fair in the chest. The soldier beside the captain snapped his musket and cursed the rain that had wet its priming. But other French muskets were firing now, though from the ragged, scattered sounds there were many others that were wet and useless. As he reloaded, the captain saw the cap fly from the head of a huge British officer. As he rammed in the ball, he watched to see the great figure stagger, topple, and fall. But the big officer did not fall. By the time the captain had primed his piece and snapped shut the frizzen, the bleeding, bare-headed Rogers, by shouting and bellowing like a great bull, had turned his startled column around. As the French captain took a long aim, all the rangers were running back to high ground across the valley. Now Frenchmen running behind gleaming bayonets were pouring into the little valley. Some were running after the fleeing rangers. Others had isolated a single Englishman and were jabbing at him until he surrendered.

But the fight was not over. On the high ground among the boles of great trees, Lieutenant John Stark had deployed his rear guard of rangers. Coolly now, they were firing into the French, and soon Rogers rallied to them with the remnant from the killing ground. Neither Langlade, Basserode, or La Granville was able to dislodge the rangers from their hopeless position. They tried to flank them, but two ranger sergeants led out a counterattack and drove the Frenchmen back. They called on Rogers by name, begging him to surrender for compassion's sake, but were cursed, shot at, and laughed at for their pains.

With the coming of darkness the French captains, short of ammunition after the three-hour fight, broke off the siege. They had counted fourteen dead rangers, taken six prisoners, and wounded others. The bodies of eleven French dead were carried back into Fort Carillon by torchlight, and the surgeon worked late that night patching the wounded, among them Captain de Basserode. In the barrack rooms at Carillon and in the huts on the shore the French prisoners rescued from the rangers told tales of their short captivity and spiced the *"popote"* of legend with accounts of their close view of the wonderful, awful, giant English captain, Robert Rogers.

There was no food, no warmth, no rest for the ranger leader and his men on the night of 21 January 1757. From the valley of their ambush, the survivors of their party of seventy-four struggled south in retreat all that long night, supporting, carrying, and encouraging their six badly wounded companions. It had turned freezing cold again; the deep snow had crusted; their snowshoes were useless, and every step of their moccasined feet was an uncertain adventure. Morning found the fifty-four exhausted survivors on the shore of Lake George, six miles below the last French outpost. There the wounded were wrapped in the remaining blankets in a cold camp while Lieutenant Stark, tall, spare, and tireless, trekked the lake to fetch sleds and help from Fort William Henry, twenty-five miles away. The French did not attack the desperate camp, and on 23 January the rescue party found them and took them off.

In the days following his return from the ambushed scout, Robert Rogers's wounds would not heal. In the cold of that terrible winter, devil's fingers clawed at the raw skin of the head wound taken at the opening fire. At night, when his head rested on a pillow of quiet darkness, the wrist wound, received on the hardwood knoll, throbbed and ached through the dragging hours toward another numbing day of restless, irritating pain. Finally he went down to Albany, where the doctors were, and where Charlotte Brown mothered the military hospital, and there was soothing adulation for the ranger hero of the war. It was because of his wounds that Robert Rogers was not with his rangers on 17 March—St. Patrick's Day. Captain Speakman had been wounded, captured, and butchered at Ticonderoga, and John Stark, now a captain, was in command of the rangers during Rogers's absence.

By the simple expedient of locking sutler Levi's store, Stark kept his men sober all during the celebration for the saint of Ireland. Three scouts were sent northward and discovered the French army coming up the frozen lake. They saw the French in three long lines, man-dragging their sleds behind them. As a light snow came on, the rangers made their return to Fort William Henry, undiscovered by the enemy.

The French did not show themselves on the 18th, but at one o'clock the next morning the alarm was given. The regulars in the fort bundled themselves in clothes and blankets before going up to the walls, and the rangers, having moved in from their own huts and stockade, went with them into the cold night. Major Eyre, engineer and officer of the old 44th, stood atop the bastion wall, listening into the dark. There was a light, a very small light, far down the lake on the eastern shore; nothing more was to be seen. For two hours he watched, keeping the garrison stood-to in the bitter night beneath the hard, crisp light of the unwinking stars. Faintly at first, the ice field of the lake took life in sound. The long running snap of cracks racing across the surface could be heard in the fort. Below the bastion where Major Eyre stood, the water soughed where the shore edges of the ice were weak and trammeled, as the weight of 1500 men bore down on the tenuously anchored mass. Listening, as the British in the fort were listening, one could believe that he heard the mouse-squeak of 3000 shoes, crunching on the slick snow. When he could sense, rather than see, dark forms moving on the lake, Major Eyre shouted the order to fire. Instantly, the stealthy quiet was ripped from the night. Hell lights danced at the cannons' mouths, while 400 Irish throats keened a wild, banshee wail. When the echoes died away all was quiet again in the starry tomb of night.

In the morning light, the many tracks of the French advance and retreat showed clearly on the unbroken snow of yesterday. Some abandoned scaling ladders lay dark-limned in the whiteness of the snow.

At the first shout and shot out of the night, Monsieur Rigaud de Vaudreuil knew that his expedition to the British fort had failed in that element of surprise on which success had depended. He had not brought cannon for a siege. He had counted on speed and the mobility of his winter-wise Canadians, in numbers unexpected by the British regulars, to carry Fort William Henry by storm. For four weeks Vaudreuil's force of 1200 marines, militiamen, and Indians had hurried down the road from Montreal. They had snow-shoed more than 100 miles, dragging sleds loaded with provisions and the canvas cloth that sheltered them at night. They had paused only briefly at Carillon to regroup and to make all ready for the last long dash up Lake George. Throughout the long march, a company of grenadiers of Royal Roussillon Regiment and 200 French volunteers had measured their pace with that of their Canadian cousins. On instructions from General Montcalm, Captain de Poulhariès of the grenadiers had kept close to the governor's brother to point out and remind him of the hardiness of the soldiers from France.

For four days the French prowled around the fort, taunting, tempting, and threatening the English who were penned up safely within the walls. At night the French crept close, to burn the outbuildings, the ships, the bateaux, and the piles of cordwood and planks stacked all about. Inside the fort, Major Eyre withstood the urge to make a sortie with his outnumbered garrison, though the temptation was great. As each night he watched the new fires starting up, all that he could do in retaliation was to set his marksmen shooting at the figures silhouetted against the flames. Anxiously, the major watched the spread of each new fire and kept a fire watch, alert to the danger to the fort.

One day Le Chevalier le Mercier was brought into the fort blindfolded and Major Eyre declined the Frenchman's polite offer of surrender. Eyre enjoyed the conversation, in the course of which he discovered that the chevalier shared his interest in the engineering aspect of the soldier's trade. One morning, it was a Tuesday, the day after the wet, heavy snow had fallen, a pack of well-trained, well-rehearsed, and well-led Canadians attacked the big new vessels on the ways, close in under the walls of the fort. It was a bold attempt by a daring officer. Lieutenant Wolf was a waif cub, abandoned to the wilds of Canada by the misfortune that befell his patron and countryman, the Baron Dieskau. On the morning of 22 March he burned the big ship, which, but for the stillness of the air, would have been a torch for the whole fort.

Wolf's raid was Rigaud de Vaudreuil's last attempt on Fort William Henry. With his whole army, the governor general's brother left Lake George by the way he had come, over miles and miles of glaring, blinding ice, all the way to Montreal.

In high pride the governor general of New France wrote to Versailles, recounting the deed of his brother and listing the achievements of his Canadians in burning the British boats, installations, and supplies at Lac de St. Sacrement (Lake George). Grandly, the Marquis de Vaudreuil claimed that his brother had completely destroyed all British capability to make an attack on Lake Champlain in the coming campaign season. In his correspondence the Marquis de Montcalm was less sanguine as to the results of the winter action, from which the army had been excluded. As for his own plans for the 1757 campaign, Montcalm prepared the army for an active defense of Fort Carillon. Piqued by Governor de Vaudreuil's bombast and spurred by Rigaud de Vaudreuil's failure to capture Fort William Henry, the general included in his plans an army attack on that place. Montcalm's aggressive defense *à la Dieskau*, however, depended largely on the rumor that "milord Loudoun" would be taking the bulk of the British army against the Louisbourg fortress that year, rather than concentrating the troops against Carillon.

Everywhere, as March moved into April, the terrible winter gave way slowly before the coming of spring. In Montreal and in Albany, the loosened snow slid from the roofs as the sleepers woke to the drip of rain off the eaves. At Quebec, the ice floes, moving with the tides, ground themselves into great chunks which isolated the south shore from the city. No longer was the ice road up Lake Champlain safe for sled or man alone. At Fort Edward and Fort William Henry, at Carillon and Fort St. Frédéric at Crown Point, the snow banks were melting. The run-off cut deep furrows through to the mud, while the men on guard took hope from the sight of a bare shoulder of earth, freed from its counterpane of snow.

In their Canadian billets, French soldiers were finding and fitting their marching gear. In the room at headquarters where lists were made and records kept, the Marquis de Montcalm counted up the casualties to marriage among the

young gentlemen of his corps of officers. Lieutenant Duglas
had made an acceptable colonial match. Only boredom
could account for the others.

At the English forts the barrack rooms were newly swept
and aired. The company women sitting with their belong-
ings in a group beside the wicket gate at Fort William
Henry were going away. The bright tatters of their skirts
and shawls gave color to the drab foreground of charred
ruins, churned mud, and last year's matted grass. From the
hillside of dark evergreens and gray-branched hardwood,
the screech of dry brakes and the shouted "haw" of the
wagoners traced the line of the relieving force, as it came
down the last mile from Fort Edward.

Major William Eyre was going away from the fort that
he had conceived and built, and that he had seen stand
strong during the days and nights of his defense of it. With
him were going the regulars whom he had commanded
during the attack, and their women who had shared that
anxious time. Two of those companies of colonial rangers
were leaving, too. Some said they were going to Louisbourg by ship out of New York; others *knew* that their
destination was Quebec itself.

The grass of Ireland is bright and fair and green in April,
when the snow still lies in the shady hollows along the upper Hudson. Major Eyre's regulars, two years out from
their Irish homeland, sat huddled and cramped in a cold
drizzle in the bateau running them downstream to the
transports that awaited them in New York Harbor. At
Cork, where the Bride and the Lee flow into Queenstown
Harbor, seven British regiments were loading on the transports in a warm shower of rain. There was wailing on the
quayside where the black-shawled women mourned each
man taken for a soldier, and they wept for their own sad

plight. For the women and children left in Ireland there was poverty, and hunger, and begging, and scant alms from the well-intended "Hibernians" and that other earnest group, "The Society of British Troops Abroad." The men —English, Scots, Welsh, and so many Irish since the regiments had gone recruiting—were off for Halifax in wild America and the bleak war the king was waging there.

Admiral Charles Hardy's 100 transports down from New York were still unloading in Halifax's great harbor when the convoy from Cork bore in around the piney headland on the eastern shore. General the Earl of Loudoun, commander of 12,000 assembled soldiers, made his dignified entry a week later. Immediately he caused a large parade square to be cleared and leveled so that the regiments could put some needed polish to the drill.

Slowly through the days of July the square-bashing progressed to simple, then to eye-catching, complicated maneuvers under the gracious eye of the noble earl. There were days, sunny days, when the general and his entourage stood rooted on the shore to watch the soldiers rehearsing with the sailors the loading of the boats, the assault landing from them, and, with foresight rooted in timidity, re-embarking from a hostile shore. Meanwhile, in the little meadows at the margin of the forest where French Indians lurked, Rogers's rangers, the finest woods fighters in the world, cut and bundled the hay.

The July days became August days and still Loudoun dallied. On 5 August he was nudged in the right direction for a decision. On that day, the French schooner *Parole* was brought into Halifax, a prize. At the moment of easy capture the French captain had thrown over the side, almost into the bow wave of the British boarding boat, a packet of letters. Fished out, dried out, spread out on General Loudoun's desk, the letters dampened the earl's hope of an easy capture of the French citadel. From the letters, it appeared that there were twenty-two ships of the line at anchor in the harbor. The garrison held 7000 well-fed, happy troops, according to the testimony of the letter-writers, who wrote down large the numbers of great guns bejeweling the rampart crown of Louisbourg. Overwhelmed by the ominous fist of words brandished under his beak, the earl lightly discarded, like a molting feather, the whole idea of the expedition.

If he was cautious in his generalship, Loudoun was decisive in the defence of both his omnipotence as a commander in chief and his exalted position as a peer of the realm. A Jewish merchant of Halifax town was thrown into the common jail for saying in the market place that the French had but five ships fit and able to sail, not the twenty-two of the *Parole* letters. The merchant's source of information lay in the gray-sailed smugglers, anchored in the coves outside the harbor. There were many who thought the French prize schooner too easy a catch and the packet of letters too easily picked up. Major General the Lord Hay, who commanded a brigade, sneered openly at the alacrity with which his general stacked his arms, and implied that a modicum of cowardice bleached the plumage of the earl.

For all his rank and family, Hay was promptly arrested, pending a court-martial. But it appeared that not even a palace mutiny could drive milord to action. Toward the French in Louisbourg the Earl of Loudoun continued for a second year his tried policy of cautious and persistent procrastination.

The French were in Louisbourg, and there they stayed. The watch boats, shuttling between Halifax and the blockading fleet, brought word on every trip that in the harbor behind the town French masts were as thick as asparagus. The inshore frigates, the soldiers were told, were counting the barrowloads of earth going into the works and redoubts that the French were building in every bay and every cove where troops could land.

The French had come to Louisbourg early that year; the British had been late in arriving at the Halifax base. Still in political turmoil which Pitt had not yet the strength to sway, the dissipated strength of the Royal Navy had not been able to prevent three French squadrons from getting away. Admiral de Beauffremont had taken from Brest, unchallenged, four ships of the French line.

After a cruise to the West Indies, he had sailed up the colonial coast to drop his anchors at the end of May in Louisbourg Harbor. Without a watch at Minorca, Du Revest on board *L'Hector*, with four ships in company, had been able to duck past Saunders in the straits of Gibraltar, to arrive all safe at Louisbourg on 19 June. The following day, Du Bois de la Motte arrived with nine big ships and two battalions of the regiment Berry. The seventy-four-year-old admiral had sailed from Brest on the heels of a gale which had driven Temple West, who had sailed with Byng, off station.

But the old man was content to rest in the safe harbor at Louisbourg, nor would he let his captains cruise out on their own. They missed their chance therefore when the Cork convoy of fat transports came close under the lee shore of Cape Breton Island to ride out a storm. Fifty-nine years at sea for France had worn thin Du Bois de la Motte's ardor for gaining new glory. Time, ability, and many successes had brought the slim, jeweled baton of a marshal of France close to his grasp. Nothing that an inferior British fleet might do could tease the venerable admiral to try for new laurels.

All through the summer weeks, fifteen British ships of the line cruised off Louisbourg in peace. On pleasant afternoons the four British admirals, Holburne the Senior, Boscawen, Hardy, and Holmes, rowed over to dine together. In the military game of balanced numbers, the Englishmen were content. The captains of eighteen French ships and five frigates dined ashore.

XII

————

Montcalm's Year

Men, French and Canadian alike, were rolling their blankets on the grass. They looked up, their faces wide in smiles, as Montcalm threaded his way through the disorder of the dismantled bivouac. Soldiers, regular and militia, carrying heavy loads down to the bateaux, stood aside in affectionate respect to let their general pass ahead. Company officers doffed their hats to the marquis and, catching the eye of the young aide-de-camp at his heels, made grimaces reflecting their high spirits, which did not escape the army commander's attention. The Marquis de Montcalm, wise in the ways of troops, read success to his venture to Fort William Henry.

He had ridden out early from Fort Carillon to the launching site at the foot of Lake George, to see the loading of the new artillery rafts. They were simple in design, being but a platform secured to strong bateaux lashed together. If the chief of his Royal Corps of Artillery was correct—he had tested them the year before—the troops could shoot their way onto the landing beach or could even bombard the British fort from out on the open lake.

All was ready with the cannon rafts when Montcalm walked among his gunners, commending them and promising them a gay cruise and targets to delight them. At the end of the gun line, where Lieutenant Jacquot's bateau, mounting the 12-pounder, nuzzled the shore, a grass fire was spreading while shouting men ran to contain it. For a moment Montcalm stopped short. Bougainville, the experienced aide, sensing a change in mood, stepped quickly to his general's side. But the order that Montcalm gave was in the earlier mood of confidence: "Let the army move out." The word heard by the gunners kindled a cheer that raced along the beach. Montcalm's expedition, launched by fire, took its flame to the enemy far up the lake.

All through the weeks of June and July, Montcalm had carefully laid the faggots and piled the logs for the blaze of his intent.

From the word passed over the back alleyways of the forest, Montcalm had learned of Lord Loudoun's plan to conduct a seaborne invasion. On the map of New France, this could only spell Louisbourg or Quebec itself. There were anxious days at headquarters, with the indivisible strength of the small French army threatened on two fronts, to the south and to the east. Anxiety and tension relaxed somewhat when word was received that the first French squadron had berthed safely at Louisbourg. With a French fleet to maneuver from its harbor, not only was Louisbourg considered to be invulnerable, but the portculis had been rung down on the St. Lawrence with Quebec safe behind it.

By early June, with all his obligations to the east satisfied by the navy and the garrison at Louisbourg, Montcalm could concentrate his attention and all his troops on the ever-vulnerable southern front. The Hudson River was a javelin, poised ready to launch against the commercial heart of New France at Montreal. While the grip, and the force to throw the javelin, was at Albany, its steel-shod head was secured at Fort Edward and tapered to the point at Fort

William Henry. Rigaud de Vaudreuil's winter raid had succeeded in dulling that point: Montcalm's intent, in the summer of 1757, was to snap it off.

Governor General de Vaudreuil readily acceded to General Montcalm's plan to eliminate Fort William Henry. Though the army's attempt at the feat in which his own brother had failed could be construed as a slight to the family honor, the governor general's jealousy had been flattered smooth again by the convincing reports he himself had read and signed, detailing the destruction achieved by Rigaud de Vaudreuil's bonfires in the snow. But far beyond mere acquiescence, the governor of New France aided his general's scheme. He mobilized a force of Canadian militia under his brother's direct command and put them all at Montcalm's disposal. He went even further, when he permitted the navy department's independent companies of marines to be gathered together as battalions to serve with and under command of the army. Vaudreuil was too deeply imbued with a sense of Canadian history and tradition, and too conscious of where lay his country's destiny, not to be sensitive to danger menacing its southern frontier.

With a Franco-Canadian army fixed in the geographical fault of the Champlain-Hudson Valley the governor was free to gloat over the Indian victory on the long western frontier. Carefully he counted each scalp taken and spread the numbers across the long reports for his liege king. From the western Iroquois' homeland, down the whole green-forest links of ranges, even into the Cherokee bastion at the far end of the mountain walls, Vaudreuil tallied the successes to which he could point with boastful pride.

But to one less eager to catch the glint of reflected praise, there was to be seen a new star of hope rising in the red sky of Indian war. There were still scalps for the taking along the Mohawk and down the rivers watering Britain's Middle Atlantic colonies. But the easy loot had been removed into and behind the fort line that, in 1757, was guarded by determined men who struck back. Gone from the frontier war were the French officers who had rallied the Nations and set the war parties on the trails to the east. Dumas of Fort Duquesne had come east to command the new battalion of the Marine with General Montcalm. Villiers, from Famine Bay, was marching with Lévis's wing of the army the day that Montcalm embarked for Fort William Henry; so were the Indians, two thousand of them.

Warriors of more than nineteen of the continent's great Nations were with Montcalm that summer. They came from the east where the Abbé Le Loutre had taught them avenging Christianity. The Abbé Picquet was there with his praying Iroquois, and St. Luc de la Corne brought in the northern tribes, while Langlade and Niverville came down from the further lakes in canoes filled with Indians painted bright for war. There were Sacs and Foxes and Sioux from the prairies. There were even ten strange warriors who came from the land of the giant trees by the shore of the western ocean.

They had all come to join in war the new French war chief, in whose eyes were the wings of the eagle. To the Indians, that summer of 1757, Montcalm stood as high as the fabled redwood of the Iroquois legend. Under the wide-spreading branch of Montcalm's fame was safety and good fighting. The long black shadow of his leadership lay over the rich English cities of the coast, heavy-laden and ripe for plunder.

As each Nation came paddling in to Montreal, Montcalm greeted them, made them welcome with praise, and hurried them south to the great rendezvous at Carillon. There Lévis, with his easy grace, melded the army and prepared it for the march to the British forts. He kept the Indians from idleness by saturating the woods south of Carillon with marauding patrols, each under the guiding (and it

was hoped, the restraining) hand of a French or Canadian
leader.

The first tally of success to the expedition's credit, however, was rung up on 21 July by a Canadian patrol of ten
men. M. de St. Ours's scout was attacked among the islands
in Lake George, but, though there were seventy-five English in five barges and 100 more on the shore at Isle à la
Barque, the fast French canoes harried the enemy and made
them give way. St. Ours brought back with him to the advance camp the body of a young cadet killed in the action.
Gently, the soldiers lifted the body out of the frail craft
that was its bier.

The whole French camp was thrilled by Lieutenant
Marin's journey to Fort Edward. With the western Indians and the Canadian woods runners, the laughing ranger
moved so fast that half his party could not keep the pace.
But the 200 swept around the British fort like the spring
flood that only that year had washed away the island huts.
The soldiers from Carillon who walked out to the Indian
camp on the evening of Marin's return saw the scalps hanging from their poles. There were thirty-two of them. It had
not struck the lieutenant's fancy to take any of the British
as prisoners.

There were prisoners aplenty for the French soldiers to
see before the expedition set sail. One hundred and sixty
wet, bedraggled, and frightened New Jersey troops, rowing
their own boats surrounded by a ring of war canoes, were
landed on 26 July. They were the *lucky* ones, as again many
of their comrades had died, shot in their boats or toma-
hawked in the water as they tried to swim ashore. Langlade
and Hertel de Chambly, with Hurons and Ottawas, had
contrived the water ambush up Lake George, where Sab-
bath Day Point juts out halfway across the lake toward
the rocky eastern shore.

General Montcalm, who had lately come from Montreal, learned from the prisoners that it was General Webb against whom he would be going. That otiose officer was expected daily at Fort Edward, where he would take command of both forts. It was well that Montcalm had come to Carillon, for it was only his fame that kept the Indians from going home with their prisoners and their scalps. Through their chiefs, he persuaded them to follow on where he himself would lead in the name of "Onioto," the French king. Long into the night the Indians danced, boasting of the deeds they would do for the great war chief their king-father had sent to them.

The Indians and their white leaders had already gone ahead when the grass fire sent the soldiers racing to embark for a hasty departure for the English fort. At nightfall the artillery rafts and the bateaux were to meet the Indian canoes under Sugar Loaf Mountain, then, together, thread through the islands of the narrows to the rendezvous with the Chevalier de Lévis and his overland party.

It had been impossible to assemble enough boats for the whole army to cross Lake George, so Lévis had undertaken to march 3000 men up the west shore of the lake. The party had set out at dawn on 30 July with Villiers's *coureurs de bois* finding the trail, scouting the passes, trying the fords and crossings, for the mountain wilderness through which they went was trackless.

At ten o'clock on the night of 2 August Lévis was at the rendezvous. With his flint and steel, the chevalier lit the three signal fires previously agreed upon to beckon the French bateaux to a friendly shore. At midnight, Lévis heard the slap of a paddle cautiously signaling out on the lake. With Villiers, he walked to the edge of the water, calling out a welcome to his first guest.

At three o'clock in the morning, the Marquis de Montcalm came ashore. Cookfires had been lighted, and the reassembled army, 8000 strong, prepared a meal and found a few hours of rest under the trees.

When, at eleven o'clock in the morning, the march by land and water was resumed, the British whaleboat which had been watching the French since sunrise hoisted sail and scudded for home. By the presence and the action of the swift craft, Montcalm knew that his coming to Fort William Henry was known and had been expected. Militarily, however, surprise was achieved, for though Webb, at Fort Edward, had sent horsemen to Albany, the time for rousing the militia had passed.

That night, while Montcalm was landing his troops in the perimeter set up by Lévis's land wing, a British whaleboat was captured and its twelve men brought to Montcalm's headquarters fire for questioning. They were cocky men of the ranger corps, who consistently told of the 1000 soldiers who had arrived from Fort Edward that afternoon, bringing with them four cannon and twenty-five loaded wagons. The captured rangers also assured the French general that Colonel Munro would attack him in the morning and that by noon the French and all their savage ilk would be cruising back down blue Lake George.

At dawn on 3 August Montcalm, undaunted by threats, sent Lévis's force forward to contain the promised sortie or, if no attack developed, to carry on with the encirclement of the enemy position, in the approved style of siegecraft. There was only scattered musket fire ahead where Villiers's and Lévis's Indians were driving in the British pickets. There was no whisper of sound to indicate they were concentrating outside the fort. Doggedly, the columns of regulars and Canadians threaded their way in single file among the trees at the mile-consuming easy lope they had adopted on the long walk from Carillon. In their soiled white coats the columns looked like threads of cotton stitching up the green waistcoat of the forest that tightly girded the fat body of the British fort.

On the hills behind Fort William Henry, Lévis's soldiers paused to round up a big herd of cattle in the swamp meadows. They were good fat beeves which the farmer-militia from the St. Lawrence and the soldiers, once herdsmen from the Garonne, appraised hungrily as they stroked with loving hands the warm brown haunches.

The chevalier set up his defenses across the brook that, at its marshy mouth, divided the tight, four-bastioned fort from the straggling stockaded works capping the other high ground to the east of William Henry. Lévis's position straddled the portage road to the Hudson. Down this road to Fort Edward, toward the Bloody Pond and the old ambush ground, the Indians were drifting. Along that road they would have their best chance of taking an English scalp.

In the afternoon, Rigaud de Vaudreuil's Canadians passed through Lévis's positions, gaily singing their *habitant* songs on their way to the belt of French encirclement. Montcalm, they shouted as they passed through, had demanded that the Scotsman, "Monrow," should surrender at once, or ————. The short, swarthy men in bright-colored toques made tomahawking motions with their hands, fools' grimaces of agony on their grinning faces. So Rigaud de Vaudreuil's Canadians passed through the regulars, singing, laughing, and playing the clown. Beyond the Canadians, small parties of Indians could be glimpsed as they moved soundlessly along the inside edge of the woods.

On the western end of the perimeter, the gun rafts had been unloaded, and Colonel Bourlamaque, the besieger of the Oswego forts, was telling off the squads of regulars making the approaches. Those who were to dig drew tools from the sappers' stores, those who would guard the workers filed off to positions on the higher ground. Even before Montcalm's herald returned with Colonel Munro's refusal

to surrender, the pioneers had thrown up the first earth
shield of their sap. The British Jack, flapping lazily at the
top of its tall white staff on the bastion, was only a little
more than 300 yards from the digging Frenchmen, when the
gloom of night fell to hide the flag from their view.

The flag was still there in the morning, but nearer now to
the line of the trench.

The Union Jack still flew from the fort on 6 August
when Mercier, the gunner, with Montcalm and Bourlamaque, made a little ceremony out of the firing of the first
gun of the first battery to bombard Fort William Henry.
The flag was there on the 7th and the 8th, with more
batteries opening as completed. Guns within the fort were
firing, too: round shot battering at the French camp and
angles of the extending lines; bombs plunging down to
burst behind the mounds of new-turned earth sheltering the
French. Sometimes a bomb fell true, and for a moment, in
some corner of the siege lines, the coatless, sweating diggers
would watch, slack-mouthed, while their cursing, groaning
wounded were led off and their dead were borne quickly
away; then the digging continued. From a point where he
could see the progress being made, Lévis estimated that at
the end of the fourth day the French were but 100 yards
from the curtain wall of the fort. This was close enough for
the storming party of grenadiers to launch their attack.
The next day the guns would concentrate to breach the al-
ready-crumbling west face of Fort William Henry.

Hour by hour, the siege developed with the orderly prescribed inevitability of a hanging. Colonel George Munro
watched from his prison fortress. On the west the parallels
rose like a gallows tree. To the south and east, beyond the
stockaded camp, a cordon of French and Canadian troops
cut him off from his friends and his general, sixteen miles
away. On the lake, French boats cruised outside of gun

range. Far to the north, a white sail caught the sun as it drew near with messages from Carillon.

On his writing table in the south barracks, in a small room not yet pre-empted as a hospital for his sick and wounded, lay the dark-stained, crumpled sheet of paper which was the final message Munro had received from General Webb. The Marquis de Montcalm's aide had delivered it under a flag of truce. According to the polite aide it had been found in the waistcoat pocket of a messenger. The stains were regrettable but unavoidable. General Webb did not think it prudent to come to the succor of Fort William Henry. There was a delay in the call-out of the Albany militia. Until all of Colonel Sir William Johnson's forces arrived, the general could not risk a sortie—or his person. General Webb suggested that Colonel Munro might seek advantageous terms.

The intercepted letter was two days old—it had lain one day in Montcalm's field desk, another on Munro's table—before the commander of Fort William Henry roused his tired officers to consider an honorable surrender. That afternoon, Colonel Munro had noticed a shifting and a concentration of the enemy troops which, not knowing the rumor of Webb's imminent approach to be but a false alarm, he judged to be the gathering for an attack on his stockaded camp across the brook. That night there had been an alarm when two soldiers had jumped over the wall. In the garden between the fort and the French trenches, there had been sounds of a scuffle where the deserters were being picked up—by French? by Canadians? by Indians? The silence that followed was broken by a long, howling war whoop that ended in a series of high, penetrating yelps. Colonel Munro heard it as he stood in an empty gun embrasure, peering out into the night. He heard it taken up in the breastworks, on the hills behind them. An Indian yell came over the water like darting swallows at evening. It spread along the slopes of the eastern mountain like the scandalous cry of the blue jay, and like the insistent mournful cry of the whippoor-will, it was taken up along the portage road and where the brook defiled out of the forest. Finally it came to rest in silence in the garden.

Montcalm's Indians were gathered close around the fort. It was then that Colonel Munro roused his officers.

At seven o'clock in the morning on 9 August, a white flag was run up on the tall flag pole. Shortly after, Lieutenant Colonel John Young of the Royal Americans, his hair neatly tied and his coat carefully brushed, marched out the main gate behind a white flag and a drummer beating the parley. Halfway to the raw earth mound of the French sap, close by the smallpox graves, he waited for Montcalm's emissary. From around the end of the sap, Major Bougainville stepped out and, with a compliment to the courage of the defenders, began discussion of the terms of surrender.

The terms were quickly arrived at, Colonel Munro bowing to the obviously inevitable, the Marquis de Montcalm granting every consideration to the honor and personal possessions of the vanquished. At noon, the British and the colonials marched out of Fort William Henry and over the bridge spanning the marshy brook, to the palisaded camp, chosen as the assembly point for the paroled prisoners, their women, their baggage, and, in the morning, the escort of French regulars who would see them safe—safe from the French Indians—to Fort Edward.

Colonel Bourlamaque, the siegemaster, marched his regulars into the fort. Men of Royal Roussillon were set on guard at the powder magazine and the storeroom. There was no need for an armed guard on the rum store. Its door stood open. Looking in, the off-duty soldiers saw the open O's of row upon row of stove-in casks, the earth floor a mire of delicious, pungent mud. Though rum was a military store, the commanders, the Scot and the Frenchman, saw no cause for complaint or explanation of wanton destruction of the British rum. Both old soldiers were horsemen of war, knowing well the unrest, under their saddle of authority, at the end of a battle, and the necessity for keeping the beast's head high, with a tight hand on the reins of discipline and a soothing hand patting the taut, arched neck of pride. On no account must the hot animal be allowed to drink.

Bougainville delayed his departure to Montreal with the dispatches of victory in order to be at his general's side during the crisis that developed late in the day. Disappointed with the leavings found in the empty barrack rooms, the Indians claimed the baggage of the prisoners, even the prisoners themselves, as their right by their rules of war. It was nine o'clock at night before the marquis could calm the tribes, and in anticipation of the morning, when the British garrison was to march away, impose responsibility on the chiefs for the good conduct of their warriors. From far down the lake Bougainville could see the glow from 1000 campfires in the sky of the August night.

The prisoners spent a restless night in their camp. Many sat up listening to the chant of the Indians dancing rhythmically around their fires. Before light several parties had slipped away, trusting their own heels above the promises of escort and French protection from their savage allies. Though they started early, there were Indians watching by the side of the road. To show friendship, masking fear, the British offered their canteens to the warriors. There was rum in the canteens, the soldiers' own private hoard.

A tribe of the Abenaki from Acadia started it. They had been bred in hate by Le Loutre; their French officer, Niverville, could not restrain them; their Jesuit priest and their interpreter could not or would not control them. Their keen sense of smell, quickened by the rum they demanded and were given, made them bold in contempt of the odor of fear. A brown hand snatched at a woman's shawl; she screamed and a man rushed to her rescue. Indians ran up to see and help. Britons and colonials were running, some toward, some away from the incident. Soon everyone was running: the prisoners in panic, the Indians to the rape, the French officers to the rescue. Only the British officers sat still in the barrack where they had been gathered apart from their men; they were powerless.

Montcalm was there, raging and struggling with drawn sword to beat his allies back from the prey he had so far held from them. An outraged man of Europe, he regained his command and quickly took back his control. But it took time to herd the sheep and collar the dogs, and in that time some fifty Britons were dead and scalped. Beyond the fringes of the turmoil 200 British soldiers ran alone, stumbling, through the forest, away from the horror; from 400 to 600 more were being pushed and shoved along by their Indian captors toward villages remote at the ends of the continent, or, in hope, toward ransom at Montreal.

For Montcalm the joy for his victory was the red welt of a dishonorable scar, as red as the cordon of the Order of St. Louis, which four days before he had received with honor and pride.

The campaign was over, and the French went home. First the Indians with their captives, leaving their havoc behind, then the Candians hurrying home to the harvest, which after two lean years was needed to feed New France through the coming winter. Next Montcalm sailed down the lakes for Montreal, his army disintegrated, himself disenchanted. Though Webb still cowered at Fort Edward, that place was beyond Montcalm's shortened reach.

Finally the Chevalier de Lévis left with the French regulars and marines. He had destroyed the British fort utterly, until no unburned log stood notched to its neighbor. At the

old burial ground where the victims of the spring epidemic
lay, Lévis reinterred the bodies which had been dug up,
desecrated, and tumbled by loot-starved French Indians.
There was retribution for the disturbed dead in the smallpox cemetery, for the Indians who had molested them in
their graves bore the darts of their disease to far lands of
many Nations.

Major General Daniel Webb rested, shaken, but again
secure, after the departure of the alien, foreign horde from
Lake George. Fort William Henry was gone and therefore
no longer his responsibility. To save the whole northern
spearhead, while giving up the keen point, Webb had acted
with dispatch in sending dispatches, one crying out to Sir
William Johnson in his capacity as colonel of the militia,
the other a long, far cry to his commander in chief and
patron, the Earl of Loudoun, presently at Halifax. The first
appeal caused Johnson to round up 3000 militiamen to go to
Fort Edward. They arrived there on the third day after
Munro, unaided by Webb, surrendered.

Lord Loudoun's dispatch from his general at Fort Edward traveled fast to reach him in Halifax on 16 August. It
told of the French attack on Fort William Henry but did
not tell the outcome, which left a void of dreadful doubt in
the studious vacuum of the earl's mind. Already Loudoun
had given up his grand design against Louisbourg.

But the drilling on the parade square continued, well-
polished brass winked in the sun. The Earl Loudoun, very
much the commander in chief, drew out a plan for an expedition up the St. John's River on the north side of the
Bay of Fundy. He was pondering this *divertissement* when
Webb's frantic letter reached him, upon which Loudoun
took two regiments and sailed away to save or rescue Albany. The Nova Scotia summer was over; a plague of little
brown field mice had annoyed the earl at Halifax, and the

swarms of mosquitoes had bitten without regard to rank or station.

With the general gone, the campaign postponed, called off, and ended, the British regiments old to Nova Scotia shuffled around, making ready for their long hibernation in the isolated forts around the peninsula. The regiments newly out from the old country watched the veterans settle in for the winter and followed suit. Cold, disease, and boredom were the enemies in the lonely forts, though there was always the threat of an Abenaki raid. The guard heard their animal cries signaling in the forest and stood alert, suspicious and quick to react. So it was on a foggy morning that a sentry challenged a dim figure coming toward him from the shore. The voice from the gloom answered in a gibberish tongue and came on. When the tense sentry distinguished a blanket cloaking the figure and long, streaming hair, he fired pointblank and screamed for the guard to turn out. Down among the rocks they found the naked white body of a boy, hair still unclubbed, lying on the rumpled plaid of the Frazer tartan. He was a Scot gone down to the water's edge to bathe. Shortly after the accident, Colonel Simon Frazer's 78th Highland Regiment, recently arrived from home, moved into winter quarters in Dartmouth across the bay from Halifax, away from the English, to whom their Gaelic language and their Highland ways were still so strange and suspect—Culloden and the Stuart Rebellion were but twelve years gone.

British ships of the blockading squadrons off Louisbourg came and went into Halifax through all of August and into the month of September. In the French port Du Bois de la Motte's fleet still lay at anchor in the roads. The British admiral knew that the French men-of-war had reached Louisbourg with sickness on every deck. But now in September the Admiral knew that soon the French fleet must sail for home or starve with the garrison. So tight had been the blockade that few supply ships had won through on the run-in down the Atlantic coast.

On an evening in mid-September the British fleet lay becalmed in full view of Louisbourg. The sea was oily and still, mare's tails streaked across the sky, and sea birds were flying into shore. Petty officers were short and sharp with the watch clewing up the running gear and lashing tight the gun carriages, and on the quarter-deck the officers were restless. At midnight the hurricane struck. Twelve hours later Admiral Holburne's fleet was wreckage floating on the sea. Eleven mastless hulks bobbed in the pitching waves. Empty gun ports gaped like the mouths of stranded fish, showing where the top-deck batteries had been jettisoned. Sloop *Ferret* had disappeared with all hands. Somehow, 175 men out of the 400 aboard 50-gun *Tilbury* had reached shore through the pounding, beating surf. The rest had foundered with their ship. French soldiers from Louisbourg had helped the survivors ashore; their act of rescue and mercy had saved the sailors from the Indians there.

XIII

Quid Dux? Quid Miles?

Until the spring of 1757, the King of England was poorly served by the enduring government of the Pelhams. In June of that year, William Pitt became the steward of the realm. Pitt's popular appeal and his greatness as a commoner in the House, as well as a strong popular reaction against the Pelham Duke of Newcastle, no longer could be denied by the Palace. Reluctantly the crotchety old Hanoverian monarch summoned the radical statesman to his service in a compromise government. The Duke of Newcastle retained the privileges and perquisites of a butler. To Pitt, the new man, was given the responsibility and hard work of management. During the last years of his reign, George II was well attended by Pitt and the brilliant men whom "the Great Commoner" could call to the king's service.

Pitt came into power too late in the year to inspire or influence Loudoun's indolent campaigning in North America. India was too remote for Robert Clive's far-reaching victory at Plassey to be attributed to Pitt's new policy. Nor could Pitt do more during his first few months of office than build the instrument of policy out of the muddle that surrounded him.

Two weeks before Pitt took control of Britain's foreign

policy, his only ally, the Prussian King Frederick II had rushed brashly into a crushing defeat by Austria at Kolin. Immediately the mighty alliance of the three women who ruled Europe moved in to destroy the rude king who had called them witty names. Calm as a porcupine beset on every side by yelping bitches, Frederick presented his quills to the "Apostolic Hag" of Russia in the east, to Maria Theresa, the "Hapsburg Mother," in the south, and to the decayed army and debauched generals of Louis's "Mlle. Poisson." Twice during the autumn of 1757, the prickly King of Prussia lashed out at his tormentors. At Rossbach, he routed the French Army; at Leuthen, the Austrians fled in panic before the Prussian mobility and field guns and cavalry. Elisabeth's wild Russians, not unlike the North American "savages," raped, tortured, and looted, then dispersed in every direction, leaving no vestige of an army.

Though the British had lighted bonfires to celebrate Frederick's victory over the French, they had done nothing whatever to help their sole ally in the western world at war. The Duke of Cumberland had ordered a British army sent to guard King George's homeland kingdom of Hanover. It had bungled through one minor battle, signed an inept "Council" with the French general, and exposed the kingdom to plunder.

Yet it was from all this that William Pitt shaped his policy. He repudiated Cumberland's Council of Klosterzevern. He encouraged Frederick to fight in Europe. With a cash grant of over a million pounds for the year 1758, working closely with Anson at the Admiralty, he concentrated the ships of Britain's navy and set the admirals and the captains of his choice on quarter-decks around the world. In Clive, Pitt had a man of the sort he liked: young, dauntless, a wise judge of other men, and, above all, with a vision of empire that kept pace with an ability to attain it. William Pitt not only had ability, he could recognize it.

From the army of the Duke of Cumberland, Pitt picked a well-nurtured young lieutenant colonel, promoted him to major general, and sent him to do the job that Loudoun had neglected. At the age of eighteen, Jeffrey Amherst had entered the army as an ensign of the Foot Guards, but on active service he had quickly risen above the stultifying court ceremonials of his regiment. While in his mid-twenties, Amherst had gone to the staff as aide-de-camp to Lord Ligonier, for whom he carried dispatches on the battlefields of Dettingen and Fontenoy. The Duke of Cumberland had taken Jeffrey Amherst into his military family for the Scottish campaign of 1745, after which the young officer was the duke's protégé, as lieutenant colonel of a battalion of Foot Guards in the Netherlands, a senior aide, a commissariat, and in 1757, a responsible staff officer. Major General Jeffrey Amherst was thin and straight at forty-one. His hair was red and his complexion florid. He kept his chin in, and the long line of his nose made him resemble a ram ready to butt. In 1758 he was ready for an important command.

Having made the selection of a general to go and capture for him the French fortress of Louisbourg, Pitt did not beggar the establishment. Fourteen battalions were put under Amherst's command, together with guns, engineers, and rangers numbering half of a full battalion. More, he gave the newly promoted major general three brigadiers of varied and useful talents. Charles Lawrence, the governor of Nova Scotia, was an old hand in the Maritime Provinces and in Acadia. A regimental colonel, Edward Whitmore, had a bent for administering conquered places. For a fighting general, Pitt gave Amherst the promising thirty-year-old James Wolfe. His hair, too, was red.

To the Army was wedded a fleet of thirty-five naval ships and 120 transports to run the soldiers up the coast from Halifax, to shoot the troops ashore, to bombard and blockade the French citadel and harbor. It was a happy marriage, for the naval commander, Edward Boscawen, was Amherst's personal friend of long standing.

Rear Admiral Sir Charles Hardy opened the Louisbourg campaign of 1758. On 5 April he left Halifax with eight ships of the line and two frigates, to set the blockade of Louisbourg. Since January, when the privateer captain, Doloboratz, made a winter passage from France, no food had come for the French garrison and townspeople, who had lived off the siege stores. Hardy sent the 22-gun *Diane* into Halifax with provisions, clothing, and arms, and he took four provision ships of the spring fleet for Louisbourg. But mostly the British squadron cruised about in the growing warmth of spring, waiting for the arrival of Boscawen and Amherst.

William Pitt had a grand design for the conquest of Canada of which the capture of Louisbourg in 1758 was but a phase, though the most important phase of that year. By seizing the underlip of the mouth of the St. Lawrence, he could hold the jaws open for a plunge up the river gorge of Canada for Quebec in 1759. In 1758 he also planned to seize the French salamander's tail at Fort Duquesne, from which point its lashings struck stinging blows at the colonies bordering the Alleghenies. Simultaneously, a British-Colonial army was finally to take the French forts on Lake Champlain, ready to thrust a bayonet into the commercial heart of Canada at Montreal. The final blow at the St. Lawrence Valley which would destroy New France was timed for 1759.

General John Forbes, a physician turned soldier, was given the task of taking the forks of the Ohio, where Washington and Braddock had failed. Forbes had two battalions of regulars: Colonel Bouquet's Royal Americans and Montgomery's wild Scots from the Highlands. The rest of his army consisted of the colonials who, for four years, had been fighting Indians along the spine of mountains that bordered their homeland.

For the capture of the formidable new French fort at Ticonderoga, James Abercromby was chosen. His merit lay in his on-the-spot seniority and in his accomplishments in administering all the details by which an army moves quickly, eats regularly, and fights efficiently. To balance the quill pen, Abercromby was sent a keen sword. George Augustus, Brigadier General Viscount Howe, a cousin on the left hand to George II, was the bright blade of the expedition against Fort Carillon.

In North America Major General James Abercromby lived, as dictated by his temperament and training, in a very small world circumscribed by high disdain. No mere colonial, with the exception of Sir William Johnson, who had been raised to "respectability" by his baronetcy, was admitted to his circle of familiars. Even the near-royal Lord Howe's ideas were suspect because of the high regard in which he was known to hold Rogers, the ranger savage. Yet, moving only in the little coterie of such very *British* British that made up his official family, Abercromby moved his army of 15,000 men with unprecedented speed and efficiency.

Two months from the time the ice had left the rivers and the mud holes had dried in the cart tracks, Robert Rogers was launching five whaleboats on the desolate shore of Lake George where Fort William Henry had stood. Major Rogers—he had been promoted—had gone to Ticonderoga with fifty men to make maps of the forts and the roads around Ticonderoga for the army, even then moving up from Albany. When he returned, after making his reconnaissance and fighting the French, Lord Howe was moving with the advance guard to reclaim the launching site at the head of Lake George. Standing beside the portage road, the two men talked as the troops marched past, regulars trimmed down for the forest war, colonials untried in European battle craft, gun teams plunging into their collars to crest the slopes, and oxen, with swaying heads and shambling gait, hauling the bateau wagons down the avenue through the trees. As the ranger major and the British lord talked, the road ahead was clear to the French fort where the Marquis de Montcalm awaited their coming.

Since the end of the 1757 campaign, Montcalm's soldiers had been inactive and in trouble. Those scattered in distant hamlets and isolated farms left untended by their officers and sergeants became soft as rotting apples. Those in the cities grew truculent in the near-famine after the poor harvest. In Montreal Le Chevalier de Lévis was forced to put down a near-mutiny, to which his men were incited by the bad types who had come out from France as replacements. In Quebec young officers dissipated their *ennui* and tried their luck in the gambling rooms of the intendant's palace. Montcalm tightened discipline, gambling was stopped, some of the mutineers were sentenced to the royal galleys, others went before a firing squad. Few soldiers saw action in the ten-month period from August '57 to July '58. The patrol activities were carried out for the most part by Indians led by the most hardy of the Canadians, who required no European food. They did well.

In November 1757 a party of 300 descended on the five forts in the German colony of the Palatine, on the Mohawk River. Mayor Johan Jost Petrie surrendered his town to the war whoop. The marines, the Canadians, and the Indians gorged themselves on the stores they found in the houses, which they burned when their hunger was sated and their packs bulging. Systematically they slaughtered the hogs, the cattle, the sheep. Then with 150 prisoners they rode off on a big herd of horses, some of which they were forced to eat on the long march home. The Indians of the

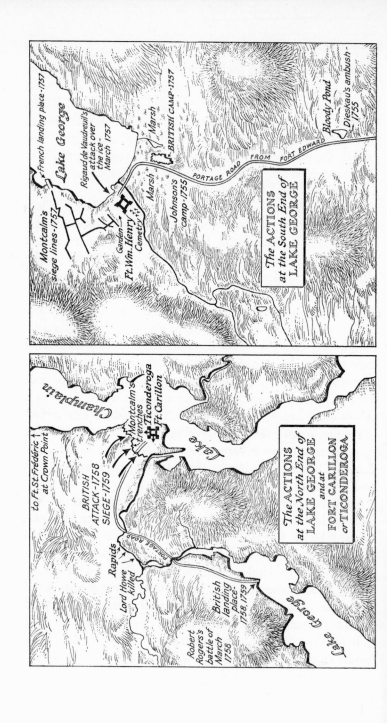

The ACTIONS at the North End of Lake George and at FORT CARILLON or TICONDEROGA

Champlain

to Ft. St. Frédéric at Crown Point

Montcalm's trenches

Ticonderoga

Ft. Carillon

Lake

BRITISH ATTACK -1758
SIEGE -1759

Rapids

Lord Howe killed

PORTAGE ROAD

British landing place
1758, 1759

Robert Rogers's battle of March 1758

Lake George

The ACTIONS at the South End of LAKE GEORGE

French landing place -1757

Lake George

Rigaud de Vaudreuil's attack over the ice - March 1757

Montcalm's siege lines -1757

Garden

Ft. Wm. Henry

Cemetery

Marsh

Marsh

BRITISH CAMP -1757

Johnson's camp -1755

PORTAGE ROAD FROM FORT EDWARD

Bloody Pond

Dieskau's ambush - 1755

Six Nations watched the raid in benign neutrality, and it was an Oneida who told the Canadian commander of all the bateaux that the British in Albany had ordered to be built by spring.

So successful had been the raid on the Palatine and so co-operative were the five westernmost Nations of the Iroquois that Lévis, with Rigaud de Vaudreuil, Longueville, and the Abbé Picquet, planned to take a large force of French and Canadians in the spring of 1758 to scourge the valley of the Mohawk, at least as far as the gates of Schenectady. The chevalier's strike from the west would divert the English from Montcalm's expedition to hold Lake George to its southern limit.

But meanwhile the winter must be lived through. The snow lay deep when Wolf, the German, raided into the lands of Massachusetts. He killed cattle, burned farms, and the Abenaki with him took scalps from the *"Bostonais"* whom they hated. The snow was deep that winter. It fell before and after the January thaw, which put the Hudson River into flood and carried away, among other things, the stockpile of snowshoes stored on the island at Fort Edward. Without snowshoes, a work-party of English near their fort was driven off the trodden path by a raiding force of Indians from Carillon. The Indians, trotting easily on their *racquets*, drove the English till they dropped exhausted, floundering in the thigh-deep snow, then scalped them as they lay gasping. It was a patrol from Carillon that found the British stockpiling goods at Saratoga, well up the road leading from Albany to Fort Edward at the Great Carrying Place.

Captain d'Hebecourt of La Reine commanded at Ticonderoga that winter, with men of his regiment doing guard duty on the stone walls of the fortress. The regulars were alert at Carillon, and at Fort St. Frédéric, for the British rangers were out against them, nagging at the work-parties, pecking at the patrols. There were rumors, too, passed by the captain's mess waiter, that the English might attempt a winter raid on one or the other of the Lake Champlain forts.

One morning at dawn, a single bullock of the meat herd that was kept outside the gate was found wandering about with a note tied to one of its horns. Addressed to Montcalm and signed by Rogers, the note was at once a receipt and a "thank you" for the rest of the herd. The slaughtered carcasses were found later that morning, the choicest steaks cut from the haunch and flank. The ranger's jaunty humor was deemed mere braggadocio by the French, who kept the receipt to collect in kind. Their chance came in mid-March.

The Sieur de Langy de Montegron, most knowing in the art of the "little war," went out to meet Rogers. The two masters of the craft met in the valley behind the bald-faced mountain west of the northern end of Lake George. Each was traveling with a strong advance party—ambush bait—a little way ahead of the main body. Rogers made the first mistake by taking the advance party in flank. When Langy, in turn, attacked with his main force the exposed right flank of the rangers, Rogers fell back, up the slope to where Lieutenant Crofton and Sergeant Phillips had been stationed as a firm base. The Sieur de Langy, running easily on his wide *racquets*, followed his men upward. Rangers were firing from behind trees, then running back to load and fire again. His own men, Canadians and Indians all, were following the English in a like manner of caution starched with determination. Higher up the mountain, stationary firing marked the stand of Crofton and Phillips against the attack being made by the detachment of Indians that the Canadian captain had ordered out to find, engage, and fix their position. Reloading his musket behind a big hemlock tree, Langy came up to the Sieur de la Durantaye. With a hand on the young Irishman's shoulder, the Canadian commander gave his orders to the lieutenant. Pressing rather than charg-

Robert Dinwiddie
Lieutenant Governor of Virginia
1751–58

George Washington
Colonel of the Virginia Regiment
Courtesy of the Museum,
Fort Ticonderoga

General Braddock's
Defeat, 1755

Sir William Johnson
Indian Leader

An Indian Warrior

Sectional Drawing of Fort William Henry

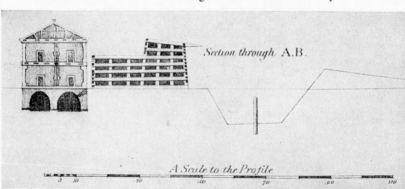

Section through A.B.

A Scale to the Profile

Daniel Hyacinthe de Beaujeu
Officer of La Marine

Chevalier Louis François
St. Luc de la Corne
Indian Leader

Robert Rogers, Major of Rangers

The Earl of Loudoun
Commander in Chief in North America
1756–57

James Abercromby
Commander in Chief in North Ar
1758

A View of Oswego

Courtesy of the Museum, Fort Ticonderoga

ert Monckton, Brigadier General
tenant Governor of Nova Scotia

Edward Boscawen
Vice-Admiral in Command of
the Fleet at Louisbourg
1758

A View of Louisbourg

James Wolfe
Major General in Command of
the Army at Quebec
1759

Charles Saunders
Vice-Admiral in Command of
the Fleet at Quebec
1759

Ruins of Notre Dame des Victoires, Quebec, 1759

Joseph, Marquis de Montcalm
Commander of the Army
in New France
1756–59

Pierre, Marquis de Vaudreuil
Governor General of New France
1755–60

A View of Quebec

Chevalier de Levis
Commander of the Army
in New France

Jeffrey Amherst
Commander in Chief in North A
1759–60

A View of Montreal

ng, La Durantaye and the thirty cadets of the Marine whom
he led worked their way between Rogers and his firm base.

The day was ending when Robert Rogers, coatless,
caught sight of Sergeant Phillips and called out to him. In
response, the sergeant called back that he could not hold out
and would have to surrender. For a few minutes, the two
rangers were forced to turn and fight. When there was another moment of calm they were separated from each other
and darkness was seeping in through the trees. Rogers
turned and shuffled away on his snowshoes. He passed bodies lying crumpled in the snow. The wide bear-paw tracks
led away from him. Once he saw the track of a big dog
running in the waffle-like prints in the blue evening snow.
It could mean only one thing: his New Hampshire neighbor, Captain Stark, had made good his retreat with his wolf
dog, "Sergeant Beaubien." Major Rogers followed, crossing
over the top of the mountain and hurrying on to the rendezvous, set the night before.

The screaming had stopped by the time the Sieur de
Langy reached the place where Sergeant Phillips's party
had made terms of surrender. At the tree trunks, held up by
the bonds that tied them, the tortured, dead rangers sagged,
headless and horrible. Shouting through his cupped hands,
Langy called his men to him. They came out of the dark,
flushed with the killing and carrying their plunder of coats
and belts, guns and knives and tomahawks. Some of them
had the Scottish bonnets favored by Rogers's rangers
crammed onto their heads. One cadet handed Langy an officer's green coat, and the wallet he had found in its inner
pocket. In the flickering light of a torture fire, the Canadian
read the commission, filled out for Captain Robert Rogers
and signed by General Shirley. Somewhere down the slope,
lying in the dark with more than a hundred of his men, the
great Robert Rogers and his legend must be dead. In this
belief, the Canadians cheered and the Indians danced their

joy at the fall of the tallest pine in all the forest. Later, at Carillon, a cooler head decided, "Rogers is killed completely, clothes, coat, and breeches!"

Three weeks after the battle fought on snowshoes, the ice had melted away from the shores of Lake Champlain. Another ten days brought the first flight of homing Canada geese to the open water below the fort. With their coming from the south, Montcalm's white-coated regulars came down from the north to begin the new campaign at Carillon. They wore the fresh uniforms that had come out earlier in the season in the eight supply ships from France. When they set to work, the men laid their new coats carefully on the young grass. With the new white uniforms and the new, bright season their morale was greatly restored. Under the walls of the big stone fortress, their hope for a victorious season against the enemy, now known to be coming against them from the Hudson, seemed sure to be fulfilled.

The Marquis de Montcalm followed Bourlamaque to Carillon on 30 June with the last of the French regiments. Lévis's expedition to the Mohawk River had been canceled, and he was coming with his troops to stand with his general against the British. Montcalm knew now, at the end of June, that the bateaux and the stores reported to him during the winter were for an expedition against Ticonderoga. He knew, too, that General Abercromby had moved north with unaccustomed and incredible speed. The English had eight battalions rated as regulars and ten battalions of colonials under their General Lyman, who was so familiar on the northern frontier. A siege train of artillery was coming, and, from the deck of a new schooner, *Halifax*, a captain in the navy commanded the escort boats. On the last day of June, the British invasion was imminent. A lieutenant of the Marine who had gone to Fort Edward under a truce had not returned, nor would he, now that he had seen so much.

To meet Abercromby's army, generously estimated by the French at 25,000, Montcalm had his fort and the six battalions of veterans. To these were added two weak battalions of the regiment of Berry that had arrived in Canada late in 1757. No new regiments had come to Montcalm in 1758, because the Marquise de Pompadour was so engrossed with her Prussian war that she could spare neither thought nor soldiers for a distant colony. When Lévis arrived with his regulars, and the Marine and the Canadians, Montcalm could expect 6000 bayonets in his battle line—each with a stout heart behind it.

By 5 July, Montcalm knew that the British in 1000 boats were coming down Lake George. Langy had seen them embarking at the head of the lake. The French regulars were stationed in depth from the landing at the southern end of Lake George to the bridge at the sawmill on the river that connected the two lakes. On the high ground west of Fort Carillon, the French engineers were driving the stakes to outline fieldworks at a distance but protected by the guns of the fort. There was a chance that the British would land a force down Lake George on the west shore to follow the long valley behind the bald-faced mountain, in a move to catch the echelon of French regiments in the flank or rear. To guard this approach, the Sieur Trepezec, a captain of Béarn, was sent with 350 good men. In the deep, trackless forest he marched over the ground still strewn with the pathetic remnants of the battle on snowshoes. Trepezec spent the night of 5 July bivouacked in the haunted woods.

On 6 July the British landed unopposed on the west shore, across the water from the French forward line of battle. Before they could deploy, Bourlamaque drew back his regiments on Montcalm at the mill. Together they burned the mill bridge and climbed the portage road to the heights of Carillon, where the 2nd battalion of Berry was digging at the line of fieldworks.

Earlier that morning, when it became apparent that the enemy would land in mass, rather than in detail, Trepezec's force was called back. The captain from Béarn, alone and without guides, found the mesh of tree trunks confusing, the folds of the hills baffling, and the summer-dry brooks appearing to lead nowhere. For twelve hours the woods held him, until, skirting a thick tangle of cedar swamp, he saw men moving at right angles to his path. The men saw him, too, but they recognized him as an enemy first. Men clad in green and brown opened fire, and Trepezec's tired soldiers began to fall. The French were rushing forward when Trepezec was hit. He stumbled, struck the trunk of a tree, and fell. He was aware of a British officer of very high rank trying to rein in a plunging horse. Someone helped him to his feet and with an arm around his waist half-carried him off through the woods. Before Trepezec died, he was told that the horseman was General Howe and that he had been shot dead, whereupon the British column had run away. Of the French force, half were missing.

All the day of 7 July the British-Colonial army wandered in indecision through the woods on the left bank of the stream between Lake George and Lake Champlain. Many of them saw the place where General Howe had died and where a part of the army's soul had died with him. General Abercromby spent the day in lonely command. Having brought the army to its destination, the man he relied upon had left him. Sir William Johnson, the baronet with his strange following of Mohawks, had not come up as yet. General Abercromby could turn to him for guidance in this terrible, alien wilderness. Close to Abercromby, wrapping him round in a cocoon of young English gentlemen, were his staff. One of them, claiming knowledge of engineering, had climbed a mountain and looked down on 3000 Frenchmen preparing their fieldworks: a ragged fence of logs, the engineer reported, easily carried by assault. There was no need to bring up the guns. On this report, Abercromby based his decision. With his 15,000 men as gillies, he would flush the French from behind their rail fence like partridge from the bracken on a Yorkshire moor.

All that day the French worked at their trenches. From the ditch that they dug in front, they threw back dirt, mounding it into a parapet. Logs and branches held the loose earth in place. In the ditch and in front of it they made an abatis of tangled branches. Beyond, the ground was open for 100 yards to the trees. By nightfall the French works crowned the highest ground, open like a chaplet to the rear. On the French left, below a steep escarpment, a redoubt with cannon was built on the shore. On the right a hedge of abatis trailed off through the woods on the low ground there. At five o'clock, permission was given for the men to boil their soup. While they were eating it, Lévis's men were arriving at the shore. Proudly they marched along the line of campfires, to taunts of the regulars, for having come too late to dig. Montcalm was assured that Lévis himself would arrive before morning.

The Chevalier de Lévis was shaken awake by the Indian paddling in the stern of his canoe. First light streaked the eastern mountaintops and, looming ahead on its high hill, seen now through a wide avenue of trees stood Fort Carillon. Along the line of soldiers at work on their defenses spread word of the chevalier's arrival. He would command on the right hand of General Montcalm, while Bourlamaque, the old dragoon, would command the left of the works.

At half-past noon the British came, climbing up the hill from the sawmill, deploying onto the heights. Behind their earth-and-log wall the French could see the red-coated regulars forming up at the edge of the forest, where the trees were thin and they had cut the underbrush for the abatis.

Though, like the others of his regiment, he had laid aside

his blue regimental coat, the shoulders of John Brainerd's red waistcoat were dark with sweat when he broke over the rise onto the heights of Ticonderoga. Colonel Johnston, at the head of the reconstituted Jersey "Blues," had set a fast pace all the way from the sawmill. Brainerd had been forced to jogtrot the whole way in the hot July sun.

On the flat ground the always-ill-tempered sergeants of the king's regulars were shouting and shoving at their men to get them into columns of march. The king's officers stood negligently by, talking with each other as they passed around their flasks. They did not deign to look at the colonial regiment crossing behind them. The "Blues" passed by the rear of two columns of regulars, then made a right turn into line. The officers were shaking the companies into loose lines of skirmishers. Two more columns of regulars were forming up beyond the gap, now filling with the Jersey men. At the head of the farthest column, at the left of the battle line, Brainerd could hear the din of the squealing bagpipes, lashing up a fury there.

They were walking east now, and Brainerd, imitating the man on his left, checked the prime in his musket and seated his bayonet firmly on the muzzle. In the direction he was going, the bright sunlight of meadowland showed beyond the trees. John Brainerd was walking toward the sound of muskets firing.

It was not until he was about to leave the woods that John Brainerd of New Jersey saw the enemy in his lines, which had been said to be no stronger or higher than the partially raised walls of a cattle shed. Now he saw them as a formidable wall, rising nine or ten feet above the plain. He saw the stakes and tangle of the abatis. Straight in front of him, the point of one of the angles shoved out toward him, like the front of a tricorne hat, and, like a hat of olden times, the prow in front of him was edged with a fringe of white-smoke feathers for all its angular length. Brainerd could see, without comprehending, the heads and shoulders and arms of Frenchmen as they rose up from behind the wall to fire at the men, like him, walking across the meadow.

Men were falling in the meadow now. They were rangers and men of Gage's light infantry, and New Jersey men too. Running, John Brainerd saw a big pine log. There were men behind it and he ran until he too could throw himself down beside them. He jostled the arm of a light infantry-man, pouring powder into the open pan of his lock, and the man swore vilely at him. The men behind the log were calmly firing at the enemy, then reloading. Calm again himself, John Brainerd followed suit and saw that all over the meadow, from behind stumps and bushes and out of little hollows in the ground, men were firing at the hats that showed for a moment above the French lines about 100 yards away. The man whose arm he had joggled told him to fire to his right front, where an angle in the wall and a rise in the ground would give him an enfilading shot. When he rose to shoot, he could glimpse through the smoke the Frenchmen, loading and shooting from behind their barrier. John Brainerd settled down to work.

On the British right, drums began to beat and the two columns the Jersey men had passed moved forward out of the trees. The firing line in the meadow slowed their rate of fire to watch in awe the tight red ranks, trudging out across the sunlit plain, the haughty little officers walking stiffly beside their men, the silly little swords they affected shiny at their shoulders. The men in the meadow turned again to their firing, aiming fast and loading fast—anything to help those proud columns forward to their goal.

The nearest column was at the abatis, a clawing mass of red-coated men struggling to get through. Some succeeded and a few men were scrambling to climb the wall of earth and logs and branches beyond. But they didn't, they couldn't, and reluctantly, sadly, the whole column gave

way. When they had gone, their coming and their going
was marked by a red ribbon of honored dead.

There were casualties among the marksmen, too. John
Brainerd saw John Hendrickson of his regiment running
wildly to the rear, clutching at his throat with fingers over
which the blood seeped. It had been John who shot the
wounded and imploring Frenchman full in the face during
the woods fight when Lord Howe was killed. On the pungent smell of powder-smoke, obscuring fact but bearing
rumor, Brainerd heard that Lieutenant Colonel Shaw of
Amboy was lying dead, and that further off, the regulars
were attacking again. Rumor had it, too, that the colonials,
New Englanders and Yorkers, were rushing forward with
them, forged by the flame of battle into one will of tem-
pered steel and angry purpose.

On the French right, the Highlanders were attacking to
their wild music, with DeLancey's New Yorkers behind a
screen of Rogers's rangers and Bradstreet's bateaumen. The
Chevalier de Lévis was there with Béarn and La Reine. In
fine order, Lévis's soldiers, three deep at the breastwork,
stood silently waiting. Rank by rank they stepped up and
fired into the skirted men surging forward to engulf them.
Lévis called up his reserve of grenadiers and the first attack of the Highlanders fell back. But they only receded,
closed their ranks to fill the many gaps, and came on again,
sliding around to the right of the French wall to bring the
regiment of Guyenne under attack. From the center, where
Montcalm commanded, Bougainville came running over to
inquire if the chevalier held. By then the Marine, in the low
ground on the right, had moved in front of their abatis to
fire into the flank of the attacking columns, a mixture now
of big Scots, rangers, bateaumen, and Yorkers. When Bougainville returned to his general with word from Lévis
that all went well with his men, the aide was hatless and was
holding a soiled handkerchief to a deep cut in his head. As

Bougainville gave his report, a surgeon dressed the wound.

On Montcalm's front, the Royal Roussillon and the 1st Berry had been attacked, initially by the Royal Americans. But as the grim afternoon wore on, that column had joined with the Scots to storm the slope where La Guyenne held the right-flank angles of the line.

It was after five o'clock, and the first British column had come in shortly after noon. About four o'clock, Colonel Bourlamaque had received a dangerous wound. Montcalm had gone to him at once, appraised the situation, and had sent the colonel back, leaving that end of the line to the commanders of La Sarre and Languedoc. They would be able to hold the little surges made by the exhausted and frustrated British troops, still licking at the left of the French line. Before returning to his command post in the center, Montcalm looked down from the escarpment to his redoubt on the shore. Earlier their guns, backed up by the guns from the fort, had turned back a British sortie by water, bent on turning the flank.

By five o'clock the fury besetting Lévis's front was also subsiding. The constant, deadly fire of the marksmen still probed in behind the too-hastily constructed angles of the French lines. Montcalm counted his casualties and found them heavy in proportion to his small force. A few Frenchmen went forward into their ditch and the abatis, looking for prisoners. The rest waited on their arms for the valiant enemy's last grand charge.

The final attack against the Royal Roussillon came within an hour. The remaining Highlanders with the Royal Americans were in the van, but the orderly flame of discipline had been extinguished. It was a searing flash of anger that drove the British up to the abatis in the face of the steady French musket fire. The strength was gone from the fury. Fatigue had withered the core of determination. Imagination took charge of tired minds. The British regulars fell back across

the meadow, stumbling over no visible object, tripping over
their own new dead and those dead who had lain there during the endless hours of the long, sunny afternoon. The colonial marksmen left their firing positions, running back to
the deep shelter of the woods, empty powder horns flapping
lightly at their backs as they ran. At the edge of the wood,
rangers and light infantry kept up a desultory fire on the
inert, immovable, indestructible creature that the French
lines at Ticonderoga had become.

Abercromby did not return to the fight next day, nor did
Montcalm pursue his beaten enemy. Both sides had taken
heavy casualties, nearly equal in proportion to the respective numbers engaged. But the British 15,000 had been humbled in their numbers, and after the headlong retreat which
did not stop until it reached the far end of Lake George,
they were shamed. The 3000 French, slightly bewildered
by their stand in the face of such acknowledged and re-
spected bravery, humbly dedicated their victory to God.
As at Oswego, the Abbé Picquet raised a great cross of
wood. In the rising and the setting sun its shadowy arms
fell long, across the grave pits both within and without the
French lines. God was the victor, but the French did not
forget their hero of the day. On posts set beside the cross
they wittily praised, in Latin, their "leader," and caused
praise for his "foot soldiers" to be inscribed there also.

After Ticonderoga, Major General James Abercromby
quietly disappeared down the dim gallery of quiet disgrace
where walked his predecessors in command in North America. But Abercromby had carried out his campaign in good
order and good time, something the others had not done.
James Abercromby was a good groom who had brought his
horse in fine fettle to the course; he lacked the hands, the
seat, the grip of the jockey to lift his mount over the impos-

sible hurdle. Lord Howe, the jockey, had fallen at the starting line.

General Montcalm sought for himself in success the same obscurity that failure had thrust upon his opponent. He entreated the minister of war for permission to return to his estates, to his waiting wife, to his children. After three campaigns in New France, the Marquis de Montcalm had had enough of the Marquis de Vaudreuil.

Because of the governor general's hostile jealousy, the army's great defeat of the English on 8 July had been a desperate thing, an act of God, as the cross over the battlefield acknowledged. The voice of the army, speaking out to the very margin of treason, accused Vaudreuil of willfully attempting to destroy the army—which had only been saved by a miracle. In the spring of 1758, the army of France in North America stood alone, unsupported by Canada, ignored by Canada's governor, bound only by duty to the king and loyalty to its general to stand against an overwhelming enemy.

Not only had the governor abandoned Montcalm at Carillon, but he had weakened him. From the army, Vaudreuil had detached the Chevalier de Lévis and the pick of the companies from the various regiments. These were to bolster the force being sent to raid and pillage from the neutral Iroquois lands on the Mohawk River. It was not unnoticed by the disgruntled army officers that Rigaud de Vaudreuil was in command of the Mohawk expedition, still seeking a victory on which his brother could build a military reputation for the family.

Vaudreuil had left Montcalm without the piercing eyes of Indians to search the forest south of Carillon, and too few of the rangers had been assigned for duty to Montcalm. It was for want of guides that Trepezec had become lost and most of his detachment wasted.

Further, the army officers blamed the governor general
for not calling out the Canadian militia in strength com-
mensurate with the ominous situation existing that spring.
To muster them meant to feed them, and Monsieur Bigot
could not find in his granaries the food to supply both the
militiamen and his own greedy sycophants.

Only at the very last minute had Lévis broken away from
the governor's court at Montreal to hasten to his general's
right hand. He brought with him the detached companies
of the regiments, and he also brought 400 men of the Marine, finally released to Montcalm. After-battle gossip gave a
poor account of the courage of the Marine during the action on the French right flank, but Montcalm gave them
much praise in his official report. Not to have done so would
only have added fuel to the army-navy rivalry existing in
New France.

Montcalm wanted to go home to France—to Candiac,
where the soft air of summer drifted gently up from the
Mediterranean Sea. It was hot on the Ticonderoga Peninsula. The lake shimmered under the sun. Into the same glorious sunlight under which the army's great victory had been
won, Vaudreuil sent his brother to bask. The Canadian militia, now unnecessary and unwelcome, came up the lake,
2000 hungry men, to encamp untidily underfoot. Six hundred Indians came tardily to voice their protestations of loyalty and to claim their right to gifts in return for the brave
deeds that they might have done.

There was talk by the newcomers of going to Fort Edward. That talk came from Montreal, where the governor's
court loudly praised Vaudreuil for his victory, and the war
map of the Hudson Valley lay unrolled on the viceregal
desk. In letter after letter, Vaudreuil urged Montcalm to
follow the beaten enemy down to the British forts below.
But the general knew the impossibility of such an action.
The French army had been pummeled; he lacked boats in

sufficient number, the food was in short supply, and no one who had not stood in the French lines that July day could know the courage or the numbers of the enemy, now pausing to catch their breath.

The steeple bells tolled the peals of victory through the busy streets of Montreal. At Ticonderoga, the carillon was in the sound of the water, rushing over the falls from Lake George. In the spring and early summer the water bells rang clear and strong. Montcalm's battle for Fort Carillon came at the height of Canada's summer, after which the green season for New France entered upon its decline.

XIV

Frontenac on the Lake, Louisbourg by the Sea

John Bradstreet was a bateau man. In the ugly, flat-bottomed boat that was the dray of North America's inland waters, Captain Bradstreet of the old 51st Foot rode to distinction as a soldier. In the period between 1755, when he took his first supply convoy up the Mohawk to Oswego, and 1758, he had regulated the water transport service and he had regimented the free and skilled agents of the rivers into the proud band of Bradstreet's bateaumen.

In almost 1000 of his craft, each with a bateauman at the steering oar, Abercromby's army had traversed Lake George. Bateaux had carried the whipped army back again, with the wounded cradled in damp straw on the thin board bottom while the bateauman plied his bailing scoop and the oars squeaked in the thole pins.

Lieutenant Colonel John Bradstreet, deputy quartermaster general to General Abercromby, did not himself wait long at the launch site by the ruins of Fort William Henry, amid the wreckage of the beaten, angry army. His own plans, sanctioned and approved by the commander in chief in North America, were pointed up the Mohawk River to the west. On the bank of that river, ranged neatly in rows, another fleet of bateaux lay ready to his purpose. Dutch bateaumen smoked their long pipes and waited for Bradstreet, coming down from the north. Many were old hands who knew the river road to lost Oswego. Now they were waiting for their old commander to take them out onto Lake Ontario and the French fort, Frontenac.

There were overturned Indian canoes on the river bank by Johnson's stone fort-house when Bradstreet's flotilla worked its way by. They belonged to the chiefs, the agents, the spies, and the connivers, who came to see the great man of politics. Beyond lay the wasted lands of the Palatine towns, and above, where Fort Bull guarded the portage landing, new walls were rising to mark Britain's return for revenge. Here the bateaux came ashore, and tall John Bradstreet strode down the planks of the unloading dock to meet old Colonel John Stanwix of the Royal Americans, and builder of the fort. From his colonel—Bradstreet's permanent rank was that of captain in the Royal Americans—he was to pick up the troops for his Frontenac expedition. He found Stanwix willing and the troops eager. In the hot sun of August it is back-breaking work to worry the big logs into position atop the ever higher walls.

It was hard work, too, that the soldiers found awaiting them at the other end of the portage road from Fort Stanwix. There Wood Creek was choked by debris left by the timid General Webb in his retreat. Bradstreet's men cleared it for Bradstreet's bateaux. Out on Lake Oneida, the journey was a pleasant cruise and in the summer season the river beyond was a lazy ride down to Lake Ontario.

On the site of the old Oswego forts under Montcalm's victory cross, the British army now mustered. There were 3000 men, all, but for a handful of British gunners and Highlanders, North American men. Except for the Scots, the 135 regulars were Royal Americans, and Bradstreet, too, had counted himself an American for the past thirteen years. The rest of the force consisted for the most part of

Yorkers, soldiers of Charles Clinton's and Isaac Corsa's regiments from the populous land down the Hudson and from Long Island. There were watermen among them, as there were in the companies of Rhode Islanders, Bostonians, and troops from Jersey, so Bradstreet's 300 bateaumen had seamen at hand to help them when, out on the big lake, the setting poles lost bottom and the jury mast needed staying. Neither Bradstreet nor his officers noticed the change of loyalty in Red Head, the Onondaga chief whose young warriors paddled their canoes on the flank of the bateaux line.

Four scouting Mississaquas discovered the English as they entered Famine Bay. In the woods they ran down and killed two of Bradstreet's rangers. At a cold campfire they picked up two crumpled bits of discarded paper. One of these was a rich find: smoothed out and carefully cleaned off, it told the commander at Fort Frontenac that Bradstreet's force, as of 11 August, tallied 2737 English. Monsieur de Noyan paraded his 110 Frenchmen and set his fort in order for an attack.

For Monsieur Payan de Noyan, the command of Fort Frontenac was the final act of grace at the sunset of a long, faithful career of service. In the rambling stone fort that handled all supplies going to the western posts, a courteous and honorable old man could acquire a modest competence for his retirement. While an attack by the British had not been foreseen, Noyan's philosophy did not permit an admission of fear. Quickly he sent the soiled general orders to Vaudreuil, with a request for aid. He then prepared to meet Bradstreet's attack. There was humor in his situation, and in his infirm little walks on the curtain wall he made the most of it with his companions, the charming Mesdames Duvivier and Barollon.

On 25 August, Noyan could point out to the ladies the

sails of the British boats close in to shore. On the night of the 26th, they woke the old man to listen to the digging-in of a battery. Before going back to bed, he ordered his mortars to annoy the diggers. Throughout the night bombardment, Colonel Corsa and his Long Island men kept at their work. At dawn on the 27th, the battery was emplaced and firing, nor was it long before the round shot had made a breach. It was time for Monsieur de Noyan to save his small garrison by surrender. Through the wide-open gates of Fort Frontenac, Lieutenant Colonel John Bradstreet walked into a treasure trove. The warehouses were filled with the concentration of matériel needed to see the western forts through the coming winter. Seventy-six cannon, mounted and unmounted, were listed by the blue-coated British gunners making their check lists of the ordnance stores. Some of these pieces belonged to the seven unrigged vessels in the builder's yard. Bradstreet had himself rowed out to the two full-rigged vessels lying at anchor. He had last seen them two summers before, flying British colors at Oswego. Now British colors flew again, and one of the vessels was fully laden with a rich cargo of stinking peltry, £30,000 of beautiful furs.

As the British sailed away, they estimated that they had destroyed £800,000 of French matériel and stores. They had, of course, done more: they had wrecked the fort and destroyed the French shipping, and out along the fort lines to the source of the Great Lakes and on the Ohio post commanders would not be able to feed their men nor hold their Indians with gifts and bounty. Indians from all the Nations had been trading at Frontenac when the bateaux appeared. They had moved away a little distance when cannon answered cannon. They had seen the French father-king's great fortress fall. Since 1672, the place had borne the mighty name of Governor Frontenac, who bound the In-

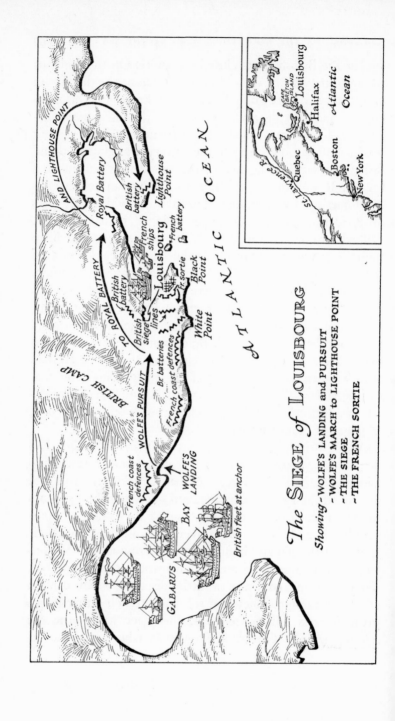

The Siege of Louisbourg

Showing—WOLFE'S LANDING and PURSUIT
~WOLFE'S MARCH to LIGHTHOUSE POINT
~THE SIEGE
~THE FRENCH SORTIE

dian flint to the shaft of New France to make the Canadian arrow. At Fort Frontenac Colonel Bradstreet had severed the old, weakened cords.

August was a month of changing moods where men waited for the news of war. In London, the bonfires set alight for Amherst, whom the couriers said had captured Louisbourg, were allowed to die out when the criers shouted of Ticonderoga, Abercromby, and defeat. In Montreal, the bells that rang for Carillon and Montcalm, called, too late, the rally to save Frontenac. Ten thousand Britons faced Montcalm's forces across Lake George, and rumor followed rumor from Louisbourg where fourteen British regiments were on shore.

The battle for the fortress harbor of Louisbourg began across the North Atlantic, where the seaman's landfall is the coast of France. In the winter of 1758, Admiral Sir Edward Hawke—"courage was his cargo"—kept the Atlantic coast with England's channel fleet. In the Mediterranean, Sir Henry Osborne guarded against the French fleet forcing the Straits of Gibraltar.

In February Admiral de la Clue made his move to take the Toulon fleet to Louisbourg. With his own ships he was safe from harm in the neutral port of Cartagena in southern Spain. He waited only for the coming of Admiral Duquesne's squadron from Toulon; together, they could brush the British aside, to sail free out into the Atlantic. Osborne boldly sailed away from Gibraltar on a west wind to prevent this meeting. The last day of the month Sir Henry sighted Duquesne's sails approaching Cartagena, and while he kept La Clue pinned in the harbor, he detached a squadron to engage the French ships from Toulon.

Early in the action, Duquesne lost two of his squadron, one a prize, the other driven onto the Spanish shore. To

save his own 80-gun *Foudroyant*, Duquesne sheered off
downwind into the open sea. Captain Arthur Gardner, once
post captain to the sacrificed Admiral Byng, turned his 64-
gun *Monmouth* in pursuit. At four in the afternoon, his
hands shading his eyes against the sun, Admiral Duquesne
judged *Monmouth* to have closed within range of *Foudroyant's* long stern chasers. He gave the captain his consent
to begin the fire. Though hit, Gardner came on, closing
fast as his bow guns accepted as a challenge the big Frenchman's warning. Gardner died at dusk on his quarter-deck,
which was by that time reduced to a shambles. Standing
where his captain had stood, First Lieutenant Carkett
pressed on the unequal attack into the dark barrel of the
night. Slowly and more slowly, the two hard-hit ships
moved on and on as the watch bells tolled the hours and
half-hours to midnight. By one o'clock in the morning
neither *Foudroyant* nor *Monmouth* was making any headway. Both lay helplessly rolling in the trough of the swell,
masts broken, sails and rigging trailing overboard, guns all
but silent. They lay thus together in the dark, a shout apart,
telling each other by the futile popping of cannon that they
yet fought on. When two more British ships came nosing
up through the night, *Foudroyant* gave in. In recognition
of a gallant foe she struck her colors to *Monmouth*.

The Marquis de Duquesne de Menneville did not, that
year or ever again, return to the New France he had once
governed, where his name still lived on the fort at the forks
of the Ohio. Nor did La Clue get to Louisbourg with his
fleet of warships. The Strait of Gibraltar was kept closed
by Sir Henry Osborne.

In March spies told Pitt in his chancery that the Rochefort fleet—cargo vessels, troop ships, and naval escort—was
ready to sail. Pitt told Admiral Anson at the Admiralty,
and a dispatch boat located Hawke in the Channel and told
him to mind the Bay of Biscay. Hawke found the French

convoy forming in the Basque roads and took his fleet right in. Like hens in a barnyard, the French ships scattered, running for the shallows close to shore. Hawke did not follow them, but in the morning when the tide was low, the prospect through the admiral's glass was of the entire French fleet aground. "Many were on their broadsides," he was able to write to Anson.

The Rochefort fleet did not go to Louisbourg. One French fleet did slip out past the British blockade that spring of 1758. It took an east wind out of Brest while the watch frigates were riding offshore north of the island of Ushant, and it got away unmolested.

Beaussier de L'isle's fleet from Brest (it was the veteran "*bleu*" Commodore come again to Louisbourg) arrived on 28 March. There were five ships-of-war, but three had their guns unshipped and were freighted and loaded with stores and troops. The latter were big, surly men, brutish, sullen, and discontented, regimented as Foreign Volunteers. They came from the Swiss cantons and the backwashes of the King of Prussia's war. They themselves called their volunteering "trepanning." Up through the snowy slush of the streets they marched, 525 strong, carrying their own sick with them from the wet, cold wooden hulls to the freezing damp of chill stone barracks. "The Foreigners" brought yet another wrangling faction to the colonial garrison town, isolated behind its deep walls set tenuously on the edge of a continent between a bleak ocean and a fearful forest mass.

Louisbourg was decreed, the site selected, and the place built as a scabbard for France's naval sword in North America, but, despite its formidable appearance, it was, in reality, little more than a sham. In principle, Louisbourg was under the navy department as an overseas base. But as a colony it was a remote appendage to the administrative territory of the governor of New France. The latter ig-

nored it, and since Acadia and Beauséjour had fallen in
1754, the Marquis de Vaudreuil had only the most casual
contact with his adjunct charge. Not so with Monsieur
Bigot, the intendant, who had a sentimental attachment to
every stone in the long walls of the fortress of Louisbourg.
Louisbourg had been the first charge of Bigot, then a new
young intendant, and his first golden opportunity to get
graft. Bigot had left the new walls of the king's great citadel, already beginning to crumble, to go to Montreal, where
he was to regulate the affairs of all New France. For the
furs of a continent, Bigot left the fisheries of the coast, retaining only the modest gratitude of the heir whom he had
designated to succeed him in the town. In 1758, one Prévost
was Bigot's *commissaire-ordinaire* at Louisbourg. Prévost
was a thoroughly detestable man, whom the military services reviled and snubbed, but who had become progres-
sively more indispensable to Governor Drucour.

A fair man and a brave man, the Chevalier Augustin de
Drucour had come to his governorship in 1754, the year
that the war began on the Ohio. By tact and precept con-
scientiously applied, Drucour kept his town steadfast
through the years of semi-starvation from the British blockade and resolved to stand firm against the annual threat of
invasion. By nature and concept, Louisbourg was ever a
garrison town, filled with a curdling concoction of civil
and military antipathies, laced with inter-service and intra-
service rivalry, constantly simmering just under a fast boil.
In his attempts to stir the mess smooth, the governor was
greatly aided by the motherly charm of his wife. To their
table came the naval officers, the gentlemen, and the near-
gentlemen. The regular soldiers of the regiments of Artois
and Bourgogne supped with the Marine on one side and on
the other a gunner with proprietary claims to Louisbourg,
as his Royal Corps was created there to man its citadel.
The ineffectual Acadian leader Boishébert came often to

dine at the governor's palace, while his ragged force of rangers indolently licked their fingers in a smoky Indian camp at Mira, fifteen miles away. In the salon, Madame Drucour patted down the rumpled ladies with a gentle but firm hand, while the gentlemen sipped their brandy in the hall under the perceptive eyes of the patient chevalier.

A shipyard sailor, Drucour faced the invasion storm of 1758 with no experience as a "guns and guts" fighting man, nor any flair for the craftiness of strategy or the cunning of tactics. Twice during the winter, the ministry in France had tried to send out a military commander to shore up the defenses of the chevalier's fortress town. Duquesne's commission to Louisbourg had been nullified by the guns of *Monmouth*, and the Chevalier Blenac de Courbon had saved the ship entrusted to him, running the blockade back into Brest in preference to the one he glimpsed at Louisbourg. Finally, on 30 May, Mathieu Henri Marchant de la Houlière arrived at Louisbourg and was presented to the land forces as their commander in chief. Though La Houlière was a veteran of nine sieges, he was now too ill actively to influence his tenth. In this he shared the predicament of the only other military director in Louisbourg in 1758. Though Engineer Franquet did bolster the crumbling walls with fascines and such other material as he could get from the niggardly Prévost, that officer, in addition to a crippling case of gout, had a propensity for getting himself wounded. So it was that Drucour, alone on top of the heap, faced the invasion, with only his wife's courage showing in her heroism at his side.

On the day that the haggard La Houlière had assumed nominal command, word came from Fort Dauphin, in the north, that the regiment of Cambis had arrived and was marching overland to Louisbourg. The next day, the British fleet entered Gabarus Bay, six miles west of Louisbourg, and anchored there.

For a week, high seas pounded the black rock coast and pebbled bays chosen by Admiral Boscawen to set the British troops ashore. For a week, the soldiers rotted in confined inaction on the pitching, rolling decks of the transports. Green-faced officers peered each morning into the bitter-tasting fog, until the white line of surf showed through. No landing possible that day. Sitting in the lee of the un-launched landing boats, the officers turned to read again the operation orders for their longed-for amphibious land-ing. There was solace in the fact that light artillery was go-ing in with the first wave, and that rescue boats were laid on, with the boats from the hospital ship to take off the wounded. Bayonets would not be fixed until the men were on the beach. Again they read the paramount order of the landing: "Assault off the beach at once; leave the beach clear for the naval beach master to bring in the second wave of infantry, and make room for the guns to get ashore."

In the 90-gun *Namur* Boscawen waited out the weather with his soldier-guest and friend, Major General Amherst, who had only joined his command at sea. He had made an unusually slow passage out from England, and Boscawen, himself late for the Halifax rendezvous, had dared wait no longer.

James Cunningham of General Abercromby's staff, who had come up from New York with the regiments which had wintered there, saw the embarkation of troops in deep harbor at Halifax. On the day that the great fleet sailed for Louisbourg, Cunningham left aboard a frigate with dis-patches for London. Clearing the harbor, the frigate met the 74-gun *Dublin* inbound with General Amherst on her quarter-deck, cloaked, packed, and ready to disembark. On board the man-of-war might be the longed-for orders that would reassign Cunningham to the army bound for Louis-bourg. But there was no hail from *Dublin*, and the frigate passed her by. So James Cunningham went back to England, and Jeffrey Amherst arrived in Halifax just in time.

The logbooks of the British fleet in Gabarus Bay marked down the weather for 4, 5, and 6 June as "a hard gale—foggy," "very foggy—a great surf," "rain, fog, high surf on the landing beaches." On 7 June the fog lifted. In the admiral's cabin on *Namur*, Boscawen and Amherst concurred that the landing would go in on the morning of the 8th.

The seven frigates with the bombardment role were under sail when the sun went down. In the early hours of the night they took up their stations, in three divisions, along the four-mile stretch of coast from White Point, a mile and a half from Louisbourg, to Coromandière Cove. By one o'clock, the landing craft were nested under the signal lanterns hung from the main-yards of those vessels marked as rallying points for the three wings of the army. There remained three hours of darkness when the boats moved out for the long row to the frigates and the beaches beyond. Brigadier Whitmore led the right wing, bound for White Point; Lawrence held the center. In a little rowing boat on the left wing, under his division flag of red, red-headed James Wolfe sat wrapped in a gray-hooded cloak. His health seemed better now that action was imminent. The first, faint light of dawn showed the beaches under the bluffs behind Coromandière Bay. A rocky islet was black in the water to the left. Close behind Brigadier Wolfe crowded the longboats, each one packed tight with the grenadiers of the first assault force. From the shore, a French cannon boomed; it was still too dark to mark the fall of its shot in the water. Wolfe's division rowed on into the cove.

For the seven days that the British fleet lay in Gabarus Bay, the French soldiers manned the earthworks covering the beaches from White Point to Coromandière Bay. The positions had been dug the year before to turn back Loudoun when he came to that only stretch of shore on which invaders could land. For seven days, the French soldiers watched in the fog and the rain and the wind. Beyond the pounding surf, which was their surest defense, they saw the frigates come in close to shore, and they looked at the picket boats, taking soundings where the gray seals sported in the swell.

On the 7th, the soldiers of Artois heard hammering out in the thick fog: it was the ship carpenters mending a rudder. They got a brief sight of two British boats reconnoitering the shore—Wolfe was in one boat, Commodore Durell in the other. On shore the regiment of Artois's positions looked down from cliffs fifteen to twenty feet high to the beaches of Coromandière Cove. Lieutenant Colonel de St. Julien, commanding there, watched the sailors bring up a 24-pounder over the rough, swampy track from Louisbourg, and, with the gunners, sight the big cannon on the bay.

St. Julien and his 1000 men were alert at dawn on the 8th, and saw Wolfe's boats in the water coming on like a wave from the sea. The first cannon shot was fired at hazard into the still, lowery darkness. Soon the daylight came, and the four 6-pounders kept the invasion boats at a distance. Beyond the boats, the two British frigates opened with their broadsides. From Coromandière Cove, St. Julien could hear the broadsides of other frigates, eastward along the coast, where Marin, the colonel of Bourgogne, held his stretch of shore and D'Anthonay lay beyond with the Foreign Volunteers.

After fifteen minutes the broadsides stopped, and the longboats made their dash for the beaches. The men of Artois held their fire. In the boats they could see the tall mitre hats of the British Grenadiers and knew that the best of the enemy was coming against their beaches. When the order came to fire, the Frenchmen's targets were the white faces of English soldiers and the broad backs of the sailors, hunched, tugging rhythmically at the long oars. Beyond the breaking surf in the last surges of the Atlantic swell, the landing boats hesitated and fell back under a cross-fire of cannon hail and a beating rain of musket balls. The British boat line was in confusion as the sailors backed their oars and attempted to turn, and the soldiers moved restlessly or sought a resting place for a wounded comrade. Into the welter dashed the little rowing boat with the big red flag, unmindful of the cannon shot that splashed at the tip of the swinging oars. Quite suddenly, or so it appeared to St. Julien, posted at the center of the French line, the little command boat bore off to the east, and one by one the big troop carriers, recovering themselves, turned to follow.

James Wolfe had seen that one of the longboats, at the extreme right of his command where it overlapped the cove, was in among the rocks. At first he could not be sure whether the boat had actually landed, been holed and beached herself, or had been carried in by the current and the surf. But when a second boat from the right-hand flight dove in through the breakers, Wolfe knew that his men had found their way ashore.

Wolfe had let his big boat-cloak drop while he crouched in the bow waiting for the lift of his boat to bring the top of the wet black-gray rock within jumping distance. The boat slewed sideways as he leapt, but he gained the rock. The general was ashore. Scrambling to his feet, he climbed in and over the bare rocks to the rising ground. In a hollow, a boatload of Highlanders were forming under their ensign; they had drawn their chunky broadswords. Above his head, at the crest of the steep, fir-tree-dotted slope, a group of American rangers was in a firing line. Lieutenants Browne and Hopkins, whose boats had been first ashore, had mounted an attack beyond the line of morning sky.

With the Highlanders following, and more and more boats coming in to land, Wolfe climbed the high hill.

To his left, all of Coromandière Bay was in view, and beyond in Gabarus Bay the ships of the British line could be seen. A line of spruce-covered hills, about a mile away, cut a saw-toothed second horizon across the blue of the sky. Into this pleasant prospect the light infantry had gone, and the position of their firing told the general on the cliff top they had found the enemy flank. As long as his impatience would allow him, Wolfe sent the troops coming out of the cove forward down the inland slope. Then he went down into the firing. Before the day was done, he and his light infantry, rangers, and grenadiers had chased the whole French line back into their citadel at Louisbourg. Tired, their clothing torn and snagged in the long pursuit through the thick, hard bush, the assault troops of Amherst's army paused, out of breath but exalted by the sight of the walls of Louisbourg across the cleared ground of the plain. The fortress guns were firing on the weary men, who laughed at the balls that fell short, and cheered the pretty bursting of the mortar bombs exploding harmlessly at the end of their trailing arc of smoke.

Wolfe did not go back to the landing place at Kennington Cove, so named for the inshore frigate. The divisions that came in over the beaches after him could do the work of getting the heavy baggage ashore. Wolfe's assault troops had won their ease, and they took it, munching at their haversack rations, and enjoying the view of the French fort, the harbor, and the town, with its girls and its grog shops waiting for them. But as they rested, they kept a wary eye on their thin, sickly, chinless weed of a general. Look sharp, soldier, when red-headed Jamie Wolfe falls silent, grows aloof, and broods.

On the fourth day after the landing, Major Scott and his light infantry and colonial rangers rolled their blankets early in the morning and moved out. Wolfe, with his grenadiers, Highlanders, and two regiments, followed soon after. They marched over the causeway and bridge at the northwest corner of the harbor. Fog hid them from the French sailors, whom they could hear talking on board the ships. They moved away from the water, up a gentle rise to high ground, seeking to get above the sea fog. But the wet, gray mass covered everything, and again the troops sat down to wait.

Louisbourg Harbor is shaped like a round Italian wine bottle lying in the grass at a picnic. On the west side of the bottle's neck is the town and its defenses. Across the narrow opening lies Lighthouse Point. In between, but nearer to the point, is a small island on which the French had a battery. On 12 June, Wolfe headed for Lighthouse Point, from which the British could control the entrance to the harbor with their guns, neutralize the island battery, and give the gunners a good pitch into the town itself. But Wolfe could not merely blunder here and there through the fog. At the bottom of the bay the French Royal Battery was situated so as to give its big guns a clear bows-on shot at any ship sailing into the harbor. The Royal Battery was a formidable work.

But Wolfe need not have worried or delayed. At two o'clock in the afternoon, when the fog had lifted, the light infantry found the Royal Battery and two small camps deserted. Four broken guns were in the embrasures. In their haste to retreat, the wardens had neglected to spike one 8-pounder. Within two hours Wolfe was standing on the up-thrusting rocks of Lighthouse Point. It, too, had been abandoned. The only note taken of Wolfe's arrival was two lazy shots from a French ship in the harbor. A little east of the point, British transports were edging in toward the beach where Wolfe's men waited to take the guns that the transports were bringing on shore.

With Louisbourg surrounded on all sides, General Amherst began the long slow task of setting up the siege of the town. While this was being done, Wolfe's target was the island battery and the French ships in the harbor. If Boscawen could get some of his ships into the harbor, their heavy broadsides would bring down the town in rubble about the "Monsieurs'" ears. By 25 June, the battery at Lighthouse Point had dominated the island battery, and five days later the five French warships were forced to move their anchorage in nearer the town, because of another English battery placed on the northeast reach of the bay.

Compressed into the crooked point of land behind the walls like tobacco into a clay pipe, the French under the Chevalier de Drucour made their defense. Any real hope of repelling the invaders had been sunk in the red surge of British infantry flooding over the beaches. Yet Drucour wore in his hat for all to see and emulate the brave feather of confidence, and his lady wore its counterpart. The governing couple set the fashion of tireless work and boundless cheer. Thus the walls were made strong and safe, the covered way repaired. Everyone in the town saw the humor and the justice in using bales of Virginia tobacco, taken in a privateer's prize, to reinforce the new powder magazine. While Amherst worked on his batteries, the French guns on the bastions were shifted, sandbagged, and brought to bear. During an evening walk among the men, Madame Drucour was invited to fire the opening gun of a bombardment directed at a wagon park. She accepted, and "Madame La Bombardière" became the toast.

Jeffrey Amherst, too, acknowledged the indomitable lady. He sent her two pineapples just received from the Azores. She returned the compliment with several bottles of champagne, which brought more pineapples and a firkin of sweet butter. At one of these parleys of exchange, an English lady discovered in the French officer a third cousin. Together they went to pick a salad from the garden which lay close under the walls. The Jacobite Chevalier Johnstone was able to use a flag of truce to send his compliments and condolences to his sister Cecilia's husband, Lord Rollo of the 22nd, on succeeding to the title. There were other less polite exchanges between the opposing forces. Deserters took their opportunity and chances, and crossed over with high hopes of sympathy and redress. Remarkable and indic- ative was the prompt desertion of the senior non-commis- sioned officer of the Foreign Volunteers, in whom rested the responsibility for the discipline in the whole battalion.

If the Foreign Volunteers were double prisoners of the fortress and of their allies, the French soldiers' resistance to the enemy without the walls was neither reluctant nor pas- sive. When Vaudreuil's Boishébert remained so distant and aloof that he did not even come in person to receive from Drucour the Cross of St. Louis which had arrived for him from France, the governor found other men eager to harass the outer perimeter of the British lines. The two brothers Villejouin were eager to protect their ancestral home of Ile Royale. On a dark night they rowed across the harbor, landed in a quiet place, and took to the bush that they knew so well. With them went twelve soldiers as instruc- tors and a band of Acadian refugees as rangers. Some- where in the hinterland were more Acadians. The Abbé Maillard was there, too, with his Indians and a cache of arms. Perhaps the Villejouins might even persuade the new holder of the Cross of St. Louis to fight.

With all his tactful persuasion, the Chevalier de Drucour was unable to get his own naval officers to fight. Since the five guns of Wolfe's battery had driven the five big ships— mounting 340 guns—away from their moorings, they had lain ineffectually at anchor near the town dock by the west gate. At low tide, three of them were aground. The Marquis Charry Des Gouttes was the senior naval officer, over Beaussier de L'isle, and would do nothing whatever after the governor in council refused him permission to take the five ships of his squadron away. So they lay, huddled and useless, sharing the bombardment of the town. All but a deck guard had been taken on shore, as had the powder and other combustibles.

One French captain and one French ship fought alone. For two weeks, Captain Jean Vauquelin kept his frigate *Aréthuse* at a strategic anchorage with her thirty-six guns bearing on the British. None of the planned work could go forward with *Aréthuse* in that position. It took Wolfe two weeks of digging and building to erect a battery that Vauquelin could not deny. His useful purpose having been served, and not being under direct command of Des Gouttes, Captain Vauquelin took his ship out through the harbor mouth, and with a flip of his coattails to the timid men-of-war's men, ducked gracefully around the blockading squadron and was hull down over the horizon bound for France.

When *Aréthuse* sailed away, the siege was five weeks old and pressing ever closer to the walls. The British siege guns had come up slowly over the swampy, dismal track from the distant landing beaches. But by early July the fire from the guns on Lighthouse Point and from the batteries creeping toward the western walls could cross over the town. The big citadel behind the king's bastion was in easy range. On one occasion, a bomb fell into the hospital. The townspeople watched silently as two Fathers of Charity were carried out with the dead, the sick, and the pitiful wounded, now wounded again. A hundred and fifty shells a day were falling on the town, ripping through the roofs, crashing down the walls where the 4000 civilians hid from their loom. The main British endeavor was directed toward the western gate at the harbor end of the wall. When the work appeared to be spreading toward the ocean end of the wall, Drucour launched his one big sally.

The raiding party of 724 men under the lieutenant colonel of Bourgogne left the east gate about midnight of 9 July. Turning left, they followed the zigzags of the counterscarp to the cliffs above the ocean. These they followed with the wind on their left cheeks until they were challenged by the French sentries, alert at Black Point. Here Colonel Marin's force divided to strike on two sides the first British post, its position marked well in the minds of the officers. Their precautions of stealth and tactics were not necessary. The British watch was asleep, and the first assault ended with silent scuffles in the dark, from which the French attackers rose victorious to wipe their bayonets clean in the British-turned dirt of the works. At the second British line, the raiders found the enemy alerted and ready. Excited now, the French rushed in with a whirlwind of bayonets before which the grenadiers broke and ran off to the safety of the rattling drums, now arousing the whole British line to the assembly.

Marin's corps of miners came up with the rear of his column and with picks and shovels fell to the job of destroying the work that the English had done. Daylight was forewarning by a streak of gray in the sky over the black ocean, and to judge by the orders and sounds from the night, at least a regiment of redcoats already was formed up.

The raid had accomplished little but give vent to the energy of the French soldiers. There were fifty French casualties in the nasty work of fighting in the dark, for an English "milord" killed, two officer-prisoners taken, and sixteen soldiers killed. Marin gave the order of recall. Back the French raiders marched across the rough terrain, muskets slung, carrying their shovels, singing loudly to wake their

comrades left behind the walls. Some of the French soldier
were wondrously and happily drunk when they marched in
under the lingering night shadow of the east gate.

The days of the siege wore on into the seventh week
time for the news to have been heard by Frenchmen aroun
the Great Lakes and Englishmen along the roads, traces
and trails deep into the Alleghenies. Day by day and step
by step, Major General Amherst methodically performec
the traditional motions by which the art of siegecraft attain
the inevitable. With helpless grace, the Chevalier de Dru
cour discharged the duties of an unwilling partner in the
dance. Slowly Amherst pressed closer, and the day of the
final polite bowing and compliments drew near. The in-
tensity of the British fire and action centered now on the
east gate and the dauphin bastion. In this quarter the impetuous, restive Wolfe commanded, while railing against
the slowness of the elder brigadiers. By 16 July Wolfe had
pushed his troops forward to a position but 200 yards from
the eastern gate. There they began work on a 6-gun battery. It was completed, ready for the guns to be brought
forward, on the night of 21 July, when a chance shell fell
on the poop of *Célèbre*, the French man-of-war closest to
the dock and town. The shell exploded fair, scattering its
jagged pieces across the deserted deck. By chance, a red-
hot fragment ignited some powder stored near a gun. Before the boat guard was aware of the fire, the flames were
leading up the tarred cordage of the mizzenmast. Sparks,
blown by a southeast wind, ignited the rigging of *Entre-
prenant*. From her, the fire spread to *Capricieux*, and within
half an hour all three ships were ablaze. The whole town
was in danger and everyone rushed forward to help keep
the fire away. The British, too, came out to watch. On the
Green Hill batteries, from which the lucky, terrible shell
had come, a pudding-faced chaplain praised and gloried in

the sight until the officers with him turned away in revulsion. The ships burned all through the night.

Next morning, the new 6-gun battery set fire to the great citadel building behind the king's bastion. The French defenders, tired from their efforts of the day before, compounded by their unending labors on the walls, could not control the fire. When smoke flooded into a deep casement in the bastion, the women and children sheltering there fled in a panic that was almost contagious. Doggedly, the exhausted garrison fought the fire under the increased fury of the British bombardment. There was no rest, for in the evening the wooden barracks behind the queen's bastion caught fire and were destroyed. As was her custom in the evening, Madame Drucour walked the bastion, picking her way around the rubble and past the broken guns, pausing to exchange quiet pleasantries with the gunners of those pieces still in action.

Before dawn on 25 July, Admiral Boscawen struck the final sharp blow that cracked the hard shell of Louisbourg. Sensing the end, he had sent up the small boats from the fleet in Gabarus Bay. Into them piled 400 sailors. In a night thick with fog, the boats made their way through the sunken hulks that blocked the passage into the harbor, where still undetected, the boats split into two divisions. In his Huguenot French, Captain Laforey of the sloop *Hunter* hailed *Prudent* and was told by the lone sentry to come aboard. Surprised in his bunk, the midshipman in command surrendered, but because *Prudent* was aground, Laforey could do nothing but burn her and get away with his prisoners and the twenty joyous British prisoners of war he had released. Captain Balfour had even better luck in boarding *Bienfaisant*, for he was able to tow away the ship as a fine, big, rich prize.

On 26 July, Boscawen wrote a letter to Drucour demanding surrender on the harshest terms. The letter still lay on Amherst's desk, while its delivery was being arranged, when a Monsieur Loppinot, under a flag from Louisbourg, was announced. He asked for terms and Amherst, reaching across his table, handed him the letter, already signed, demanding surrender at the Britisher's discretion.

At Drucour's council, M. Loppinot, who in 1749 had taken Louisbourg back from the British, was poorly received with his harsh terms. The army officers leapt up, vowing they would revolt before they would surrender. D'Anthonay, of the Foreign Volunteers, went out to attempt to treat with the British, but Amherst was adamant. Brigadier Whitmore would not even let the French colonel through the first outpost. In the streets outside the improvised council chamber, the soldiers were milling about on the verge of riot. In the room with Drucour, the unctuous Prévost was pressing the civilians' case, underscoring the hardships of the women and weeping for the plight of the children. Prévost prevailed. In the street, the soldiers roared in anger, an anger turned to anguish as they smashed their muskets against the walls. The men of Cambis took their colors from their ensign and burned them.

At high noon on 27 July, the leading grenadiers of the 1st, or Royal, Regiment of Foot, halted at the far side of the ditch outside the dauphin gate. When French laborers had laid the last planks on the new bridge, the English marched into Louisbourg. With one company each of the 15th and 40th, they marched to the esplanade where Brigadier General Whitmore waited to accept from Drucour the governorship of the town. At the same hour of noon, Major Farquhar entered the west gate and posted guard. The turnover of the town was made quietly and without confusion.

Monsieur and Madame Drucour would not be ready to leave Louisbourg until 12 August, when their troops, so very courageous, were also ready to go. On the eve of their departure, Amherst dined them on board Captain Rodney's *Terrible*. Four nights later, he dined the useful Jacques Prévost; the younger officers at table found the boldness of the intendant's wife most amusing. As the month of August wore on, British detachments were swarming out all over the eastern limits of France's North American empire. The island of St. Jean, in the Gulf of St. Lawrence, surrendered; the restless, roving Wolfe took the settlements on the Gaspé Peninsula and looked up the river toward Quebec, where stood another citadel.

On 30 August, Jeffrey Amherst sailed with his troops for New York, to turn his attention to Lake Champlain and the unsolved problems left there by the defeated Abercromby.

XV

The Forks of the Ohio

Since June, Colonel George Washington had had his 1st Virginia Regiment at Fort Cumberland, ready to march on to the Ohio. He knew the road well, having built it as far as Fort Necessity and further, to the glade where was Jumonville's grave. In 1755 Washington had followed the improved road as far as the high ground beyond the second crossing of the Youghiogheny, where the bones of Braddock's soldiers lay unburied in the bush. All during the summer of 1758, he stood ready to march over the last miles of the old road to its end at Fort Duquesne.

It was at the very end of August that Colonel Washington, still at Fort Cumberland, gave a *feu de joie* for Jeffrey Amherst and his regulars who had captured Louisbourg. By then the Virginia colonel knew that Brigadier Forbes's army, of which he was the elder veteran of the way, would not be taking the old road to the French fort. Washington pleaded with the British general and his second-in-command, Henry Bouquet, to take Braddock's route, but he failed to make his point, and on the threshold of autumn, with every good grace, he marched his troops from Cumberland to join the new road at Raystown in Pennsylvania Colony. Colonel Henry Bouquet, the Swiss-born profes-

ional sword commanding the 1st battalion of the Royal
American Regiment, had Forbes's main army at that place.
With Raystown as its base, the army was projecting the
new road westward along the routes used by the pack
trains of the Pennsylvania Indian traders. From the head
waters of the Juniata the track crossed the watershed,
passed through Edmonds Swamp and over Laurel Ridge to
Loyal Hannon Creek, where an advance post was to be
built. From Fort Ligonier, on the Loyal Hannon, it was
fifty miles over Chestnut Ridge to the forks of the Ohio,
and forty-five miles back to Raystown. Starting out from
Fort Cumberland in September, George Washington had
doubts that Forbes's expedition would ever cross Laurel
Ridge. Already, the campaigns of Abercromby, Amherst,
and Bradstreet had been concluded, while the expedition to
Fort Duquesne was still at its base on the shady side of the
terrible mountains.

Brigadier General John Forbes, however, could rest content with his efforts, in the horse litter that, at the end of
August, was carrying him forward to join his troops at
Raystown. The grave illness which compelled Forbes to
travel by litter forced him to halt his journey at Fort Loudoun, in the eastern mountains. But the presence of the general in person was not needed up front, where Bouquet was
the strong horse that pulled willingly and knowingly at the
army's wagon. General Forbes's job had ever been that of
the co-ordinator. His trials and his skill had been in building
the wagon, loading it, and keeping the herd of colonial
governors, legislators, merchants, and suppliers tied to the
lead ropes of his army's purpose.

Commissioned in March to drive the French from the
Ohio by seizing Fort Duquesne, John Forbes took up the
reins and immediately slapped them tentatively over the
backs of the various colonial governors on whom the expedition depended for men, transport, supplies, and money.

His team did not start off at a careening gallop. Governor Sharpe of Maryland replied at once to the general's letter. He said that the political situation was such that he could do little more than send 200 or 300 men and a garrison for Fort Cumberland, which, after all, was in Maryland. Governor Arthur Dobbs of North Carolina promised militia, and eventually sent two companies, with a major. But Dobbs did a good service to the expedition in securing a strong war party from the Cherokee Nation. These fine warriors were ever ready to fight with their Indian enemies on the Ohio.

Forbes counted on and received good help from the Huguenot Francis Fauquier, who had replaced the wrangling Scot, Dinwiddie, as governor of Virginia. Though Williamsburg contributed little in the way of supplies, the two regiments of Virginia militia it sent to the frontier were well led. The young George Washington, who commanded the 1st regiment, had recovered his health and was much wiser now in military ways. The injury to his pride was mollified, too, by Pitt's decree that colonials ranked in grade with regulars. True, there had been a rush to upgrade the acting-commanders of British regiments so as to rank the colonials, but Washington could walk a colonel among colonels, and majors and captains obeyed his orders promptly and without question. With energy and devotion, the Virginia men with Forbes strove to end the years of Indian terror on the Allegheny frontier.

With Pennsylvania troops holding the longest line and suffering most on the bloody frontier, General Forbes expected much and required even more from Governor William Denny. To meet head-on the quibbling and equivocating that he expected in the Quaker Woods, Forbes moved his headquarters to Philadelphia. There he stayed for two and a half months, fighting the battle of the bureaucrats and skirmishing daily with the wily merchants. In his siege of Pennsylvania and its government, Forbes had his triumph.

To it he brought all the stubbornness that birth between the Tay and the Forth had given him, all the experience of a regimental and staff officer, all the patience learned as a doctor of medicine, and all the charm of a very handsome and attractive man. In Philadelphia, General Forbes shaped his army, fed it and moved it, and won his right to fight it. On the cobbled, shady streets of the city, he concurred in the plans for a new road over the mountains, which would be a hostage to Pennsylvania in the days of peaceful trade to follow the conquest of the Ohio.

Henry Bouquet had worn many gaudy uniforms as a professional soldier in Europe, but none fitted him better than the purposely plain red and blue of the 60th, the Royal American Regiment, which he put on in January of 1757 and never afterward took off. From the fierce independence of his native Switzerland, he found an affinity with the Royal Americans growing, hardy as an Alpine flower, in the garden of the colonial Englishman. Bouquet's Protestantism found a home in the regiment and a parish in the colony of Pennsylvania, to which he came in 1758 to serve as cannoneer to General Forbes. From South Carolina, he brought the contingent of regulars to stiffen Forbes's army of colonials. Bouquet had only half of his own 1st battalion of Royal Americans with him when he arrived in Pennsylvania. The others were with Abercromby.

The 1100 Highlanders of Colonel Archibald Montgomery's regiment did not arrive from Charleston until the second week in June. Forbes met them in Philadelphia, and before the plain people of the city could gape at the "fancy women," he sent them swinging their kilts in pursuit of Bouquet, who was advancing on Raystown.

Including the Virginians at Fort Cumberland, Colonel Bouquet had 6000 troops on the back frontier between Carlisle and Raystown. He had supplies for three months, no guns, few tents, some wagons, enough horses to pose a problem regarding fodder, and a plague of rats. Bouquet also had the loyalty and respect of the colonels under his command: Washington and William Byrd III, the Virginians, and Armstrong, Burd, and Hugh Mercer of Pennsylvania. Colonel Bouquet, in turn, gave his talents without stint to his general, absent in Philadelphia where he was finding and getting together that army which his second-in-command held in trust for him out in the safe fastnesses of the western mountains. Henry Bouquet was less lucky in his attempt to hold the loyalty of the army's Indian allies.

On 14 June, Bouquet held council with his Indians at Fort Loudoun. The Cherokees were growing restive. They had come over a long trail to make war at the side of their English brothers, who had not yet begun to fight. It was but two months since the French and their Ohio and Mingo Indians had led the white woman captive close by this very fort. No white man had gone to rescue or avenge her. Through the trees Mary Jemison had seen the stockaded walls, a last glimpse of a once familiar life. The Cherokee warriors had been too late to save her from a life among the Senecas, though they had caught up with and waylaid other French war parties from the Beautiful River. By June, the young Cherokees were scornful of the fort-bound, road-bound English—who also had failed to bring out the expected presents.

Abraham Bosomworth, their white captain, brought 100 Cherokees in off the western trails to the conference. With them came twenty-seven diffident Catawbas. The Swiss colonel met with the chiefs in the big room of the pleasant summer-house by the river, where the heavy June air might be expected to circulate the smell of bear grease and dirty blankets. Bouquet's oratory was correct, addressing the Indians as branches of the same tree. Colonel Bouquet was pleased with the Cherokees' promises to stay with him, to go in the English soldiers' time to fight the French and the

dians in revolt against the English king. Bouquet was in-
erested when a young warrior was brought forward who,
ith the point of his scalping-knife, carved out on the table-
p a map of the route to the forks of the Ohio. Leaning
orward into the pungent smell of rancid grease, the sol-
ier of European kings pried the secrets of the unknown
ountain ranges from the swarthy young warrior of the
orest. With his guide he crossed the bed of each stream
nd saw the steep slopes down which the cannon must be
wered. This was the value of the Indian ally.

Out in the full June air, with a thunderhead backing up
gainst the stirring of a breeze, Colonel Bouquet brought
ut the gifts. Carefully, he distributed them as far as they
vould go among the Cherokees, and those others, the
Catawbas.

In the matter of gifts to entice and bind the Indians to his
rmy, General Forbes had been caught between a limited
var chest, the parsimony of the Parliament, and the cost-
nd-profit accounting of Sir William Johnson. Ethically
nd economically, the Cherokees had their own Indian
gent, John Stuart of the Southern Department, on whom
either Johnson nor his deputy in Pennsylvania, George
Groghan (late of Dublin), saw profit in trespassing. While
Bouquet was struggling by his oratory to keep the able
Cherokees loyal, Forbes and Groghan were playing to win
ver the Nations in the Ohio country from their allegiance
o the French.

Needing an emissary to go boldly into the Ohio towns,
Forbes made the happy choice of Christian Frederick Post,
a Moravian lay-missionary. Post, who spoke little English,
had an Indian wife, a profound knowledge of the Bible,
faith in prayer, and a brave countenance. The last two at-
tributes were the salvation of his secular mission. The tall
German, sitting straight on his horse's back, needed a strong
prayer to ride unchallenged under the walls of Fort Ve-

nango. While Post, in his prayer, reminded the Lord th.
the enemies of Lot and Elisha had been blinded, the Frenc
did not see their enemy as he passed by the gate of the
fort. Later, when the one-eyed Captain de Ligneris sent in
the Indian towns to take him for a spy, Post's wife's relativ
delivered him safely from his enemies. The Shawnees an
the Delawares listened to him as he journeyed among the
during the summer days of 1758, and when October cam
they went as Post had asked them to do, to hear the prom
ises of the British king at a great conference at Easton, i
Pennsylvania. Even the Senecas and other western Iroquo
grew curious, and drew cautiously near to hear the English
man's talk. After four fat years, the voice of New Franc
in Canada was as monotonous as the song of the whippoor
will receding into the night.

On the steeply tilted side of Laurel Hill, the coloni
roadbuilders stood aside to let the Highlanders marc
past behind their blow-cheeked piper, screeching music t
still the jaybirds. Behind their proud major, five companie
marched up to the blank end of the road and halted. Fron
the right, the companies filed off into the narrow trail be
yond. The driver of a skid-horse, stroking the soft muzzl
and soothing the nibbling lips, heard the bagpipes far up
the trail on the mountain. When the last regular hac
marched on, the man gave his "Haw," the log chains rattled
and, heaving into his collar, the big horse snatched the log
into place for a revetment to the road. The soldiers woulc
have need of their cannon, where they were going!

Ahead of Major James Grant's kilted Scots had gone
Colonel Burd's Pennsylvanians and Adam Stephens's Vir
ginians. They had slipped quietly past the roadbuilders with
a jeering word for the "soldiers with shovels." The march
ing men were dressed without breeches, in shirts and leg
gings, in a fashion suited to the woods. Regulars and colo
nials, they were the hard point of Forbes's army, and they

rived at the Loyal Hannon on 3 September. Four days
ter Colonel Bouquet, with an escort of his Royal Ameri-
ins, rode into the bivouac on the bluff above the creek, to
nd the work on Fort Ligonier well in hand and the im-
atient major of Highlanders with a plan in mind.

Grant wanted to take his Highlanders raiding into the
wland haunts of the savages, in their camp outside the
alls of Fort Duquesne. According to the woods chatter of
ie scouts and spies, the Indians were harkening to the mis-
on of Christian Post and would run at the approach of a
dcoat. There were not enough Frenchmen or Canadians
: the forks of the Ohio to sally out of the fort against a
rong raiding-party. Colonel Bouquet gave his assent to
ie plan. On his arrival at the Loyal Hannon, he had been
reeted by an Indian scare, and the sight of a scalped Scot
eing sewn into his great plaid with the pipers all wailing
ie mournful "Lament." A raid such as Grant proposed
ould satisfy the blood revenge of the Highlanders and
alm the rattled nerves of the others. It would also serve as
n engineer's reconnaissance of the road, and might well
rain off the war parties that were picking at the fringes of
he British army. Bouquet, however, did not let Grant go
lone into the forest. With the Scots he sent a woods-wise
ontingent of American rangers, under Major Andrew
Lewis, who had been with Braddock in '55.

After two days' march beyond the outpost of Fort Li-
onier, referred to by the soldiers as "Grant's Paradise,"
he 800 raiders were close to Fort Duquesne. They had ar-
ived without detection. On the night of 13 September,
Major Grant set in motion the elaborate, detailed plan
vhich he had drawn up and expounded and fussed about,
vith much recourse to his pocket snuff-mull. In the black
iight the attack force of 400 Virginians and Royal Ameri-
:ans was hopelessly fouled on the trails within a mile of the
rench fort. The men fell back on the hill, where Grant

stood cursing the cowardly colonials who had brought h
plan to naught. With a scowl, Grant sent Major Lewis bac
a mile with his disgraced Americans to wait with the ba;
gage guard.

Still there was no sign from the French that they kne
the British were so near. With the rising of the Septemb
morning mist, Grant's anger at the Americans changed t
contempt. In the full light of the new day's sun, contemp
led the colonel to brashness and into foolhardiness. Gra
sent the engineer officer forward with a hundred men t
make a plan of the garrison from a place where he coul
look into the Frenchmen's beards. With fifty of the be
cattle thieves from the Highlands, Archibald Robinson an
Alexander McDonald went forward to attack a house. Th
two lieutenants found the house and set it on fire. Back o
the hill, they pointed with pride to the smoke rising abov
the trees at the edge of the fort clearing. To underscore h
presence, Grant gathered all the company drummers an
pipers about him in the center of the line and called for
tune of impudence. There was no doubt that reveille, a
played on the bagpipes, would wake the "Monsieurs" sleep
ing in Duquesne. The Maryland and Pennsylvania troop
on the right of the Scots looked over at the defiant majo
and his music. One by one the men from the colonial fron
tier blew the old priming powder out of the pans of thei
muskets or rifles. From their powder horns they poure
fresh grains, which they knew to be dry.

A mile to the rear of Grant's battle line on the hill, Majo
Andrew Lewis had set an ambush along the chosen trail o
the force's withdrawal. Lewis himself sat, spraddle-legged
up against a hardwood tree, digging idly in the loam wit
his sheath knife. Good Virginia blood, once as red as th
turning leaves of autumn, was mixed into the black eart
that he churned with the bright steel blade.

The distant, smothered popping of musket fire was lik

n echo of the old battle fought on this ground. Major
.ewis sprang to his feet, clutching hard on the handle of
is scalping-knife. On the trail, other veterans of Brad-
ock's march were standing clear of their "hides," listening.
he new man and the very young men looked up at the
lder men. They, too, saw the old ghosts and heard the dis-
ant firing. Quietly they gathered up their weapons and
heir gear. The Major whistled sharply, once, through his
ingers, and his Virginians came alive. They were jogging
lown the trail now, strung out under their officers and
ergeants, all behind their major. It was half an hour since
he firing had begun. As heard by the Virginians, the firing
vas no longer concentrated. It was scattered and sporadic,
.nd very deadly. Quite suddenly, a wild-eyed Scot came
:harging up the trail like a great red bull. Lewis grabbed
he frightened man, swung him hard against a tree, and
hook him. But all the man could say was that he had seen
)onald MacDonald crawling through the mud, with all
he skin off his head. Leaving the blubbering man, Lewis
ook up the trail. The Virginians were moving cautiously
10w, as other fugitives from Grant's forces straggled into
he column. The Scots had been surrounded, rushed, and
roken. The Pennsylvanians had been sliced off from the
Highlanders and had gone away. The main body of the
·egulars had fallen back—fled, in fact—on other trails that
.ed to the rear guard. For a long moment, Major Lewis and
his relief force hovered, undecided, on the main trail. They
were too late to reinforce, their positions unknown for a
rallying-place for Grant. Then the French and their Indians struck from the forest in a swirl of bayonets and the
glint of tomahawks. In minutes it was over, the Virginians
scattered. Major Lewis found himself held and pinioned by
a mixed group of Indians and swarthy little Canadians,
who were ripping the clothes from his body. He was naked
and helpless when a Frenchman, an officer, to judge by the

gorget he wore on his bare chest, claimed him as a prisoner
of the king.

With his savior, Andrew Lewis walked, stark naked, into
the fort at the forks of the Ohio. The women jeered at him
and the Indians threatened and menaced him. Quickly the
French officer hurried his captive into his own quarters,
gave him clothing, and told him to lock and bar the door.
All the afternoon Lewis heard the cheers greeting the prisoners as they were brought in by ones and twos. That
night the Indians tortured seven or eight soldiers outside
the door where the major had been hidden. Neither the
scar-faced, one-eyed commander of Fort Duquesne nor the
officer of the Marine who had saved Andrew Lewis could
keep the Indians from following their ancient customs.

In another cabin in the fort, Major James Grant sat, a
prisoner of the French. They had brought him pen and
paper with which to write his report. Carefully, he set
down the minutes and the action of his disastrous day. He
did not know then that he was one of almost 300 dead or
taken prisoner. Major Grant was concerned lest, as a prisoner
of war, he might forfeit his place in the promotion list.
He asked General Forbes that he be exchanged as soon as
possible.

A month after Major Grant lost his army, his freedom,
and his dream of glory, the French counterattacked on the
Loyal Hannon. The fine French sense of logic of François
le Marchand, Sieur de Ligneris, had been bruised by the
presence of the bold Scotsman on the forest trails of Pennsylvania. It was impractical, and therefore illogical, for the
British not to use Braddock's route, the existing road, the
traditional way, which patrols from Fort Duquesne had
watched all summer long. But now that Grant had drawn
the line of British march directly from Fort Ligonier to the
Ohio, rather than around by Fort Cumberland, Ligneris

accepted the British illogicality with a Frenchman's practicality.

On 12 October, 440 French Canadians, with 150 of their Indians, raided the English on the Loyal Hannon. Neither the Sieur de Ligneris nor the expedition commander, Charles Phillipe d'Aubry of the Louisiana government and the leader of the western Indians out of the Illinois country, expected to throw back the English in their thousands. The Frenchmen's purpose in the raid was to nick the edge of British morale and delay the enemy's advance in the face of the oncoming winter season. In the latter, D'Aubry almost succeeded.

Colonel Burd of Pennsylvania, in command of Fort Ligonier during the temporary absence of Bouquet, twice misjudged the French strength. At the first report that the French had come, he sent out sixty rangers to drive them away. When these were swallowed by the ominous woods, he sent 500 more, whom the French drove back. From the safety of the log fort on the bluff and the log palisade on the slope, Colonel Burd made his defense with cannon. All afternoon and into the night, his mortars and howitzers pitched their shells into the treetops, searching for the enemy below. Under the scattered, harmless rain of bombs, D'Aubry sent his men to search out horses. They found them in the little forest clearings, wandering close to the forest trails, and in the paddocks near the fort. They were poor creatures, for the most part, worn out by the long, hard haul over the laurel ridge, but they were the power to tote the packs and roll the wheels of Forbes's army over the last fifty miles to Fort Duquesne. D'Aubry took them with him in the morning, a pitiful herd, not many, but enough to give the British pause.

General Forbes, sick and wasted, came up to Ligonier on 2 November. The blaze of autumn colors had dulled to brown, and cold, hard rains were falling, chilling the sol-

diers in their worn clothing and cutting little gullies in the
new fill of the road, gullies that grew into washouts. On 11
November, the general called a council of war. All his colonels attended: Bouquet, Montgomery of the Highlanders,
and the testy quartermaster, Sir John St. Clair. Washington
was there, with William Byrd III of the 2nd Virginia Regiment, and the three Pennsylvania regimental commanders,
Armstrong, Burd, and Hugh Mercer. They were good men
and good officers, and they balanced carefully the gains
against the risks—not the risks to themselves, but to the
cause and purpose of the expedition. In the end, they decided against going on, and walked out into the cold drizzle,
sniffing the air for the snow that soon must come. Before it
came, they must be back over Laurel Hill—or in Fort
Duquesne.

But the next day the decision of the council not to go
forward was put at naught by a little skirmish in the woods,
where George Washington was finishing off the season's
work on the road ahead. Somehow, a strong French patrol
got caught between two converging parties of Virginians.
The engagement was brisk, bloody, and short. A Canadian
prisoner was the prize. He was an Englishman, an unwilling
volunteer, happy to be again among his own kind, and sensi-
ble in his talk. With a glass of English rum in his hand, he
told General Forbes that, at Fort Duquesne, the western Indians had gone home after D'Aubry's raid. For want of food
(since the sack of Fort Frontenac no supplies had come up)
the garrison had been sent away. The prodigal Englishman,
cramming good Virginia tobacco into his pipe, said that
when he left there were less than 300 Canadians at Fort
Duquesne, of whom only a third were well enough, or strong
enough, to fight.

On 14 November, Forbes issued orders for his army to
advance in three brigades to the Beautiful River. Under
clear skies, the British-Colonial army moved out the next

day to Chestnut Ridge and the last slope down to the forks of the Ohio.

On 19 November, with the enemy close on him, it was the Sieur de Ligneris's turn to call a council of war and to expound his logic to the few officers still in Fort Duquesne. The French council, like the English, took a negative view. But there was no last-minute drama to give hope to Ligneris. At the little council in the commandant's room, standing before the big fireplace, Ligneris gave the order to evacuate and destroy Fort Duquesne. During the next four days the French dismantled the fort, tearing down the stockade and loading the fleet of bateaux in the river. On 24 November 1758, in the space of three short hours, the French left the forks of the Ohio. Food and the artillery went down the river, the food a gift to the future friendship of the river Indians, the artillery into safekeeping in the Illinois country or, if necessary, to Louisiana. The garrison went up the river in their boats to winter and wait in the other forts, perhaps to return in the spring. Alone, the Sieur de Ligneris made his last tour of the deserted fort. The parade square was empty, the windows of the barracks blank. An eddy of dust whirled down the long reach of the curtain wall. The door of his house, near the main gate, stood open. A drift of dry leaves had blown in and lay, brown as rotten apples forgotten in a barrel. François le Marchand closed the door of his home. Inspecting carefully as he went, he followed the long train of powder to where it ended on the river bank in a laid bonfire. With a burning bit of artillery match, the commander of Fort Duquesne blew a fire onto the torn square of a letter. Bending down, he gently tucked the brave little flame under the pile of sticks and twigs and driftwood logs. He waited to see the big flames licking upward, then went quickly down the bank to the boat waiting for him on the shore. There were tears in the Sieur de Ligneris's one good eye, which was logical, as the smoke from the pyre of Fort Duquesne had blown back into his seamed and scarred and weather-beaten Canadian face. The boat carrying its last French commander had rounded a bend in the river when Fort Duquesne exploded with a roar.

The morning after the French left, a troop of colonial light horse rode out of the forest. The horses were restless, tossing their heads and dancing sideways on their quick hooves as their riders urged them around the smoldering ruins. On the triangular point of land where the three rivers met, the officers ordered the men to dismount. The horse-holders took the mounts down to drink from the Beautiful River.

If Major Grant of Montgomery's Highlanders, who wished for an early exchange, had any fond hope of being released by the oncoming army of his friend General Forbes, he was soon disabused of this hope by his French captors. Before the British army was over the last high ridge between it and the Ohio, the Sieur de Ligneris had sent away to safety all his prisoners of war. They were far too valuable as coins of exchange to be risked in the tottering Fort Duquesne. Besides, they ate up precious rations. Either the Scottish Major of the Virginians, Andrew Lewis, or a group of the junior officers might be worth Ligneris's friend Beletre, captured after his successful raid on the Palatine towns along the Mohawk River. The French commander opened a correspondence with Colonel Bouquet on the matter. It appeared, according to the Swiss colonel's reply, that Beletre was a highly prized captive of the Cherokee Nation. Perhaps the Cherokees placed a value on him even greater than the sum offered by the French to their Hurons for the unfortunate Ensign MacDonald of the Highlanders.

So the negotiations stood when Forbes supplanted Ligneris as commander at the forks of the Ohio and gave orders for the building of Fort Pitt on the still-warm ashes of Fort Duquesne. The negotiations were to continue past the untimely death of the sick and weary General Forbes, and into the next year's campaign. Whenever a messenger passed, under a herald's flare of truce, from one headquarters to another, he carried letters regarding the exchange of prisoners.

The French ranger Wolf often acted as such a messenger, and in the autumn of 1758 he concluded a mass exchange, acting as conductor to the British who were being returned. The prisoners returning home made a straggling, tattered, burdened line as they came out of the woods into the clearing and saw the Union Jack flying high on the bastion of Fort Edward, with the falls of the Hudson a white line of churning foam. Women, their skirts fastened high for forest walking, were at the side of their men. The children, those who could escape their parents, walked stiff and bold, mimicking the dignity and grandeur of Wolf, the Frenchman, and of the man beside him, Peter Schuyler, former colonel of the New Jersey "Blues."

Since his capture in 1756, Colonel Schuyler had been living in open arrest at Quebec. Not until 1758, a garland year of victories, did the British general in North America have French prisoners whom the governor of New France wished to exchange. As the British representative strode out to meet him at Fort Edward, the long-absent Colonel Schuyler stood for the aged Monsieur de Noyan, taken at Fort Frontenac and released on strict parole. The return of the two officers to duty occasioned a general exchange. The British released from their oath not to bear arms all those whom Bradstreet had caught in Fort Frontenac. The French had sent back all the people now flowing out of the forest to eddy in behind the bulwark of their colonel.

These were Peter Schuyler's people, regulars from the disbanded regiments of Shirley and Pepperrell, and many whom the New Jersey colonel had ransomed from their Indian captivity and slavery. Schuyler had done more than save his fellow captives during the long months that he awaited his exchange. In the cliff City of Quebec, he had acted as a spy. For a man of Schuyler's position and experience, an Indian courier usually could be found to pass a message about the arrival of a convoy and its cargo, or about a significant change in the garrison. In October of 1757, one Robert Morse took off across lots to New England with a letter from Colonel Schuyler that the general in North America found useful in making his estimates for the campaign of 1758.

But Peter Schuyler's return home did not leave the British without an agent in the City of Quebec. Robert Stobo, the hostage given up by George Washington at Fort Necessity in 1754, was still there. His status, however, had changed. When the map that he had made while a guest at Fort Duquesne was found in General Braddock's captured field desk, Captain Stobo was jailed as a spy. When, in 1756, he escaped, only to be recaptured for a flattering £6000, his status was changed yet again, this time to that of a prisoner condemned to be hanged. The Scotsman's luck then returned to him, as the necessary confirmation of his death sentence did not come from France. While he waited for the ship that he hoped would not come, Captain Stobo kept himself busy. His condemned cell was a locked room in a house on the ramparts of Quebec. There was a barred window with a dizzy high view, and a door to which the prisoner looked for the *Quebecoise* who cleaned for him and brought his food.

The girl brought, too, a generous portion of sympathy, that became friendship, which gave to the prisoner hope of help and escape. As she swept and changed the bed-linen, the girl chatted of the famine, ever-present in a country

regulated by "that *salaud* Bigot." A few questions on
Stobo's part changed the chatty gossip of the town to news
and intelligence of Canada. To the prison cell came the
story of the good Montcalm's gesture to end his quarrel
with Vaudreuil, for the good of Canada, France, and the
king. The girl who brought Stobo the firewood could not
know of the governor's false pride, how he consented to
Montcalm's sending Doreil and Bougainville to Paris to
mediate the difference, then nullified the mission by a secret
letter. But, like most of the *habitants*, the girl sensed that the
governor's vanity, wounded by the defeats of the year 1758
and stung by the victory of his rival, had caused Vaudreuil
to lose touch with reality.

In March, the ice in the St. Lawrence River at Quebec
broke into floating islands that drifted back and forth with
the tide. There were days when windows could be opened.
It was time for Captain Stobo to go, before the ship from
France arrived.

Stobo was helped by Lieutenant Stevens, a ranger captured at Fort Beauséjour, who shared with the Scotsman
the friendship of the girl. On the dark night of 30 April
1759, Stevens was waiting below the high window of the
captain's cell. He caught Stobo as he dropped the last few
feet from the too-short rope. Stobo's ribs felt thin and bony
to the ranger's hands. Quickly, the two men made off
through the streets of the lower town. Upriver at a little
cove, Clarke, the Nova Scotian, was waiting with a bark
canoe. With him were his wife and their children. He and
Stevens had chosen the time well; the canoe coursed down
the St. Lawrence in an ebbing tide. Traveling only at night,
they saw no one, but the lights in the farmhouses warned
them of the coming dawn. When the canoe became too
leaky to patch with gum, Stevens stole a rowboat. Clarke
vowed to Stobo that, when the river widened, he would get

them a sloop so that the captain could enter British Louisbourg in a style befitting his rank and the importance of his news. He did better: he acquired a schooner, in which the escaping party sailed into Louisbourg Harbor with a makeshift Jack at the peak of the gaff.

XVI

The King Must Be Obeyed

Condemned Robert Stobo made his escape from Quebec
with little time to spare. On his first night of flight, the
canoe had passed a ship at anchor in the St. Lawrence. She
was just in from France and waited only for the tide and
the daylight to make the dangerous traverse east and south
of Ile d'Orleans to find safe harbor in the Quebec roadstead.
On board the ship was Bougainville, recently promoted
colonel, hastening back to his general, with discouraging
news of French apathy toward New France. Further downriver Stobo's boat passed the spring convoy from Bordeaux.
It was a poor convoy, representing the near-abandonment
of Canada by King Louis of France and Madame de Pompadour. There were a few soldiers aboard the ship, replacements for the eight battalions of regulars with which Montcalm was expected to hold a continent.

Captain Stobo arrived at British Louisbourg just in time
to accompany the invasion force back to Quebec. On the
day that he first felt the bar on his window move free, the
fleet from England had made its landfall. Governor Edward
Whitmore had gone to the seaward bastion to watch as the
chalk-white sail scrawled a "Hail! Well met!" across the
slate-gray sea. But shore ice still blocked the landing stages

in Louisbourg Harbor, so, with a "We'll soon be back," Admiral Saunders coasted up to Halifax's open harbor.

For the first two weeks of May 1759, Halifax was the host and rendezvous for the 25,000 British soldiers and sailors, sent to storm the citadel and river line of the capital of New France. In the rim town of America that spring, with the summer's work to do, ships and regiments, companies and crews forgathered. Each unit of the whole held fast to old traditions, and all the men were greatly bound by a heritage of achievement which it was their duty again to prove true.

At a modest mooring beyond the big ships rode *Centurion*, a 50-gun ship which, with *Sutherland*, was the smallest of the twenty-two ships of the line that made up the Quebec fleet. *Centurion* was a famous ship, having carried George Anson on his four-year cruise around the world, and Lord Anson to the seat of First Lord of the Admiralty. She was small beside the 90-gun *Neptune*, but the admiral of all the fleet, men-of-war, transport, victualers, almost 200 sail in all, had stepped up from the deck of the fourth-class *Centurion*.

Charles Saunders, vice-admiral of the Blue, was a seaman, a man-of-war's man, and a shipmate and protégé of Anson. He had a small, unfierce face, with a jaw that was deceptively narrow for a firm will that knew when he had to be right. Pitt had picked Saunders to command afloat in the St. Lawrence, and to steady the new, untried, fighting general in his first independent command of the army on shore. Rear Admiral Phillip Durell, who had wintered at Halifax, was second-in-command to Saunders. Charles Holmes was third-in-command; he had come to this coast in 1755, and favored frigates. Edward Hughes was among Saunders's captains, and aboard the little *Porcupine* a twenty-four-year-old lieutenant, John Jervis, commanded. Working on the charts of the St. Lawrence passes and shallows was Captain James Cook, the navigator, whose job under Saunders was to bring the fleet safely to Quebec.

With the fleet from England came Major General James Wolfe and with him to Canada came Guy Carleton, colonel and deputy quartermaster general. The Honorable George Townshend was one of three brigadiers aboard the fleet. He was tall and somewhat disdainful, as became the eldest son of a peer. Townshend had a younger brother taking the lake route to Montreal with Amherst that summer. Robert Monckton and James Murray, who commanded the other brigades, were sons of peers, like Townshend. Lieutenant Colonel William Howe was a grandson of the king under a bar sinister. His brother had died the year before in the dark woods near Ticonderoga. Colonel Howe and Captain William Delaune were attached to the light infantry, on whom Wolfe relied to out-ranger the rangers, who, as mere colonials, were disliked and mistrusted.

When the whole expedition had assembled, Wolfe had twelve battalions of regulars, plus his ranger companies and three companies of grenadiers from the regiments left to garrison Louisbourg. All the regiments but one had been at the siege in 1758, and knew their general as an explosive soldier, in periodically poor health.

While the regiments were gathering at the rendezvous, and before the expedition moved off to stage at Louisbourg, Admiral Durell sailed to stopper the St. Lawrence. Under his flag he took thirteen ships with Colonel Carleton and his troops to augment the ship marines on forays ashore. Though Pitt had ordered him to be there in April, the admiral was late on station, so he missed Bougainville on the frigate *Chézine* and the nineteen ships of the Bordeaux convoy. Durell cruised off Rimouski and Bic, and off the high, black mountains at the mouth of the Saguenay River coming down from the arctic lands where Englishmen of the Hudson Bay Company lived and traded in isolation. On the cruise upriver, Durell lost his son, taken prisoner in a small-boat action close to the shore. Cautiously, the admiral moved up the river, observed but unchallenged, to Ile aux Coudres, where the river's main channel ducks in behind the island and the north shore.

The importance of the sergeant major of the 40th's company of the Louisbourg Grenadiers had drawn a group of privates in the bows of the transport *Harwood*. The great man, affable for the moment, was pointing out the ships of Durell's squadron, strung out in a watch line across the river. Though frigates of Saunders's main fleet were ahead of them, the grenadiers' transports led the troops, for, as befitted grenadiers, they would be first to storm ashore. On *Neptune*, Captain Stobo stood watching the island coming up under the bows, the silent, peaceful houses on a hostile shore, and the flights of long-necked geese and skimming duck, disturbed by the commotion of the vast fleet pushing into the tranquil river. Major Patrick MacKellar, General Wolfe's engineer, stood beside him. Like Stobo, he was returning to a city that had been his prison, and he too had come out with valuable intelligence of Quebec: the map that he had drawn was in the general's desk.

For two more days the reunited fleet shepherded the transport up the river, the shores drawing in a little closer each day. On 25 June the boatswain told the sergeant major that the land ahead was the eastern tip of Ile d'Orleans, and the sergeant major set the men to cleaning their equipment. The men grumbled, for they had heard from the sailors that the landing was yet two days off.

For those two days the river ahead of *Harwood* was bustling, busy with the goings and the comings, the seekings and the probings, of little rowing boats. Captain Cook sent them to find and to mark the channel of the traverse, which the "Monsieurs" counted impassable to big ships unless a Quebec pilot was at the wheel. On 27 June, Admiral Saunders's fleet started through. The Louisbourg Grenadiers, accoutered for landing, looked down from their high-sided ship and exchanged banter with the sailors in the flagged and anchored buoy boats. Under the eye of a frigate, the grenadiers peeled off to their landing on the eastern tip of Ile d'Orleans. They were in ranks and ready to march inland when General Wolfe came ashore with his engineer, MacKellar. The two men stood for a time studying a map, while some light infantry came ashore. Then, like a thin red hound, the general loped off inland. His escort, already struggling to keep up with the grenadiers, followed up the hot slope. There was a distance of eighteen miles to go, and they could expect some light opposition before they reached the western point of Ile d'Orleans. From time to time the grenadiers had a glimpse of the southern channel with the British fleet spilling through the "impenetrable" traverse.

From their citadel, their palaces, and their bureaux in the high town, the important people of Quebec could see only a part of the British fleet, men-of-war and transports. Most of the fleet was hidden to the city by the high cliff of Point Lévis. For two days the vessels had been there. They had survived, without serious mishap, two squalls of rain and wind, and in surviving, had won an acceptance of their place in the river. At his cathedral, His Grandeur the Bishop had prepared to care for the souls of the militia by appointing five chaplains to the levies. Vaudreuil was in Quebec with his court, to supervise and direct the defense of his capital. Bigot's fortune was safely invested in France, so he could afford to lose a final hand at the game table in the intendant's lofty palace. Montcalm was in the upper town, from which he could see the long line of defenses that he had erected on the Beauport shore. They were strong, holding to the high ground to cover with fire the foreshore and the mud flats. The trench line ended six miles down the north shore at the great cascade of the Montmorency River.

In the lower town, on the third evening after the arrival of the British fleet, the Sieur de Louche, captain of the merchant ship *Americain*, was readying seven fireships for the night's cruise. It was agreed by the wits that young Louche had a "flare." Tar puddled the once clean decks, barrels of explosives were lashed to the gunwales, and old guns were shotted and loaded. In the empty holds, pine boughs and pitch wood were tumbled. Adzes had cut deep furrows in the planking of the seven ships, to hold the powder trains running in wandering paths forward from the stern. At the stern of each fireship, there was a towed boat to bring off the volunteer crew. At ten o'clock that night, the harbor boom swung open and Louche sailed out the St. Charles River with his six captains—Grand Mont, Leseau, Berthèlot, Marchand, Sourmeau, and Du Bois de la Multièrre—the heroes of a watching city. The weather was passably good for the venture; the tide was running out; and there was a low, fresh wind from the southeast. The fireships had every prospect of a fair cruise down to the British ships, moored neatly in rows off Beaumont with its gilded steeple.

Off Point Lévis, with the British still two and a half miles away, the seven French captains had their vessels all abreast. There was still an hour to drift under shortened sail before the captains need light the fuses. From his ship's position second in from the end, Du Bois heard shots and voices from the commodore's vessel at the center of the line. Stepping to the quarter-deck rail, he saw the torch flare up on Louche's quarter-deck, and he could see by the light that the crew, in panic, had already taken to the boat. Now all the French were shouting in the night, and as Du Bois turned to steady his own crew, a second fireship started to burn, then a third. Soon Du Bois's ship was the only one of the line not burning. For half an hour longer, Captain Du Bois held his crew, along with their deserted, fiery escort.

Now the ship to port and the one to starboard were bearing in on his course. Far ahead, Du Bois could see lanterns flitting about on the British vessels as the longboats were dispatched to grapple with the fireships and tow them away. Soon the explosive engines on the decks of the burning ships would be going off. Du Bois could wait no longer. With his pistol he fired his torch and plunged its flaming end into the powder train beside the lashed wheel. Deliberately, almost carefully, he flung the brand in a high arc toward the main deck. He watched it hover for a second, then plunge down through the big, open hatch of the main cargo hold. Then he slid down the rope into the waiting arms of a crewman in the boat below the stern. The others had the oars out and were pulling away before Du Bois had recovered his balance.

The Marquis de Montcalm watched the display on the river from his field headquarters at Beauport in the center of the river line. The following morning he sent a mild rebuke to the Sieur de Louche.

Major General Wolfe had arrived at the western end of Ile d'Orleans on the day the fireships went out. On that day he saw for the first time the citadel of Quebec perched high on its eyrie. Wolfe saw, too, the long line of newly turned earth on the north shore, and through his glass he picked out the strong points at all the places where he would choose to put his soldiers ashore. Montcalm, who had adopted the Beauport line defense while Wolfe was still a regimental commander, had anticipated the place of a British attack and had forestalled it. James Wolfe, now without a plan, spent the night of 29 June implementing a maneuver forced on him by his naval commander.

Admiral Saunders had tactfully pointed out to the general that the anchorage of the fleet was in the shadow of Point Lévis. Wolfe had agreed to send Monckton to seize the heights, and on the night of the fireships, the admiral

was busy. The confusion caused by the flaming hulks drift
ing down on the fleet was handled without panic. Young
officers in the ships' boats rowed up to the burning vessel
and cast the grappling hooks. Despite the bursting guns and
showering sparks, the sailors pulled at their oars to haul the
fireships to the inshore shallows. Of all the vessels in the
roads, only the old *Centurion* was discommoded. She was
nearest of all to Quebec and was forced to cut her anchor
cable to drop back out of harm's way.

Billy Howe crossed from Ile d'Orleans to the south shore
while the light from the burning fireships still made silhou-
ettes of the British fleet, swinging calmly at anchor in the
low ebb of the tide. With him was his British light infantry,
eager young men, and the companies of American rangers,
dour in this army of Englishmen. Immediately on landing
they had rushed a farmhouse, which they found empty, and
quickly burned it. When the light infantry heard the
screams from the cellar, they dashed back, but the flames
had engulfed the building, and the inhabitants perished.
Sobered, the men pushed on toward the village of Beaumont. Howe hurried his soldiers on when he heard the firing from where the rangers were closing in. When Brigadier
Monckton arrived with four regiments, the rangers had the
bodies of seven soldiers of the Marine laid in a row beside
the cemetery fence. Seven rangers wore new scalps in their
belts. Two others, slightly wounded, guarded five frightened Frenchmen, squatting on the ground as they had been
told to do.

The sun was on the church spire when Brigadier Monckton stood on the steps as a drummer nailed a proclamation
on the door. At ten o'clock, the brigade marched for Point
Lévis, through the back woodlots of the riverside farms.
During the frequent halts, the leading companies were deployed to drive back Canadians in blanket coats, who stood
for a moment, then were gone like the white puffs of smoke

from their muskets. The brigade climbed up a twisting trail through thick underbrush and reached the heights, where there was fine, cultivated land and a good road, on which the sergeants could march the men in proper ranks. The officers were satisfied. The British did not have to fight for Point Lévis until the sun was low over a copse that lay in the line of march. A mixed force of 1600 Frenchmen waited in the copse and on the hill behind the church and parsonage on the south side of the road. Monckton stood in the middle of the road, watching his regiments deploy into the fields. With his staff he waited until he heard firing in behind the high, rocky ground where Howe had gone with the light troops. Then he sent the Highlanders scrambling up over rocks, and the whole brigade moved forward to the beating of the drums. The French fell back and did not return.

Brigadier Monckton stood out on the top of Point Lévis that evening and watched the lights come on in the city across the way. The artillery officer accompanying him had gone leaping off to look for gun positions, with the general's admonition to beware of skulking Indians and lurking *habitants*. Behind him, Monckton's brigade was going into bivouac. Howe, his light infantry bedded down with pickets out, joined the brigadier to view the city on which night had fallen. Colonel Burton joined them, having just brought up reinforcements. The city on the other side of the river was speckled with light, from the edge of the black water to the deep blue sky above the battlements and spires and roof trees.

Montcalm had not expected Captain Joseph Chaussegros de Léry to hold Point Lévis. The general had hoped to fortify the place, but the governor vetoed the idea. Vaudreuil had fuzzy confidence that Léry's Marine and militia, stout-hearted good Canadians all, would hold back the red-coated tide from Europe—they were defending their

homeland, and none more than Léry. In the city acro
the river were the wife and the children that he had left t
go west again in 1754. Léry's father, three years in the city
cemetery, had built Quebec's great wall, the one that face
the Plains of Abraham.

Joseph de Léry, poised with his musket behind a rocl
saw the Highland regulars climbing up the steep slope. T
his right, he had been told, those regulars, dressed in th
little round hats that rangers wore, were approaching in
wide skirmish line, running from tree to tree, in the tactic
of the "little war" at which his own Canadians were s
adept. In the five years of the long war, the British regula
with their "light infantry" had adopted the tactics of th
North America woods: the Indian fighting, the *"peti
guerre."* They had added this new type of soldier to th
left of the traditional regimental line, as an armorer braise
a new cutting-blade onto an old halberd. With the Britis
light infantry coming on in short rushes on his flank, an
the battalion companies advancing behind their volley fir
and bayonets, Léry left the tenuous shelter of his rock. Th
time had come for him to fall back behind the ancestral wall
of stone, and make his stand at the hearth of his Canadia
home.

The Marquis de Montcalm's victory over General Aber
cromby, in early July of 1758, had been fought as a clos
defense. For the two years preceding that engagement, th
marquis had successfully carried out a swinging, slashing
aggressive defense of New France. The campaigns agains
Oswego and Fort William Henry had been at a time wher
the number of French regulars in the interior of Nortl
America equaled that of the British. At Carillon in 1758
Montcalm had concentrated all his regulars against a nearl
equal number of British regulars. General Abercromby ha
had sixteen battalions of colonials, who, that afternoon, ha

roved their competence as soldiers and their bravery as
men against the abatis and the trenches. With God's help,
Montcalm had thrown back the enemy. Though the gov-
rnor general of New France had "suggested" that, follow-
ng that victory, he should go over to the offensive, Mont-
alm had held to his tight defense of Fort Carillon, and
ad been criticized as wanting in initiative, boldness, and
ourage.

For the rest of that campaign season Montcalm and his
regulars had been pinned down on the Ticonderoga Penin-
ula by a still-formidable British army, that remained poised
nd capable of attacking again. All through the days of
uly and August and September 1758, the little war of
angers and Indians had flashed and rumbled like a summer
storm through the woods and mountains of the no-man's-
and between Ticonderoga and the Hudson River. Under
he hot sun, the two opposing armies worked at their mili-
ary building. The French strengthened Fort Carillon, and
on the ashes of the fort Montcalm had burned, the British
rebuilt the advance position on Lake George. But they did
not try again for the prize of Ticonderoga on Lake Champlain, though they sent more regiments to the Hudson
River. These new troops were fresh from their victory at
Louisbourg.

Autumn winds ruffled the lakes when General Amherst
himself came to see Fort Edward at the Great Carrying
Place, and to inspect the troops on the northern frontier.
Amherst, the conqueror of Louisbourg, had replaced Abercromby, conquered at Carillon, as the commander in chief
in North America. The new general's tour included a ride
on a crisp morning up the portage road to the new installations building at Lake George. Before the road began to
climb out of the Hudson Valley, the inspection party
paused and the general dismounted. While the servants prepared a little picnic, Amherst walked, through scuffling

leaves, to see the big boulder that the French claimed as th
southern boundary of New France. At staff talks with hi
ranger officers, with his naval advisor, Commodore Loring
with his supply and transport experts, and with the troo;
commanders, General Amherst laid his plans for the 175
campaign against Ticonderoga and Lake Champlain. Ther
with the white frost lingering in the shadows of the walls
Amherst sent his regulars into winter quarters, the colonial
to their homes, and secured the northern forts for winter

With Amherst and his army gone from his front, Mont
calm could give up his vigil over the lakes and turn his ful
attention to his army's role in the next year's defense o
Canada. There was, in fact, little for him to do but wait th
coming of spring and the return of the British to their clos
siege of New France. Many of the general's schemes an
plans rested on the outcome of Bougainville's embassy to
the Court at Versailles: what reinforcements he would
bring back, what diversions France would make, and how
the king would adjudicate the dispute between the civil and
military authority in New France.

The defense of Canada, after Britain's successful campaigns at Louisbourg and Fort Frontenac, had become a
naval, rather than an army, consideration. Even the one
French victory in an otherwise disastrous year had pointed
to a naval solution for the defense of Lake Champlain, by
demonstrating the precarious tenability of Fort Carillon
when faced by an enemy in the numbers Britain now could
send against it.

Among the Marquis de Vaudreuil's honorary and com-
plimentary titles was that of *capitain de vaisseau*. Though he
had never captained a navy ship, the rank echoed of broadsides and gave him confidence in an element where an army
general might have been dismissed as ignorant. During the
winter of 1758-59, Governor de Vaudreuil decreed the
building of two fleets for use in the spring. One was for

ake Ontario, to carry men and supplies to Fort Niagara, and beyond to the portage post at Venango, where Ligneris waited to return to the forks of the Ohio. The other fleet, to e built at the northern end of Lake Champlain, Vaudreuil ave to Doloboratz, the naval captain who had dared the winter passage to bring his ship into Louisbourg on 6 January 758. Captain Doloboratz was a Mediterranean sailor, and e built three lithe xebecs to row and sail in the inland ake. With these three vessels and the converted merchant chooner *Vigilante*, he could command Lake Champlain, whether Fort Carillon and Fort St. Frédéric fell or were by-passed, until the British built a bigger, better fleet.

Louisbourg had been the visor of the helmeted head of New France at Quebec. With this outer defense struck off, he capital city of Canada, bare-faced, looked down the wide St. Lawrence estuary to the Atlantic Ocean. At Quebec the river narrowed and the naval defense of New France returned to the land. The confident governor was sure that the batteries of the city could prevent those British warships which had made the difficult passage of the traverse from going further upstream. Montcalm was less sanguine. In his request to France, he had made an appeal for more guns and competent artillery officers to site them into the river defenses of Quebec.

Both the general and the governor were at Montreal, still unreconciled to each other, when Colonel Bougainville returned from France. Not finding his general at Quebec and finding the city calm, the aide-de-camp immediately realized that no one in New France knew that Wolfe and Saunders were on the eve of attacking the city. Without pausing, Bougainville hurried up the river to find Montcalm. At his journey's end, where it had begun, in the private chamber of the Marquis de Montcalm, Colonel Bougainville told his news of the British, of the Court, of France, and of the western world in tumult.

The embassy of the young soldier-diplomat-mathemat
cian had been a personal success for him and for his genera
Bougainville had been promoted to colonel, given the Cro
of St. Louis, and had been well received and complimente
by Madame de Pompadour. Montcalm was raised to lieuter
ant general, a military rank which was senior to the sam
grade held by the governor general on the colonial list o
government protocol. Further to underline Montcalm
ascendancy over Vaudreuil in matters of the defense o
Canada, a letter had been sent to the governor, orderin
him to accept the general's judgment in all military matter
and to keep out of the way. Having apparently won th
struggle for control, Colonel Bougainville had taken it upo
himself to recommend, in Montcalm's name, that the Gran
Cross of the Order of St. Louis be given to the governo
general. Only one so devoted to Montcalm and so loved b
him as was Bougainville would have dared arouse the gen
eral's anger by making such a tactful and magnanimous ges
ture to a rival so despised, though beaten.

In other areas of his embassy the general's confidant me
with no spectacular success. The king was remote and apa
thetic to all but the light pleasures provided by Madame d
Pompadour. Though gracious and lavish with the bauble
of honors, she was interested only in keeping the king's at
tention on herself. The others at the Court of Versailles lis
tened to the young soldier from New France, were sym
pathetic, generally alarmed at the agony of Canada, anc
helped where they could. The minister of war sent 40c
infantry soldiers to fill out the ranks of Montcalm's eigh
battalions, forty gunners, and munitions. He could send nc
new regiments to Canada that year as La Pompadour wa
jealously pressing her war against the spidery little King
of Prussia. The minister of Marine sent but four small ship
to the St. Lawrence in 1759. Together, the army and th
navy turned down Montcalm's proposed diversion; on

laimed that the Prussian War prevented them from divert-
ng troops, the other, that England's blockade threatened
ne French coast, and both, that they themselves were too
ccupied with a proposed invasion of the British Isles to
issipate their energy, attention, or resources elsewhere.
Iontcalm's scheme had been for an amphibious attack,
rom bases in the French West Indies, on the unprotected
oast of Virginia and the Carolinas, to draw Amherst's
egulars away from Lake Champlain.

In fact, William Pitt had forestalled such a plan before
Bougainville presented it. Though he was castigated by his
ld rival, Newcastle, for denuding England of troops in the
ace of an invasion—46,000 British soldiers were overseas in
759—Pitt still had the power to persist in his policy of
triking at France in her colonies. That winter, while
France built invasion barges and David Garrick lampooned
he effort as he sang the rousing "Heart of Oak," Pitt sent
nore troops onto the transports. Following up the success
n French Sénégal in 1758, 4000 men took Gorée, further
lown the West African coast. The year of 1759 was young
vhen eight British regiments went ashore at Guadeloupe in
he Windward Islands to begin gathering in the rotting
ruits of France's West Indian colonies. There was little
iope for a diversion for Montcalm by a governor and an
idmiral besieged in their own homes and, like Canada, for-
aken in the halls and boudoirs at Versailles.

What hope there was for New France, or the West In-
lian colonies, to survive Pitt's onslaught in the new year
ested on the diplomatic and political efforts of an ill-
eatured, small, sturdy Frenchman, whose services to Ma-
lame de Pompadour had favored him with a dukedom and
he portfolio of foreign minister. Étienne François, Duc de
Choiseul, inspired the plan to invade the British Isles, but
iis real threat to Pitt's England lay in his rare ability to
contrive the implementing treaties which would give the

invasion a chance of success. Choiseul and Pitt clashed
head-on in a struggle to dominate the Estates General and
the ten-year-old Stadholder of the United Provinces (The
Netherlands). Pitt, aided by a British princess who was
regent, kept Holland neutral, though Choiseul had been
prepared to give all Acadia for the help of the Dutch fleet
in invading England and protecting the mouth of the St
Lawrence.

In Canada there was hope that England's armies would
be called back from the ramparts of New France, and that
the tincture of time and the essence of patience would heal
the severe wounds inflicted by England during the campaign of 1758. There was balm in the tale related by three
British soldiers, taken prisoner on 12 May. Though a scruffy
trio out of the 3rd battalion of the 60th, each swore that
England had been invaded, and one of the three had it from
an officer's servant (always a reliable source) that a French
army was in London. The third man, an Irishman, had it
straight that peace had been made.

But Bougainville's return quenched the fires of the winter's dreams, and the colonel's long report showed clearly
the cold gray ash of facts. Wolfe and Saunders were coming to Quebec, there lay the army's duty, and there, perhaps, the army could defend and delay the British while
Choiseul invaded the enemy homeland.

On 21 May, the Marquis de Montcalm left Montreal for
Quebec. He left with his sense of duty pure, his resolve
high, his soldiers gay, and his weariness as private as the
locket miniature of his wife. In the last days at Montreal,
he wrote her of his love, but his request to return to his
home had been denied. The King of France could not bring
home the hero of Fort Carillon, though that place was
doomed.

With the spring thaw, Montcalm had sent the literal
Bourlamaque to Carillon with three precious battalions of

regulars, eight companies of the Marine, and 1200 militia-men. They were given little discretion. Hold unless at-tacked; if pressed, retreat on Ile aux Noix in the river out-let of Lake Champlain. The four-vessel navy of Doloboratz would keep the lake for France.

XVII

———

Sailors and Soldiers

For three years, Captain Joshua Loring, Royal Navy, had been scuffing leaves in the forest instead of stalking on the planks of a quarter-deck. He was Boston born, and therefore a rare colonial fish in the senior service. He was a natural selection by Admiralty House for the odd duty of commanding water transportation for Lord Loudoun's campaigns into the interior parts of North America. Loudoun had not used Loring, promoted captain in 1757, on the inland lakes that year, and the captain's talents had no chance to show under Abercromby. Under Jeffrey Amherst, the landlocked captain could expect to "go to sea" again on Lake Champlain. Lake George, which Loring encompassed in his title of "Commodore of the Lakes," had never been a naval problem, because the French had never maintained a big-ship navy on its waters. In building up the bateau service, Colonel Bradstreet had usurped from the navy the duty of transporting the army over water. The gunners of the Royal Artillery had undertaken the close defense of the bateau fleet afloat on Lake George by manning the cumbersome radeaux or floating batteries, craft which any decent sailor would look upon with contempt. Robert Rogers, the ranger from New Hampshire, used his fast, armed whaleboats on both Lake George and Lake Champlain more as coast-scavenging corsair than as a true, bluewater sailor. In 1759, however, Lake Champlain and the army's drive on Montreal had become a task for the British navy. With four French vessels sailing its waters as a fleet under command of a naval officer, neither Bradstreet, nor the gunners, nor Robert Rogers could move north until Loring's big warships captured Lake Champlain.

The Commodore of the Lakes breakfasted by candlelight aboard his flagship, the sloop *Halifax*, on the morning that General Amherst's army embarked at the head of Lake George to go to Ticonderoga. For Joshua Loring the soldiers were going to capture Carillon, so that he could have a dockyard and a launching site into Lake Champlain. From his breakfast table he could reach across his tiny cabin to the racked shelf where he kept at hand the rolled plans of his two big ships. In the hold of *Halifax* were big bundles of sails to dress the masts and spars still growing as trees in the forest near Ticonderoga. Stowed below were blocks and tackle, coils of rope, barrels of spikes, and boxes of chandlery. He had made the long trip to New York to purchase these against the day, now fast approaching, when he would build his fleet.

The light of dawn was faint in the stern window when Captain Loring put down his serviette, buckled on his sword, and took the single step that brought him to the door. The door stuck in its frame. The whole vessel was still wet and stank of the damp. *Halifax* had been fished up, only ten days before, from the bottom of the lake, where she had rested since Montcalm's "visit" in 1757. But Loring had seen fit to raise her for the sake of pride—the pride of the navy on Lake George.

In the breaking light of dawn, Captain Loring could see the other elements of the two ships with which he would sweep the French from Lake Champlain. The boats carrying the cannon and carriages were already loaded, in spite of the rickety dock which had collapsed under the weight of a mortar. Forming up in the lake were the provincial troops, all but the Jersey "Blues," New Englanders whose woodsmen would cut the timbers, knees and planks for the ships. The ship carpenters, for the most part, were with the tool boats and the artillery rafts. A shipwright, whom Loring wanted and had been promised, was serving with Montgomery's Highlanders up where a din of bagpipe music horribly scarred the dawn among the bateaux of the regulars. Loring's second boat would be captained by another Scottish officer, Grant, who was still with his regiment. Scattered among the boats forming parade lines in the lake were 120 seamen who, when the time came, would scramble up tall masts, instead of tugging at oars. All the elements of two ships-of-war set out from old Fort William Henry on the morning of 21 July 1759. Bringing up the rear of the army armada came *Halifax*, with Loring on her quarter-deck, and the knowledge and the ability to make, sail, and fight the ships under the sailor's cocked hat that he wore slightly askew.

Leading the four orderly columns of boats, with the light infantry's whaleboats in line to right and left, General Amherst sat in the stern of his own private boat. He was two weeks behind Abercromby's schedule on the march to Ticonderoga. It was a delay that would cost him dear at the end of the campaign, for he knew that once the French forts at Ticonderoga and Crown Point had been taken, there would be a long wait while the naval types built their ships. Colonel Roger Townshend saw that the general slept, slumped in his nest of cushions. The work load of the commander in chief had been heavy all spring, and there had been exasperations and worry. Principally, Amherst had worried about Colonel Prideaux's expedition to Fort Niagara. He had given the colonel two of the regiments that had been with Abercromby in '58, as well as the 4th battalion, 60th regiment, to stay at Oswego under Colonel Frederick Haldimand. All the New York militia had gone west with Prideaux under command of the doubtful Sir William Johnson. Amherst had given the big Irish baronet £3000 from the war chest, with which to buy the Indians. Still the general worried about the west. Before he had gone to sleep, he had determined to send Colonel Zacheus Lovewell's New Hampshire militia to Oswego, where Haldimand had been annoyed by Canadians and Indians. They could go after the landing at the north end of Lake George.

As a thorough staff officer, Amherst was confident of his own ability to capture the French forts. He had six good regiments of regulars, three of which had been with him at Louisbourg. In the ten battalions of colonials were many men and officers who had been with Abercromby to "Boges," as they called Ticonderoga. They had fought well in the charges against the French trenches, and they wanted their revenge. The problems of transport had delayed the army and exasperated the general. Colonel Bradstreet's slowness in organizing the bateaux had called forth Amherst's anger. For over two weeks, he had watched while Loring struggled to get the sloop up from the bottom of the lake. Even Orde, the gunner who had built the radeau, took four days after the launching to find that the gun ports had been cut too high for the gun carriages. But on the 21st day of July, with the army underway, Major General Jeffrey Amherst could sleep in the stern of his boat. Colonel Townshend watched the wild shoreline go by and looked up at the high green mountains, scraping the clouds in a blue sky.

By the next day Jeffrey Amherst was alert once more, standing in the bows of his vessel as the first troops went ashore. They were Rogers's rangers and Gage's light infantry, who quickly shook themselves out and soon were swallowed by the woods. The light infantry and grenadiers of regiments were forming the first tight perimeter, when Amherst himself rowed in to the beach. There was no enemy opposition. After dark the rangers brought in two meek French prisoners as a curiosity for the general. Private Robert Webster of the 4th Connecticut saw them as they were marched by the fire where he was stacking 12-pound cannon balls from the artillery boats. Much later, when Webster sat eating his supper at his company fire, he told the clerk, a timid man, that they were huge, savage Papists, who would eat a Connecticut Protestant as quick as a grasshopper.

In the morning all the regulars moved out, down the portage road to the lower falls, the mill there, the bridge, and the road up onto the heights. By early afternoon they had sealed off the Ticonderoga Peninsula, on the tip of which stood the French fort. Gunners went with them, dragging light field pieces over the two miles of road. Seeing the guns, so noticeable by their absence the year before, the French holding Montcalm's trench system fell back into the embrace of the stone walls of Fort Carillon. From the embrasures on the west wall and demilune, big guns opened fire, wafting round shot out toward where the British were.

Down at the sawmill, Commodore Loring was busy. His crew of carpenters was set to repair the machinery, while he looked to the road for the smith to come with the traveling forge. He had sent trusted men into the forest to spot trees for keels and ribs. It was not until the following day, 25 July, that the first of the whaleboats and the general's boat arrived from Lake George and were launched in the pool below the mill. They had been brought over for Robert Rogers and his rangers. His role in the siege, which was set to open with a cannonade at dawn on the 27th, was to cut the boom across the lake, get up above the fort, and play the corsair with French boats of any kind moving on the water. He was too late.

At ten o'clock on the night of 26 July, a French deserter came in to one of the batteries ready and waiting to begin fire. His story was that M. Bourlamaque and all the French had left the fort, mining it before their departure. Rogers was on the lake, making a quiet approach to the boom, when the fort blew up. For a blinding instant the crisp, straight lines of masonry stood out, clear and sharp on the hill crest. The flag was flying. Smaller explosions followed, and fires picked out the detail of a broken barrack wall in silhouette. Sometime during the night a British volunteer had gone into the fort, taken down the French colors, and delivered them to General Amherst as he stood watching the conflagration.

Fort Carillon was still burning on 1 August when word was brought to General Amherst that Fort St. Frédéric had been abandoned, and the French fleet, two sloops and a schooner, had sailed north, away from Crown Point. The old troubles that plagued the commander in chief on the Hudson and at Lake George had returned to Amherst on Lake Champlain. Bradstreet, Loring, and Orde were wrangling over priorities for building bateaux, ships, or radeaux. Amherst was impatient of anything that delayed getting boats—all types of boats—ready to move the army safely down the lake so that he could get at Montreal. There was a disconcerting rumor that Prideaux had been killed in the west. Giving credence to the report, Amherst sent Colonel Thomas Gage of the 80th Light Infantry, who had been in America since Braddock's day, hurrying toward Fort Niagara to take over the command. If Prideaux were dead, Amherst could count on a dispute in seniority between the inflated "Baronet of the Mohawk" and the dogged Swiss professional soldier, Frederick Haldimand. Four days later,

Amherst, still fretful over the western campaign, sent the 42nd Highlanders, from the reserve, to Oswego. He ordered them and the regiments already there to put pressure on Montreal from the west.

On Lake Champlain, the commander in chief could only walk the pleasant shore, and wait for the building of the fleet. To keep the army from idleness, he set the men to building a great fortress at Crown Point, which the general had selected as the main British defensive position and forward base on Lake Champlain.

In all the ruck of duty that he had to do, there was one personal obligation—a relict of the almost bloodless siege of Ticonderoga—that must be met. On 25 July, a chance French shot with a heavy ball, all but spent, had hit and killed Roger Townshend. Late at night when his other work was done, General Amherst wrote Brigadier Townshend of his brother's death. The letter went in a pack for Wolfe and Saunders at Quebec.

Brigadier General George Townshend's wit was as acid as his pen was facile. He had opportunity to sketch, in his languid way, between the time he settled in his brigade on the western tip of Ile d'Orleans and the next time Wolfe called on him to do a job. Townshend had a fine target in his gawky, thin general, who had arrived to take Quebec without a plan for doing so. To be fair to Wolfe, which did not concern the lordly son of a peer when fairness dulled a witticism, it must be said the general had had a plan, but not an alternative to it.

On the map, and in fact, the only obviously feasible way for an army to attack Quebec was for it to land east of the city and to storm it from the landward side. Both Mac-Kellar and Stobo, the latter having been in Quebec as recently as 1 May, could report to General Wolfe that the French had made no attempt to fortify the vulnerable downriver stretch of the north shore. Since Montcalm's arrival in Quebec on the evening of 22 May, however, the calm face of the riverside east of the city had been changed from a welcoming smile to a forbidding grin. For six miles, from the St. Charles River end to the high cliffs over which the River Montmorency poured in a cascade of breathtaking grandeur, French trenches, breastworks, and redoubts ran the crestline of the high ground facing the St. Lawrence. By 1 July, the beaches where Wolfe would land were a killing ground for well-protected French and Canadian musketmen. The mud flats, which at low tide carried the shoreline far out into the river, and the shallows beyond, were a wide abatis covered by French cannon, into which the British warships could not venture to give effective counter-battery fire in support of a landing.

The Marquis de Montcalm had made his military appreciation for the defense of Quebec during his first week in New France, when Wolfe was a lieutenant colonel without prospects. Then, and on a later reconnaissance, Montcalm had found the palisades west of the city unscalable to an army, had foreseen the probabilities of a landing east of the city, and had decided on the defensive policy of preventing the enemy from coming ashore. In five weeks during the spring of 1759, Montcalm built the Beauport lines with a labor force of five battalions of regulars and militia companies, amounting in all to 10,800 men. This did not include the city garrison of gunners, sailors, and militia, or the Indians, who were not much given to digging. When the British fleet came into the basin and the redcoats spilled out over Ile d'Orleans and the south shore, the Marquis de Montcalm took up his field headquarters at the village of Beauport, in the center of the line. Bougainville commanded the French right, while Lévis's responsibility for the left included the upriver ford of the Montmorency River.

Major General James Wolfe had first seen the astonishing sight of the Beauport lines from the western tip of Ile d'Orleans. At the time the fleet was negotiating the traverse and the grenadiers were carefully clearing the island from east to west. Wolfe had thrust forward impatiently with his light infantry, to be among the first to reach "his" city. In the mounded earth of the river line, he saw the grave of his plan to attack Quebec from the landward side. Like a colt thwarted by the closing of a gate to keep it from its mother, he backed off, kicked out irritably, and looked in every direction for a way over or around the obstacle keeping him from the achievement of his ends. The frustration brought on a colic.

Wolfe's irritability showed in his criticism of Brigadier Monckton's position on Cape Lévis, which he visited. His temper spilled over in sharp anger at Saunders, who had not taken prompt action against the French gunboats which had pushed out from the city to bombard the British brigade on the Point Lévis. Wolfe felt again those sharp, downward pains, deep in his abdomen. For the young general, there was always the sovereign remedy of action. With an escort of light infantry, Wolfe left the safe perimeter of Monckton's position for a westward dash to see the north shore above Quebec. He returned ebullient with a wild scheme for a pincer movement on the city. But the landing of two brigades ten miles apart was too wide a stretch for the leverage of the movement. Wolfe gave up that scheme for one calling for a concerted jump over the outside end of the gate, through which, originally, he had planned to walk.

On the night of 8 July, the languid Brigadier Townshend had his brigade down on the north shore of Ile d'Orleans, ready to go into the boats. He himself and all his troops were briefed and efficient, set to cross the north channel of the St. Lawrence and make a strong point on the cliffs and on the plateau along the east bank of the Montmorency

River. But the fun and the excitement had been taken out of the brigadier's orders. General Wolfe, leaving St. Peter's Church shortly after midnight, had already gone over with the grenadiers, light infantry, and American rangers to fight for and secure the brigade's objective. There was little opportunity for glory for a brigadier in an army whose general chose to act like a regimental officer. Townshend's river-crossing was a boat ride, and in the next days Murray brought over his brigade, and fifty guns came too, so that the bulk of the British army hovered menacingly on the French left.

The Marquis de Montcalm, secure in his Beauport lines, reacted calmly to Wolfe's taking station across the Montmorency. His concerns were elsewhere. The governor general, in spite of his orders from Paris, still rankled the general's southern temperament and continued to veto the general's military plans. The loss of Point Lévis to Monckton had largely been due to the inertia of Vaudreuil. For some time, Montcalm had doubted the ability of the Chevalier de Ramezay as a gunner and the ability of the French guns to cover the whole wide expanse of the St. Lawrence between the city and the south shore. On the night of 18 July, Captain Rouse, a Bostonian, easily ran the 60-gun *Sutherland* up past the Quebec batteries. This ship and the ones that accompanied her put a strain on the city's supply lines, for the town lieutenant and the civil authority had sent the stores upriver to safety with the French frigates. Each night a convoy of boats brought the necessary food back down the river. The British squadron threatened the city's life-line, and on 21 July Colonel Carleton gave further cause for French concern by raiding the village of Pointe aux Trembles, eighteen miles west of Quebec.

For the civilians confined in Quebec, there was the excitement of gossip in the details of Carleton's raid. The Sieur La Casse, who had resigned from the reserve because of weakness in his legs, had been captured by the British while abed with Madame de Landry. Confinement breeds rumor and there was much rumor floating between the upper and the lower town of Quebec. The French had re-taken Louisbourg! The King of Prussia had lost 20,000 men in a single battle. This news, brought into Quebec by a de-serter, was true, as was the tale that the Queen of Hungary (meaning Maria Theresa) had retaken Silesia. As they gath-ered to view the bomb damage to their city—the British cannonading of Quebec had begun in earnest on 16 July—the *habitants* took consolation in the discomfort of the British king, who, according to gossip, had lost his Han-overian homeland to Louis. And another rumor was passed about, while the cathedral burned and the rosaries clicked. If true, and there was reason and logic in it, the decisive battle for the city was at hand with the advantage in favor of Montcalm. Deserters had said that Admiral Saunders had given "Le Général Wolfe" until the end of July to take Quebec. Then the fleet must leave the river.

The battle for which Montcalm was ready was fought on the last day of July, almost as if to confirm the rumor. Wolfe had had numerous plans for his July battle. Hardly a place along the whole river bank, below, at, and above the city, but had been considered by the general in his frustra-tion. For a day, or even a few days, while the current plan was revolving in the general's mind, a flurry of preparation and movement stirred the British troops in the camps at Montmorency, at Ile d'Orleans, and at Cape Lévis on the south shore. Then the plan would be dropped for another. At one time, Wolfe was going to scale the palisades west of the town. The French had even expected such a brash attempt. Le Mercier, the gunner, built a battery at the most likely place near St. Michel, and the western hero, Dumas, was sent with militia, most of the Indians, and 200 cavalry-men to patrol the Heights of Abraham. It was the experienced eye of Admiral Saunders, who had first gone to sea in 1727, the year that Wolfe was born, that detected the weakness in the amphibious role of that scheme, and irked the general when he blew cool on the naval side. With the current plan for an assault landing in the lower town, it was Saunders who refused the support of a naval bombardment. He was irritatingly correct when he demonstrated that the deck guns of his ships could not elevate to shell the French batteries, shooting down from the high town.

The plan of attack that was to become the battle of 31 July matured from an unsuccessful raid, and from the simple idea of seizing a waterfront battery. The raid to the upriver falls of the Montmorency, led, of course, by the general himself, proved, at the loss of forty-five British casualties, that the French left could not be turned in that direction. The French had two redoubts on the shore beneath the cliffs at the Montmorency end of the Beauport lines. The one furthest from the river mouth was to be the target for an attack by four companies of grenadiers from Ile d'Orleans. It was almost an inspiration, certainly an undigested afterthought, to support the limited-objective attack of the grenadiers with a full-scale assault on the nearest redoubt from across the estuary ford of the Montmorency. The strategy was to tempt Montcalm down from his heights to a general battle on the shore.

The expanding plan of attack, which by the time it was executed involved most of the troops of the three brigades, discommoded the navy to a very slight degree. To carry the first wave of four companies of grenadiers in close to the west redoubt, two cat-built armed transports were detached from the fleet. They, *Three Sisters* and *Russell*, had the additional role of bombardment. As the plan grew in scope, Admiral Saunders himself volunteered to take *Centurion*, of fond memory, opposite the eastern redoubt, to help shoot Townshend and Murray across the ford below

the Montmorency Cascade. Ships' boats, of course, would
be used to ferry Monckton's two regiments over from Point
Lévis. Captain Alexander Schomberg, who had run his
command, *Diana*, ashore the night the British squadron
came up the river, went with Monckton's brigade as naval
beachmaster. All the details of the overwater attack were
predicated on the soundings on the north side of Ile d'Orleans by the scientifically painstaking Captain James Cook
of *Pembroke*. Captain Cook had led the two captains to
believe it possible to get within a hundred yards of the shore
redoubt at the high tide. But they were still 500 yards from
shore when they felt the mud grip their keels, and slowly
squeeze the forward motion out of the hulls. Before she
finally stopped, *Three Sisters* glanced off an underwater
obstacle and came to rest in the bed of mud, with neither
broadside able to bear on her target. As a bombardment
ship, she was worthless.

Soon after the transports grounded, a boat came up
astern of *Russell*. Wolfe stood in the bow calling through
cupped hands for permission to come aboard, while still
two jumps and a run distant. Ile d'Orleans, where the other
grenadiers were loading, was too far removed from the action for James Wolfe. The action came as the French
gunners on the heights felt out the range. Wolfe had not
been on deck long when an enemy round shot struck the
walking stick from his hand. Seemingly gone with the first
broadside from *Russell* were the pains and aches of the indecisive month of July. In the opening fire of the fifty
British guns at Montmorency was an elixir of health and
hope for August.

It was high tide, it had to be, when the armed transports
were run in over the mud flats to ground. It had to be an
hour from the low tide before Murray's and Townshend's
men could cross the Montmorency ford. During the hours
of the ebb, the four companies of the first wave of troops

at in the heat of the between-decks of *Three Sisters* and *Russell*. As he paced on deck, judging the effect of the bombardment, James Wolfe was twice hit by flying splinters. Further out in the stream, beyond the range of the French cannon, the second wave of grenadiers sat, crowded on the benches of the assault boats. Sergeant Edward Botwood of the 47th tried to write a rousing verse to the tune of "Hot Stuff," but even his favorite pastime could not take his mind from the rolling motion of the boat. In the early morning, from under Point Lévis, a long line of ships' boats had started to row the 15th Foot and Fraser's Highlanders to the rendezvous with the grenadiers' boats. Under the cliffs, the leading battalion of Townshend's brigade waited in the hot sun for the mud flats to emerge from the water. In late July, the roar of Montmorency Falls is only a whisper, as the tumbling water subsides to a mere trickle. The rumble, heard by the men sitting quietly under the cliff, was that of their own guns above them, and the more distant sound of thunder.

Before four o'clock in the afternoon, Wolfe signaled from *Russell* for the grenadiers' boats to start in. At the signal the men under the cliff were also on their feet, ready to move out. But Townshend's men were halted by a second signal, and they could see that the boats were huddled together and were not moving forward. Standing in the mud, Townshend and Murray could surmise that something had gone amiss. There was small-boat activity around *Centurion*, which meant that the admiral and the navy, and not Wolfe alone, had caused the foul-up.

An underwater field of big boulders edged the channel west of the Montmorency River outlet, and this had not been detected by Captain Cook's sounding. At low water the boulders formed a wicket through which the grenadiers' boats could not pass. The boulder-field held the soldiers for an hour and a quarter, while Wolfe himself, in his rowing boat, found a way around and through the obstacle. It was a very precious hour and fifteen minutes—fighting time cut from the heart of Townshend's and Murray's schedule of tides. If Montcalm did not come down from the heights to fight, the two brigades must hurry back across the ford before the water rose again.

The sky was darkening to a black thundercloud, when the grenadiers' boats moved in past the armed transports. Sergeant Botwood's poetic soul danced with the lightning playing over the City of Quebec. When Lieutenant, Acting-Captain, David Ouchterlony's flatboat grounded in the mud, he was over the stern in an instant, calling to his Royal Americans to follow. He was surprised to find the water waist-deep. At the bow, as he struggled forward, stood Henry Peyton, cursing in a cheerful mood at the grinning men who were sliding into the water. A stink from the riled mud filled their nostrils. Ahead, where the four companies of the first wave were forming up, field music was playing the Grenadiers' March. With a splashing, stumbling rush, the grenadiers of the 60th dashed forward to the concert. Ouchterlony and Peyton ran with them. Grenadiers from other boats, too, were charging through the shallowing water. At the top of his voice, Sergeant Botwood was singing his own song; the grenadiers were in their own wild charge for the redoubt. Wolfe snatched at a running officer and ordered him to hold his men in hand. The plan was to form up and all go forward together when Monckton's and Townshend's and Murray's troops were ready. The detained officer went racing up the beach after his grenadiers, to bring them back, or to lead them on.

The first wave of grenadiers had taken the redoubt in a swirling rush of bayonets. For a moment they paused, while the second wave deployed and came forward. In that short time the officers might have regained control. But the music of the march—their march—behind them, and the sight of Frenchmen's backs before them, rekindled all the pride of "Hot Stuff." Ned Botwood died in the next rush forward, falling, his arms flung wide, just beyond the redoubt, halfway to the steep, high sand cliff that finally halted the charge of the British Grenadiers. For twenty minutes 800 angry soldiers struggled and scrambled and clawed in an effort to climb the yielding sand. For twenty minutes Canadian marksmen calmly fired on the Englishmen below them.

The grenadiers of the 60th had held together and with their officers had drifted off to the right, where the unmanned eastern redoubt was. Behind it, a fault in the palisade offered a chance to climb up and come to grips with the French and Canadians above. It was there that a crossfire caught David Ouchterlony and sent him, hard-hit, reeling off to a dead angle of the redoubt, there to sink down and, he knew, eventually to die. In the same angle Ouchterlony found Peyton with a smashed knee and a flask uptilted to his lips. The captain shook off the offer of a pull, pointed to the red, oozing hole in his waistcoat, and sat down near his friend. The first drops of rain were falling, big drops that fell faster and faster. There was a squall wind on the river, and with the wind came the rain in sheets. The water was cool as it ran down the faces of the two wounded men in the angle of the wall. Ouchterlony tilted his head back and let his mouth hang open to fill with the sweet, sweet drops. Looking at him, Peyton wondered if he were already dead.

Above the thousand yards of river shore, where 7000 British soldiers mustered in the torrential rain, the Canadians of the Montreal militia eased back their muskets from the parapet and waited for the storm to pass. They grinned at each other as they waited to begin again the pigeon shoot on the red-backed birds below. Some of the men were hold-

ing up empty pouches and calling to their officers for more
cartridges. It had been a busy twenty minutes, for which
they had waited and watched through all the heat of the
stifling day.

The Montreal men were better off than the militiamen
from Trois Rivières who had marched from the St. Charles
end of the Beauport lines. Montcalm had sent for the Trois
Rivières men about noon, when he was sure that the British
attack would fall only on his left. Thereafter the general
had not been seen by the men in the lines. Lévis commanded the French left, and the marquis general had not
interfered, beyond sending reinforcements to the gay
chevalier.

Lévis was pleased with his troops. The regulars had taken
with fortitude their casualties from the British guns across
the Montmorency. Up the river above the falls, rangers and
Indians were patrolling and keeping him informed. But the
Montrealers had shown up beyond expectations. Attacked
by the finest troops of Europe, the picked men of the British Grenadiers, the Canadians had held their fire, cool to
the hot charge. Before the rain came, a group had gone
down the cliff and remanned a small battery. The guns were
so placed that they could worry both Monckton's men
forming behind the western redoubt, and those of Townshend and Murray, across the ford, standing ranked and
ready on the mud flats. No longer could *Centurion* bring
fire on this French battery, for British troops were in the
line of fire.

For fully half an hour the storm's fury hung over the
battlefield, drenching alike friend and foe, dead, wounded,
and whole. Then, like a great, blind bear, it went roaring
and snapping and careening down the St. Lawrence Valley
to the distant sea. On the shore where the English stood exposed, the storm had left the men wet, indecisive, and in a
mounting state of despair.

For Wolfe, too, many things had gone wrong: the sunken rocks, the mad insanity that had swept over the usually steady grenadiers, and the squandered time; an hour and a quarter lost before landing, the half-hour of blinding rain, and now the inexorable rising of the tide to flood the ford. Wolfe ordered back the brigades from Montmorency and sent part of the Highlanders with them. The rest of Monckton's men re-embarked, leaving some boats to help bring off the wounded. The bedraggled grenadiers returned from the foot of the cliff with a truculent pride that brooked no criticism. They carried their wounded with them, and many carried the dead bodies of friends, to save them from butchery by Indians. There were 430 casualties in the short duration of the attack.

Captain Schomberg, with the grenadier who had carried him all the way from the redoubt, helped lift Ensign Peyton into the stern seat of his own boat. The wounded man was white of face, in pain, and perhaps quite drunk with the brandy from the empty flask clutched in his hand. He was weeping a bit, tears of parting mingled with tears of fury and of hurt from spasms of pain. But he assured the navy captain, who cradled him and supported him, that he had left an escort for his heaven-bound friend. He had shot with his pistol one dirty red savage who was trying to scalp the wounded Ouchterlony, and with his bayonet had stabbed the other one.

A French officer found the wounded grenadier captain with two dead Indians at his feet. The Frenchman called for a cart which took David Ouchterlony safely into the hospital across the St. Charles River. For two days he seemed well enough, but no doctor could mend the hole in his vitals. When the fever took hold, he died, but not before politely expressing his thanks to the French soldiers who had brought him safely off the field.

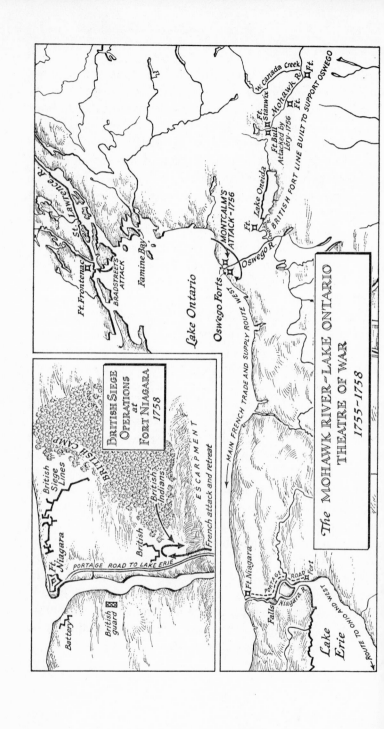

The MOHAWK RIVER~LAKE ONTARIO THEATRE OF WAR 1755~1758

BRITISH SIEGE OPERATIONS at FORT NIAGARA 1758

XVIII

The Avenue to the West

"*Celer et audax*" was the compliment paid by a fond young general to the 60th Royal Americans at Quebec in 1759. "Swift and bold" was General Wolfe's own label when the battle flags tipped forward and the drums tapped fast. But on 31 July, when he stood on the shore in the pelting rain, James Wolfe was sluggish and hesitant. He even condemned the bold dash of the British Grenadiers as "strange behavior."

On the next day, 1 August, Wolfe accepted full responsibility for the hastily and poorly planned battle which had failed so utterly. Wolfe also had reason to call in his personal physician. The pains of the indecisive month of July had returned. With another decision to be arrived at in August, that month, too, would be one of torture for the wispy, tall general.

The Marquis de Vaudreuil, with the enthusiastic optimism inherent in his nature, declared the Battle at Montmorency a significant victory. It was the first battle that the governor general had ever witnessed. He viewed it from his headquarters on the St. Charles River, from where he could have seen little, even if he had gone outside

to look. On the day after the repulse of the English, Vaudreuil was extravagant in extolling the Chevalier de Lévis
as the hero of the day. He even spoke of his admiration for
Montcalm's second-in-command in writing to Colonel
Bourlamaque, who presumably was still holding closed the
southern gateway to Canada at Carillon.

The Marquis de Montcalm, too, wrote to his staunch
friend Bourlamaque. The soldier's view, expressed to another soldier, was that the affair represented but a small
prelude to that which would follow. The day after the
battle Montcalm visited the wounded and sick in the hospital. He walked humbly beside the Reverend Mother
through the neat wards, and took time for a word with the
dying British captain with the outlandish name. On leaving
the long gray building on the St. Charles River plain without the city walls, the marquis ordered wine to be served to
all the patients. Nor did Montcalm forget the Reverend
Mother de Sainte Hélène, Superior of the Hospitalers.
Standing all of six feet in her flowing habit, she was mem-
orable; as the sister of the Chevalier de Ramezay, Lieutenant du Roi of the city, she was important; and as a woman
of the world, she appreciated a good wine at table. She wept
when her big hands closed in death the heather-blue eyes of
Captain David Ouchterlony.

In his own headquarters, Montcalm poured himself a
goblet of *vin ordinaire* and passed the decanter to Bougainville, who sat opposite him. The colonel, graduated from
aide, had drawn his first assignment to an independent command. Since the British had put a squadron above the town,
Montcalm was anxious for the safety of the western approaches to Quebec. With the Beauport lines tested and
proved strong, Montcalm could spare from the trenches
troops and a trusted regular officer. Colonel Bougainville
was the officer, 1000 men, regulars and militia, were the

troops of the new upriver command. Bougainville's mission was to prevent or counterattack any British landing on the north shore. His headquarters would be located at Pointe aux Trembles, a village eighteen miles west of Quebec and a likely place for the enemy to land.

Montcalm correctly estimated the British intent. Before Bougainville could bring his whole mobile counterattack force together, Admiral Holmes was setting Murray's brigade ashore at Pointe aux Trembles. First of the French to arrive were the dragoons, who dismounted and engaged the soldiers on the shore, and particularly the sailors of the boats. When the regulars came up, the dragoons attacked from behind the church, and Murray and the sailors were glad to get away with only 140 casualties. For most of his busy day, Bougainville rode and controlled a wounded horse.

The colonel found congenial quarters and company in Pointe aux Trembles. He was there on 18 August when Holmes and Murray struck again, ten miles further up the St. Lawrence at Deschambault. In that village the French regulars had stored their personal and private kits. Though the French dragoons had galloped ahead at the first alarm, they could do nothing to prevent the plundering of the baggage. By the time Bougainville arrived with his regulars, the sleek, quick English cat was back on its big ship.

After Murray's second raid on the north shore, Montcalm reinforced the upriver force with more companies of grenadiers from the regular regiments. For all the time Colonel Bougainville remained west of the city, following on shore the restless movements of the British squadron on the river, he had under his command the very best troops in Montcalm's army.

The Chevalier de Lévis, too, went to an upriver assignment in the days following the battle of 31 July. Unlike Bougainville, who was an integral part of the defense of

Quebec, the chevalier was dispatched to the far reaches of
the St. Lawrence. There, among the islands where the
Canadian west began, Lévis took over command from St
Luc de la Corne. The regular officer found the ranger leader
of Indians lying on a bivouac bed, a deep thigh wound
smelling sweetly of the wild herbs with which it was bound.
The wound was a relic of a two-day attack on the new
British fieldworks at Oswego. St. Luc had attacked with
1500 Canadians, Indians, and marines, in the traditional
raiding style of the wild frontier. It had been of no avail
against Colonel Haldimand, the traditional European regular, safe in a well-dug redoubt, manned by soldiers trained
to their work, and supported by artillerists who knew their
pieces. The old ways of the forest war were over, done
with, as surely as the homely forest medicines with which
the Indian woman had bound and healed St. Luc de la
Corne's gashed thigh.

At the bedside of the Canadian whom he was to super-
sede, Major General de Lévis represented the formal soldier
in the European tradition. He had been sent to the upper
St. Lawrence to change the ancient Canadian ways. He
was to make a tight defense. For this the Marquis de Montcalm had said farewell, in parting with the friendship, wis-
dom, and comforting council of his second-in-command.
As Montcalm himself stood to the east, and Bourlamaque
looked south into the eyes of the enemy, so the keeping of
the west was given into the hands and brave heart of Lévis.

The danger that threatened out of the west was couched
at Oswego, the place which Montcalm had taken by formal
siege and then erased on his first Canadian campaign. Jeffrey Amherst had resurrected the place as a British base in
the spring of 1759 and set on it a pendulum of force, swinging first to the west for Niagara, then, on the backswing
(which Lévis was sent to stop) eastward into the St.
Lawrence.

Early that spring, before the British reoccupied Oswego, Pierre Pouchot went to Niagara to ward off the blow expected there. Captain Pouchot was yet another of those French regular officers dedicated, under Montcalm, to saving New France for an indifferent monarch. He was an officer of the regiment of Béarn, with previous experience as a military engineer. Montcalm recalled this skill at the time the general first became disillusioned with the coterie of grasping builders feeding on the naïve governor and bountiful intendant. In 1756, Pouchot was sent to Niagara to make strong the decaying, neglected ruins of the old fort. The captain of Béarn made the place his own. Pierre Pouchot had come back with his regiment for the campaign of 1758, and fought with it in the fieldworks he had helped build at Ticonderoga. 1758 had been the year that Vaudreuil's jealousy had reached its peak of spite, and no army officer was allowed to rest in a command outside the ranks of his unit.

But early in the following year, the command of Fort Niagara was returned to Pierre Pouchot. The captain wintered at La Présentation, above the rapids west of Montreal, where the Lake Ontario naval squadron was being built. As soon as the corvette *Iroquois* was launched and the ice was out of the river, Pouchot sailed for the fort like a homing bird in spring.

There was work to do on the bastions of the wall that cut across the peninsula to make the landward defenses. Screening walls were needed on the lake and river angles. To do the job engineer Pouchot had just under 500 troops. There were men and officers from four regular regiments and some militiamen, handy with mattocks and spade. The largest group in the fort was that of the Marine, but these normally competent troops were swollen with a draft of German jetsam from the eddies of the war in Europe. For the defense of his fort, Commandant Pouchot staked his

security on Lieutenant Bonnafoux and his twenty-one a
tillerymen of the Royal Corps, to whom had been seconde
a hundred of the most alert of the soldiers to train with th
guns.

Pouchot had not finished the work on his beloved Fo
Niagara before the invaders came. Seven British gunboat
appeared on the lake on 7 July, while Pouchot was sti
bolstering the bastion parapets before, and shoring up th
blindage behind. Lieutenant Bonnafoux drove them off wit
a defiant salvo that acknowledged the beginning of the sieg
of Fort Niagara.

For a week after the British appeared, the soldiers o
both sides worked with mattocks and shovels, barrows an
sandbags. The French made stronger the landward sid
while the British, working only by night, projected thei
sap in a zigzag line from the woods out into the cleare
plain. Each morning the French officers sighted over th
tube of their cannon at the mole-hill line, drawing neare
and yet nearer. It was not long before Bonnafoux could fir
at the Britons' work. It would not be long before the British
in turn, could mount first their high-angle mortars, the
the big guns to batter down the fort walls.

Captain Pouchot did not spend much time on the ram
parts that first week of the investment of his fort. H
stayed in his office in the big, chimneyed building that ha
been the first fort, or he went down by the river shor
where the Indians had their camp.

Through all the days of the siege no one could be certai
on whose side the Six Nations of the Iroquois or their satel
lite Nation, the Delawares, would fight. Some walked wit
the British, some stood with the French, all passed freely
back and forth between the warring armies, in friendly
visits to the other's camp. The brothers Joncaire, one a
Indian and the other a Canadian, were with Pouchot in th
fort their French father had once commanded, and wer

ounted on by the French to use their influence with the
nighty Seneca Nation to bring the other Iroquois back to
eel. Sir William Johnson had nine hundred warriors in
amp at La Belle Famille on the portage road. He was
lways sure of the loyalty of his once-so-savage Mohawks,
nd Britain's apparent military might and success would
keep the other Iroquois true. Perhaps the Joncaires' Senecas
vould at least remain neutral.

In the late afternoons, before the British soldiers again
esumed the night's digging, and when the French cannon
vere silent in an angelus of peace, Cadet Moncourt of the
Marine would meet his friend. The Indian boy would
come down the portage road, one of Moncourt's white
andkerchiefs waving from a stick carried over his
houlder. The two youths would meet at the fort gate,
called "the Gate of the Five Nations," and together would
amble off to the river to talk of their friendship and of their
future. The Indian worried for Moncourt's safety, should
he French fort fall. In the camp of Johnson's Indians and
vhere the regulars pitched their tents, talk was of the massacre of prisoners at Fort William Henry, and the words that
passed shaped the image of revenge.

Less innocent than Cadet Moncourt's friend were the Indian messengers sent by Captain Pouchot to Frenchmen at
posts further west. One of these found the Sieur de Ligneris
at Fort Venango, on the portage road from Lake Erie to
he Beautiful River. He had with him the troops from
burned-out Fort Duquesne and was waiting with them at
Venango for reinforcements from Vaudreuil—reinforcements which would never come—to take back the forks of
the Ohio. But with Fort Niagara besieged, the French
troops he so hopefully expected could not come through
to him. So the old, one-eyed fighter saw his duty in helping
Pouchot raise the siege, thereby reopening the lines back
over Lake Ontario on which all the west was nurtured.

Ligneris sent Pouchot's messenger back to the fort with his word that he was coming with his marines and his Canadians. Ligneris also said that the Chevalier d'Aubry, from the Illinois lands, was with him with a big war party from the western Nations. They would come in all haste, boldly down the portage road. So Captain Pouchot should look for them, 1600 strong, toward La Belle Famille, under the cliff where the Niagara exits from the gorge.

In his tent headquarters, Brigadier General John Prideaux was as well informed of Pouchot's doings as the Frenchman was of his. The Englishman from Devon had security in numbers and resources that need not depend on gossip. On the lake side, he had his three regiments of regulars and the York and Jersey provincials. Their job was to push the sap forward until the gunners could get within range. Later, if the siege went as far as that, the regulars would storm the breach in the enemy's fort made by the pounding of the British guns. On the river side, Indians had their camp and were the concern of the bluff, hearty baronet. The Indians were watching the portage road around the great falls for the French troops coming from the west.

Slowly, methodically, inevitably the British siege-works moved forward. On 13 July a mortar battery opened on the French fort. The next day another was set up and began firing. Working in the rain of 16 July, and aided by a rare morning fog on the following day, Prideaux sent a section of guns across the Niagara River, which were in action when the fog lifted. These British guns bore on the wooden sheds and bakeries, and armorers' huts behind Pouchot's wall. Fires sprang up, and the French soldiers, red-eyed with little sleep, added fire-fighting to their other duties of digging and fighting from the wall with cannon and musket. The French Indians moved from their camp on the river bank, crossing over to a safe distance away on the other shore. Pouchot was glad to see them go. He was waiting for D'Aubry's western warriors, who had fewer relatives and clansmen so near at hand. In the French fort, the German recruits in the Marine were growing sullen. In the hospital there were French casualties, tended by the two ladies Douville.

There were casualties, too, in the British camp. In the late morning of 18 July, Colonel John Johnston of the Jersey Regiment was killed in the British trenches by a blast of grapeshot from an exploding bomb. Two hours later, Brigadier Prideaux walked in front of a coehorn mortar at the moment it fired, and was decapitated.

The blast that hoisted Brigadier General John Prideaux's head from his shoulders pitched Sir William Johnson into the high seat of over-all command of the British expedition to reduce Fort Niagara. It was not a clearly defined, obvious step from Indian leader to military commander. No move made by the "Politician of the Mohawk," who had ousted the formidable Governor Shirley from his ambitions on this same Lake Ontario frontier, could be thus described. On the death of the general, the senior lieutenant colonel claimed the command as senior regular on the spot, until Colonel Haviland could come up from Oswego to rank the colonial in grade. But Sir William was able to invoke an obscure clause in his commission as Indian agent that made him a king's "Colonel of the Six Nations."

William Johnson, in over-all command at Niagara, did not impose his colonial ways on the professional soldiers from England. He left to them the projection of the formal siege line, zigzagging across the plain toward Pouchot's fortress walls. Johnson's method of siegecraft was the even more devious way of Indian diplomacy, politics, custom, and tradition. In this, his kind of fight, Johnson of the Mohawks at long last triumphed over the Senecas' brothers Joncaire. He won in a battle in which promises were missiles, because in July 1759 at the mouth of the Niagara River, the English were fair to make the promise good. Johnson told the Iroquois that in return for their neutrality he would give them the French fort to pillage. The shining prospect of rape and plunder drew the Senecas out of Pouchot's fort, leaving the Joncaires fishing with dead worms.

The fort was now under British cannon fire, which, in spite of Bonnafoux's counter-battery work, persisted in nibbling away at the walls. To fill the chinks that appeared Pierre Pouchot ordered the warehouses opened and the bales used for fill. At night, Frenchmen and Canadians, who had been musketmen and cannoneers all day, turned workers carrying the bundles of peltry to the crumbling walls. A weariness dragged at the heels of the French defenders, to whom an hour's sleep was worth all the beaver, otter, and arctic-fox skins that they dumped into the latest breach. Though the Germans were growing sullen, Pouchot remained confident in his hopes. Ligneris and D'Aubry had left their rendezvous at Presque Isle. The canoes of the mighty western warriors darkened the waters of Lake Erie like water bugs on a pond-lily leaf.

For William Johnson, the second battle of his Indian war of councils began with the arrival at La Belle Famille of four arrogant ambassadors from out of the sunset land. Their figures were imposing and their demands imperious.

Sir William Johnson had lain too close to the Indians for too long a time to refuse to entertain even the most outrageous proposal of the embassy. To deny the right of an ambassador to talk was not written on the leaves of forest etiquette. Then, too, these were western men, who, when the French had gone, would be looking to an English market to do their trading. Even in the trappings of a soldier Sir William was a trader, known to all Indians as "War-rac-ji-ja-gay" (He-who-does-much-business), and after the war there would be much new business in the west.

Besides, there was a strange, new gathering-together of ll the red men, like the salmon of the river school in the ıst pool below the insurmountable dam. Molly Brandt, the brown Lady Johnson," told of it in the set of her head s she graced the foot of Sir William's table. Joseph Brandt, er brother, showed it to the "Colonel of the Six Nations"— nd of all the soldiers—lying on their arms at Fort Niagara. The four ambassadors epitomized the new Indian creed, vhen they told Johnson's Iroquois to stand aside, for the vestern people come to fight the English had no quarrel vith their brothers of the east. But the new day was not up ıut of the Eastern Ocean when all the Indian Nations could tand together against the white man's vital surge. When the :onfrontation came at Fort Niagara, it was the western Indian who dropped his lance point and drew away on softly ıadding feet to watch the destruction of the French. "War-ac-ji-ja-gay" still controlled the Iroquois, and the purring ıf his trader's voice stirred, too, the Siouxian peoples.

Above the sharp turn in the Niagara River, where the leek rushing water plummets over the falling step into the vhite, wild tumult of the gorge, the Sieur de Ligneris grew ımpatient of the Indians' talk. In the fort across the portage, ınder the falling bombs, Captain Pouchot waited for his 'riend. Ligneris had listened, and he had heard enough; he ırdered his men to march. The army from out of the west vas a tattered-coat band of 800 frontier-wise Frenchmen ınd Canadians. The marines and the militia were a year or nore's travel from the comforts and luxuries of Montreal, Quebec, or Paris. Their uniform coats were gray rags carefully patched and worn proudly with the elegance of unconcern. Lieutenant d'Aubry's "Frenchmen" wore the trappings, garb, and war paint of the Indians, and they ran the woods with a light and silent step. They were the *coureurs de bois* who came at D'Aubry's call from their adopted land to answer the cry from the past.

The marching pace of Ligneris's army quickened as the roar of the great falls receded. Ahead, down off the escarpment under the white, puffy clouds over Lake Ontario's water, British cannon fire thumped like the warning beat of the hare. At that still-distant sound the Frenchmen's pace behind their one-eyed leader quickened again. Unnoticed by D'Aubry, whose long legs were striding beside the leader at the head of the pack, the 1000 western Indians he had brought were holding back.

At the mouth of the gorge, the *coureurs de bois* surprised a boat guard of twelve Britons. These they killed, and, chopping alder staves, stuck a severed head on each one. With the twelve grizzly banners borne on before them, the Frenchmen jogged on down the portage road in their easy forest gait. The woods were thinning out, there was sunlight on the river through the bushes on their left, and in the wide-spaced trees of this forest, the light was bright in the fort clearing to the front. Earlier, on the high edge of the plateau, the French leaders had met and parleyed briefly with a party of Iroquois, sitting idly in the woods. Neither Ligneris nor D'Aubry feared the lazy eastern Nations, though their own proud western men lagged hesitantly behind.

One hundred yards ahead of the running Ligneris, a line of brush, still leafed as though just cut by fascine-makers, screened the portage road from the end of the forest beyond. A brush line angled out and forward right and left on the road, making the interior angle of a "V." A marine called out that he thought he saw the lilies of France, all gold on white, above the fort—it could have been a wisp of cloud. It was then that the brush heap blossomed red with points of fire.

The fight in the angle of the "V" was brief. The British regulars and the colonials, standing, their bodies protected to the shoulders behind the brush-screen logs of a barricade,

measured out controlled volley fire. The Frenchmen, surprised and trapped on the portage road, milled about in a
confused moment of bafflement, then turned to run out of
the snapping jaws of the ambush. Aroused by the angry
sound of firing, inflamed by the running flight of the
French, the Iroquois, no longer indolent, rushed in from the
forest flank, to kill, and to kill, and to kill. Few of the western red brothers accompanied the road-bound column of
the French. The western warriors were back on the high
ground, moving toward the falls and their beached canoes
beyond. Iroquois there fell upon the Frenchmen as they
paused to catch a breath after climbing the hill. The warriors of the Six Nations followed and harrassed the fleeing
men along the lip of the high gorge, until they tired of the
hunting and went back with their scalps, their guns, and
their snatched finery. When the bodies of the French
floated ashore, further downstream, they were found to be
broken and shattered from the high, screaming fall from
the cliff and the churning in the wild waters of the gorge.

Ligneris was felled by an early volley from the barricade,
with a wound that proved fatal. D'Aubry was captured by
the British, as were more than a dozen other French officers,
both wounded and whole, who, rather than fall to the Iroquois, sought the kinder customs of the English.

From the bastion at the Gate of the Five Nations, on the
river side of Fort Niagara, Captain Pouchot could see the
back, or inside, of the British barricade across the portage
road. He was there with Lieutenant Bonnafoux on 24 July,
and unknowingly watched the defeat of Ligneris's column,
coming to his relief. From his lookout, he watched as the
British fired their volleys. A hard summer shower swept
across the plain, and as he shook the water from his head,
Pouchot could see the British redcoats climbing over their
barricade with bayonets fixed, to pursue the French "Indians" who looked as though they had made the skirmish.

To the captain, the action on the portage road looke
like a small affair. This opinion was confirmed when Cap
tain de Villars, of La Sarre, led out an attack party of 15
men to test the British sap, snaking along the lake shore. N
sooner did Villars show himself on the plain, than the Brit
ish lines spewed out naked men. Muskets in their hand
wet shirts stripped from their backs, the diggers climbe
up on the parapets to taunt the volunteers. When a com
pany of grenadiers defiled from the end of the trench, Vil
lars called his men back. Surely the English would not ma
the right of their line in such strength if Ligneris's arm
was attacking its left and rear.

Thus Captain Pouchot had grave doubts of the Britis
emissary, a Major William Hervey, who came out to hin
about four o'clock in the afternoon to inform him of th
defeat of the western troops and to suggest capitulation. A
Hervey's invitation, a captain of the Royal Roussillon wen
into the English camp and there, in an arbor, spoke with th
captives, D'Aubry, Marin, and the others. Ligneris he saw
too, lying pale and listless under opium on a field bed nex
to Johnson's tent.

There was one more sleepless night for Captain Pouchot
as he negotiated the terms of the surrender of his fort. Un
der a truce, the exhausted defenders slept soundly afte
twenty-two days and twenty-two long nights.

On 26 July, the French garrison marched out through th
Gate of the Five Nations. As a mark of their brave defens
and honorable surrender of Fort Niagara, they hauled wit
them two cannon. Each gun was loaded with grape, anc
Lieutenant Bonnafoux himself had lighted the slow matcl
on the linstock poles at both ends and had waved them unti
the spark glowed. Every Frenchman on that march carriec
his musket loaded and primed, and he walked alert anc
looked warily at the crowds of Indians, waiting to go in by
the Gate of the Five Nations.

The arming of prisoners was less a mark of honor to a
beaten foe than a measure of precaution and defense for a
helpless, weaponless man. For the time had come swiftly, as
the scavenging crow comes after the hawk kills, when Sir
William Johnson must make good his promise to his Iroquois. The fort was theirs to pillage. Not even Johnson of
the Mohawks, nor the captive Joncaires of the Senecas,
could be sure that the rape of the place would not include
the persons of the prisoners of war. It had happened two
years before at Fort William Henry on Lake George. Massacre could happen again at Fort Niagara on Lake Ontario.
So the prisoners went out armed, and the British escort went
with them, their enemy. The foe was ally, the ally suspect.

On that tense July day only one man, an Indian acting
out of love for a friend, crossed the strange street of suspicion to the side of action. Cadet Moncourt, marching with
the rest, looked back as he heard an anguished cry of farewell from his Iroquois friend. He turned to greet the young
Indian rushing toward him. No one noticed the tomahawk
until it flashed up and then down into the skull of Cadet
Moncourt. By a quickly delivered death, the Indian thought
and acted to spare his friend the day-long hours of torture
that were a brave foe's lot. For an instant of hours the
white men, French and British, braced for an onslaught. But
the moment passed.

The Iroquois—save for Moncourt's mourning friend—
rushed in through the open gate to plunder the deserted
fort. The French cortege of defeat—bearing now the freshly
killed body of a comrade—defiled down to the lake where
the waves broke along the shore. The wind blew a dirge
through the stay-wires of the masts, as the French stacked
their arms before climbing into the boats.

Sir William Johnson, having taken his leave of Captain
Pouchot, watched them as they moved away across the gray

waters. Behind him the old fort rang to the din of looting
Indians. The soldiers, regulars and colonials, were breaking
ranks in their camps. Walking back to his tent, Sir William
stepped for a little way along the wide, fair avenue to al
the west. It was a way to travel later, in the leisure time of
peace. The soldiers of Johnson's army were moving now to
the east where more Frenchmen stood.

XIX

---

13 September 1759

The ninth month is the time of hurricanes on the northeast coast of America. Admirals and captains of vessels, remembering Louisbourg in 1757, should be homeward bound from the storm-track coast, sailing into the rising Pleiades, away from the northern ice. The dog days come in September. Like the woodchuck, generals and colonels commanding troops in that month should seek the safe hibernation of winter quarters, while the aurora borealis blazes out the crisp stars in the rising winter firmament. The September moon is reckoned as the harvest moon.

Jeffrey Amherst, commander in chief of all the British forces in North America, read the portents of the changing season. At his field headquarters at Ticonderoga, he sought the shade of a tree by day and the comfort of the hearth fire at night. As a commander in chief, his campaigns should have harvested their victories. New conquests should be stored in Britain's barn, the soldiers in their winter quarters, and the ships for the expeditions plowing hasty furrows back to England. But as August changed to September, General Amherst had yet to reap what his army had sown.

On Lake Champlain, the army that Amherst himself commanded waited for the escort fleet to be built. Commodore

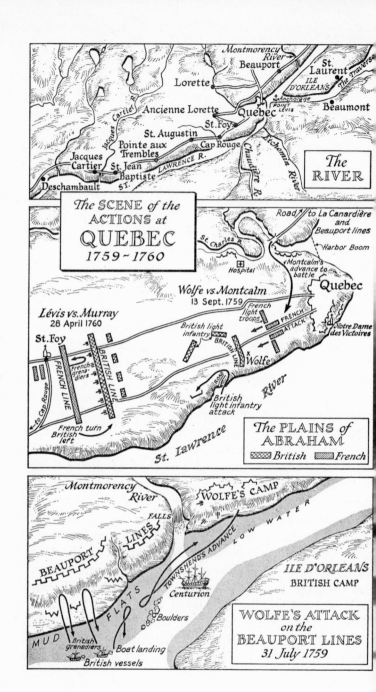

The RIVER

Montmorency River
Beaupré
St. Laurent
ILE D'ORLEANS
The Traverse
Lorette
Quebec
Beaumont
Anchorage
POINT LEVIS
Jacques Cartier R.
Ancienne Lorette
St. Foy
St. Augustin
Cap Rouge
Chaudière River
Etchemin River
Pointe aux Trembles
Jacques Cartier
St. Jean Baptiste
LAWRENCE R.
ST.
Deschambault

The SCENE of the ACTIONS at QUEBEC 1759~1760

Road to La Canardière and Beauport lines
St. Charles R.
Harbor Boom
Hospital
Montcalm's advance to battle
Quebec
Wolfe vs. Montcalm 13 Sept. 1759
French light troops
FRENCH ATTACK
Notre Dame des Victoires
Lévis vs. Murray 28 April 1760
British light infantry
BRITISH LINE
Wolfe
St. Foy
French grenadiers
FRENCH LINE
BRITISH LINE
to Cap Rouge
ROAD
British light infantry attack
French turn British left
St. Lawrence River

The PLAINS of ABRAHAM
⬜ British ⬛ French

Montmorency River
WOLFE'S CAMP
FALLS
LINES
LOW WATER
BEAUPORT
TOWNSHEND'S ADVANCE
FLATS
MUD
Centurion
ILE D'ORLEANS
BRITISH CAMP
British grenadiers
Boulders
Boat landing
British vessels

WOLFE'S ATTACK on the BEAUPORT LINES 31 July 1759

oring could report on 2 September that the brig was almost done. On the same day he started to build a sloop. A
clumsy radeau was building, and Captain Orde of the artillery was constructing "fire darts." When screwed into the
sides of enemy vessels by bold swimmers, these would destroy them by fire. A Sergeant Hopkins of Rogers's rangers
had volunteered to place Orde's darts on the French fleet.
If the sergeant succeeded in destroying Doloboratz's ships,
Amherst need not wait for the building of Loring's navy.
The army could sail down Lake Champlain and storm the
southern gate to Montreal before the snow came.

The army Amherst sent west under Brigadier General
John Prideaux had achieved its first objective, the capture
of Fort Niagara. Scant reports from further west, after the
British seized the Niagara portage, were favorable. The
French who escaped the ambush battle at La Belle Famille
had burned behind them the fort chain leading to the Ohio.
Of all France's western empire, only Fort Detroit and the
lesser ones beyond remained, alone, cut off like a lily to
wither in an untended vase. At the forks of the Ohio, Brigadier General John Stanwix, unmolested by Frenchmen or
unfriendly Indians, was building Fort Pitt at the western
end of Forbes's Road from Pennsylvania and Washington's
and Braddock's Road out of Virginia. In September, Stanwix
wrote to Amherst of the progress of the "Pentigon" fort as
"adequate to the great importance of its several objects."

But the second objective of the western army, the descent
into the St. Lawrence toward Montreal, was not achieved.
Brigadier Thomas Gage, who had been sent to take prece-
dence over both Johnson and Haldimand in succession to
Prideaux, was not the coursing type of British general officer. He worked like a gun dog, rock-like on a stylish point
to game, and with an ear cocked back to catch the nuance
of his master's whistle. So, as the sumac bushes on the old
burned-out ruins at Oswego turned to red, Gage watched

in his new camp, but did not dare to enter the defile of Lak
Ontario into the St. Lawrence. There in the river the Che
valier de Lévis rested on new defenses built on a midstrean
island. For his grand strategy against Montreal in Septem
ber of 1759, General Amherst could better have used a ter
rier general, like Wolfe, who would go into the hole an
drag the enemy out.

At the eastern end of the St. Lawrence, Major Genera
James Wolfe, the terrier general, was just up and out of a
sick-bed. Wolfe had taken to his room on 19 August and
was not seen again in the camps until the last day of the
month. When he finally reappeared at the door of his headquarters house at Montmorency, the commander of the
British army at Quebec was very tired and deeply de-
pressed. The old sickness and fever had further robbed
Wolfe's body of its meager flesh. The defeat and losses of
the July battle and the stagnation of the whole operatior
had stolen the energy from the general's mind.

From the number-one gun of the cliffside battery at
Montmorency, the pale, stooped general had a fine view
of all the river. Through his spyglass, propped against the
fascine basket on the corner, the general could see, beyond
the Ile d'Orleans, part of Admiral Saunders's large fleet riding to anchor. More ships-of-war and the many transports
were hidden from view by the jutting tongue of the island.
Wolfe purposely kept his eyes above and beyond the
burned-out hulks of the two transports, lying stark on the
mud flats below the cliff—debris of the battle of 31 July.
Somewhere beyond the cliffs of Point Lévis and the hump
of Cape Diamond, Admiral Holmes had the upriver squadron doing desultory mischief in a small-boy way. For two
months nearly fifty sail, three admirals, and over 13,000
sailors of the Royal Navy had lain "growing barnacles" in
the river. Admiral Hawke, keeping the close blockade in
the foul Biscay weather of Le Havre, Brest, Ushant, the

Saints, and Quiberon Bay, could have used Saunders's twenty-two ships of the line and all the frigates—particularly the frigates—to watch the long coastline of France.

There were generals in Europe who could have employed the regiments that Wolfe kept idle at Quebec. Brigadier Townshend, with his brigade, held the Montmorency position where the general lay sick. At Point Lévis, Monckton commanded, while the guns there fired across the river into the City of Quebec. Further west, toward the Jacques Cartier River, Murray, the mad Scotsman, helped Admiral Holmes harass the Frenchmen that Bougainville had set to patrol the north shore of the river.

General Wolfe, however, needed no spyglass to look from his Montmorency position into the trenches a quarter of a mile away, across the awesome cliff of the great cascade, behind which were Montcalm's French soldiers. But Wolfe had thought of no plan that would bring those soldiers and their general out from their defenses to fight in the open.

During his convalescence, General Wolfe had prepared three different schemes for attacking the Beauport lines. When he was again on his feet, though despondent, in pain and tortured by uncertainty, Wolfe spread his plans before his three brigadiers. These noble sons of peers—Monckton, Murray, and Townshend—who did not enjoy the confidence of their general—nor give him their own—rejected the plans that attempted once more to force the Beauport lines. After consulting among themselves and with Admiral Saunders, the brigadiers framed and presented their own scheme—an attack from the south on the north shore at a point above Quebec. The purpose of the attack was to cut the vital supply line into Quebec City. The merit of the brigadiers' plan lay in that it concentrated Wolfe's widely dispersed forces, and it had the additional merit for a fighting general in that Montcalm surely would have to come out with his whole army to reopen the roads into the hungry city. General Wolfe, who, as commander in chief, had the veto and the responsibility accepted the plan proposed by his brigadiers, and the implementation began at once.

The first step was the evacuation of the guns and troops from the strong British position at Montmorency. The move, begun on 1 September, was completed on the third. Wolfe, reluctant to the end to admit failure, tarried with five battalions in the abandoned fieldworks. Quietly, the men hid behind the logs and turned piles of earth, eating cold rations, their muskets loaded for a volley. The bright, sharp bayonets were fixed. They waited through the last day, hoping—expecting—that curiosity to inspect the old menace to his left flank would bring Monsieur Montcalm across the ford. But the wise marquis was not tempted. He merely waited until all the British regulars had gone, then moved his five regiments of regulars to the right of the Beauport lines, close to the bridges leading to the west side of the St. Charles River.

By 7 September, Wolfe had made his disposition of troops, to protect the base installations on Ile d'Orleans and the siege batteries at Point Lévis, and to make the river-crossing. To cross the river, about 4000 men were crammed into the vessels of the upriver squadron or at the embarkation point of the assault boats. Admiral Holmes had received General Wolfe aboard *Sutherland*, the headquarters ship. The point of landing had been selected, midway between Pointe aux Trembles and St. Augustin. From the deck of Holmes's flagship, lying off Cap Rouge, the admiral and the general had glimpses of Bougainville's cavalry patrols watching from on shore. Both the sea and the land commander planned to drift upriver with the night tide and to make the landing in the dark.

At nightfall, however, rain began. Ever restless with a

battle imminent, Wolfe took a boat and went downstream to appraise the situation. The rain continued steadily all through the night. The troops on the ships hunched in wet misery through the long gray day of 8 September. At half-past one o'clock in the morning of 9 September with the men ready to go, a string of lanterns hoisted on *Sutherland* gave the order to stand down. Before the night was over, another signal scrubbed the brigadiers' whole plan. At dawn, the soldiers who had been aboard the naval vessels began to go ashore to dry out, sleep, and eat some hot food. Wolfe went off on another reconnaissance.

Brigadier General Monckton accompanied the general. The company sergeant major of Hobson's (40th), forming his company with the Louisbourg Grenadiers for a march through the rain puddles to St. Nicholas, saw the brigadier away. Monckton had borrowed a watch-coat and a colored mitre cap, a size too large, and thus disguised as a grenadier, went riding off to the rendezvous on the River Etchemin, opposite Sillery and St. Michael. He met Wolfe at the mouth of the river, at the post named for Gorham, the "Yankee" ranger, to use the new derogatory name for a colonial. Wolfe, too, was dressed as a simple grenadier, but was wearing the usual black scarf tied to his left sleeve, in mourning for his father. With him, also in disguise, were Admiral Holmes, Brigadier Townshend, set for a lark, and MacKellar, the sapper. Other officers were there, too, and aides and grooms and orderlies. Monckton noted that Murray was not of the party. He was upstream, toying with Bougainville, chasing him about like a kitten.

From Gorham's post, the general led his distinguished party downriver to a point he had discovered on his trip in the rain the previous day. From a lookout, the officers could see, across the river, the long line of cliffs on the north shore. They could also see their general's great discovery: a narrow path climbing up through a fault in the palisades. MacKellar, the expert on Quebec's geography, named the places at either end of the ascending path: Anse-au-Foulon (the expert called it "Toulon"!) below, and above, the Plains of Abraham. These names, these places, were the fulcrum and the lever of Wolfe's new plan to come to grips with Montcalm, and to pry his way into Quebec.

Across the river at Sillery, a French officer watched the reconnaissance party through his telescope. Even at that distance, the innocence of those grenadiers was not convincing. The Frenchman reported the group on the south shore as high-ranking officers, probably, since the regiments had gone from Montmorency, laying out a new camp.

At the village of Cap Rouge, where the two main roads west from Quebec met and continued as one, Colonel Bougainville watched the British upriver squadron. Cap Rouge was a good town, through which passed the traffic between Quebec and Montreal. There Bougainville heard all the news, and at night could invite to dine the wittiest and the prettiest of the colony. Since the rain of 8 and 9 September, the British ships had lain inactive in the river. The 60-gun *Sutherland*, flying an admiral's flag, was off the town on 12 September, her sails furled. She showed no signs of activity. Nearer to the opposite shore, the frigates *Leostaff*, *Sea Horse*, and *Squirrel* lay, with the sloop *Hunter* and the transports. On that day there was some activity of boats between the frigates and the shore. Bougainville was watching the big *Sutherland*, his cavalry horses tethered in the square, his 1200 troops ready to march, should the big ship move. Before the rains he had been anxious, as had Montcalm. The general had thought to reinforce with the regiment of Guyenne. Lieutenant Colonel Launay had marched the regiment out to the Plains of Abraham, but had been recalled to the east side of the St. Charles River. At sundown of 12

September, the British squadron was still off Cap Rouge, and Bougainville, who had watched the boats so long that he almost counted them with the units of his command, closed the door of his quarters for the night's entertainment and repose.

Montcalm was up and on the alert through the night of 12 September. From his headquarters at La Canardière, east of the St. Charles River, he kept watch on Admiral Saunders's main fleet. That day there had been an air of activity, hovering with the gulls over the British fleet. The suspicions of the marquis were aroused. As night fell, the general waited, prepared for alarming news. An hour after midnight it came: Monsieur Dumas, the onetime hero of the Indian war out of Fort Duquesne, had heard a great noise of boats in the basin. Montcalm confirmed the Marine officer's order to man the trenches. At three o'clock, on the morning of 13 September, a Saturday, a patrol canoe came ashore having seen the image of boats in the black of night. They lay off the mud flats by La Canardière. The French army and all the militia stood to in the Beauport lines that night. No one had warned the elderly governor general of the danger of an attack on the mouth of the St. Charles River. At dawn, the Marquis de Vaudreuil was in bed in his field headquarters at La Canardière.

The Chevalier de Bernetz, too, spent a restless night. He was commandant of the lower town, and on the night of 12 September, he had been told to expect a convoy of foodstuffs by boat from the upriver supply dumps. Later, the convoy had been canceled. The sailors who manned the batteries could hear the British, out in the darkness of the basin. Two soldiers of the Royal Roussillon had stolen an Indian canoe and deserted. It was a very black night.

On the top of the cliff—up which no army could make its way—at the head of the path from Anse-au-Foulon, Louis du Pont du Chambon de Vergor spent the night of

12 September as usual—relaxed, indolent, and bored. As a captain of Marine, he had been given 100 militiamen of Quebec and set to watch the path up the cliff. It was four years since Captain de Vergor had had an important command. In 1755, he had commanded Fort Beauséjour in Acadia, and in June of that far-off year, Vergor had surrendered that distant place to Lieutenant Colonel Robert Monckton. That same Britisher, a successful brigadier general, was now on the river below the cliff where Captain de Vergor slept in his tent, a dark lantern glowing by his camp-bed.

The only order that Vergor had for the night of 12 September was to let pass a convoy of commissary boats going to the city. He had no concern for the safety of his post. Obviously, no one expected the British to come up the face of the cliff. As to the path, it was clogged with a formidable abatis. If he were alert, the sentry on the cliff would hear the boats go by, but there was no need for him to hail the convoy. There were other sentries on the river bank who could better challenge the boats, and half a mile away, a battery of French guns covered the north shore route to which the convoy would hold.

Four sentries west of Anse-au-Foulon heard the scraping of rowlocks and the chunking of oars in water. Four sentries upriver from Vergor's hundred militiamen called their "*Qui vive?*" out into the blackness of the night. Each got back over the ebbing black river a reassuring answer to the question. The sentries let the convoy pass, and returned to their little shelters for protection from the pre-dawn chill of a September morning. No one had told them or their officers that the provisions convoy would not, after all, be coming downriver that night. The sentries could not know that the boats allowed to pass in the dark were filled with British light infantry.

In the lead boat was Captain William Delaune with twenty-four volunteers of the light infantry. With him came the beachmaster, James Chad, Royal Navy, captain of *Vesuvius*. Their responsibility was to judge the current, the drift, the time, and the silhouette of the landfall, so as to bring the light infantry boats into the beach on the west side of Anse-au-Foulon one half-hour before daylight. The signal to drop away (two lanterns, one above the other) had been run up on *Sutherland* at two o'clock. For over two hours, the sailors had rowed down the hostile north shore. They had been hailed by the sloop *Hunter* and had been challenged by the French shore watch as they came close inshore. The cliffs were high over their heads when Chad gave the whispered order to pull for shore. The other boats of the light infantry, close on the stern of Captain Delaune, turned in, too. As the lead boat touched the shore, twenty-four volunteers poured over the side and ran swiftly through the darkness toward the black shadow at the base of the cliff. There was no sentry, no alarm: only quiet, disturbed by the scraping of the other flatboats as they came ashore.

Delaune and Chad stood in the shadow, wondering exactly where they had landed. A soft hail from the shore was answered, and William Howe, lieutenant colonel commanding the light infantry, joined them. Crouching down, the three officers studied the line of the cliff against the sky and judged themselves to be downstream of their intended landing. In the pre-dawn blackness, William Howe, the grandson of a king, made the decision to attack from where they stood. He sent Delaune and the volunteers west, to find and try the path to the top of the cliff. With the light infantry, Howe himself assayed the face of the cliff. At thirty years of age, the steep climb of some 175 feet offered no problem to the colonel, nor to the young, active men who followed him. The brush that covered the steep slope offered good handholds. It also tore at the dangling equipment and muskets, slung across the backs of the men. It was hard to smother the curses against the nagging clawing of the brush, with the unknown danger hovering above.

Suddenly the tilted world of the endless climb turned flat and in surprise the men crawled out of the pit on their hands and knees, hesitating to stand erect on the level land of the plain. Still there was quiet. When all the men were up, Howe turned to the left. He marched over rough ground until he was challenged by Vergor's sentry, whom they put off guard with a story, then quickly subdued. But Vergor's post had now been warned, perhaps by Delaune's party on the path, and a flurry of musket fire greeted the light infantry. In the first light of dawn the fire was without effect, and Howe's men pressed on, to find the French camp a-tumble with empty blankets, the defenders fled. It was light as the volunteers spread out to thrash through the cornfield at the back of the post, in search of hidden Frenchmen. Among the shock-headed rows, they found the French captain and his drummer, and for a few minutes they stalked, and were stalked by, Captain Fraser's company of Highlanders. The rest of the army was arriving at the landing place and on the plain.

When Delaune got back to the cliff with his prisoner, the other troops of the first wave were debouching from the path. The high-ranking officers were assembling there, Wolfe, standing straight and tall with Monckton and Murray. To one side, Howe had assembled his 400 light infantrymen. They were lounging on the ground taking a good soldier's advantage of an opportunity to rest, yet by their casual insolence, letting all the late arrivals know that they were on top of the cliff by courtesy of Billy Howe's light infantry.

Looking back over the cliff, a long line of ships' boats

nd flat-bottoms could be seen making their way toward
he vessels anchored in the river. The three frigates, the
loop *Hunter*, three armed ships, and two transports had
ollowed the assault boats down the river. On board, and
lready loading into the boats, Brigadier Townshend's sec-
nd wave of 2600 troops was set to join the 1700 men al-
eady ashore. With Townshend would come the light field
uns.

But as the idle light infantry looked, the water by the
hips and the returning boats mushroomed with white
plashes of cannon shot, falling close. The soldiers watched
xcitedly and turned their attention in the direction of the
unfire. They judged it to come from half a mile up the
liff, from what someone called "The Samos Battery."
Those cannon would have to be silenced, or else the second
wave of troops, and the third from Point Lévis, would never
et ashore at Anse-au-Foulon. The light infantry half expected the order when it came. The capture of the battery
was their kind of work.

The first French troops that the English saw were a
picket of the regiment of Guyenne. They came along the
St. Foy Road, the inland road on the heights, from the direction of St. John's Gate, and did not tarry on the plain
but withdrew into the woods. They had seen the red-
coated regiments arrayed in line of battle, and had then
spotted more regiments coming from where they had
camped at Vergor's post the week before.

It was about six o'clock in the morning when a courier
from Captain de Vergor crossed the St. Charles River
bridge, and warned the commander of Guyenne, before
hurrying on to Montcalm at La Canardière. The messenger
found Montbeillard, the artillery officer, just going to bed
after a night of alarms—which were Admiral Saunders's diversion for Holmes and Wolfe. Montcalm was roused, and
the whole French camp. By the time the marquis was

booted, in the saddle, and down to the bridge, the whole army was pouring across and climbing up to face the British on the Plains of Abraham. The Chevalier Johnstone, whose brother-in-law, Lord Rollo, was in Louisbourg in 1758, rode with Montcalm as aide-de-camp. In his haste, the marquis had not thought to warn Governor General de Vaudreuil of the alarm.

Beyond the St. Charles River, Montcalm took charge of his army. He sent Dumas and his militia to flank the British on their left, in a country covered with low brush—ideal sniping country. Some militia and Indians were sent off, single file, to perform a similar mission against the British right. It was one of the latter who, from a juniper bush at the cliff's edge, pinked General Wolfe on the wrist. As the sniper slipped away to a new firing position, he saw a British comrade tying a white handkerchief around the hand of the tall, thin, red-haired officer.

Montcalm assembled his army in the woods. He chose as his axis of advance the road from the St. Louis Gate to Sillery. On the road he put the regiments of Béarn and Guyenne in column, flanked by La Sarre and Languedoc on the right and the Royal Roussillon on the left. At both ends of the line were the militia from Quebec, Montreal, and Trois Rivières. Two field guns were firing from each flank and were being answered by the British guns. Somehow, Monsieur Wolfe had managed to get his cannon, and virtually all his army, up the impossible cliff.

In numbers, General Montcalm had a fine army. But on the morning of 13 September it was a weak army. The marquis stood alone, without the comrades of Carillon, Fort William Henry, or Oswego by his side. In the absence of gay Lévis and solid old Bourlamaque, two colonels acted as brigadiers—good men but new to higher command. Nor did the marquis have close to him his amiable young friend, Bougainville, the paragon of an aide, diplomat, and bold oldier. With Bougainville were the five best companies of egulars in the whole French army: the grenadiers. It had passed nine o'clock in the morning. The British were still arriving onto the battlefield. Montcalm had to attack at once, before they were all there against him. The order was given, and the white-coated troops moved off through the rees heavy with the old leaves of the summer gone past.

In the open, the soldiers paused to pick up their dressing again, and the officers studied the ground across which they must take their men. On the right there was much brush to break the symmetry of a charging line of infantry. But in front of Béarn, Guyenne, and Royal Roussillon, the field showed clear up to the steady-standing ranks of the red regiments. Grenadiers moved on the British right, with another regiment forming up *en potence* beyond. Next in from the British left, where La Sarre probably would engage, the Jacobite exile, the Chevalier Johnstone, saw the bright splash of the clan Fraser's tartan in the kilts of the Highland regiment. The French regiments were moving forward. The right was tangling and buckling slightly in the scrub bush.

The infantry of King Louis of France attacked with a shout and a rush and a clatter of musket fire. It was their way. The French left was muttering as it moved out across the Plains of Abraham; here and there an old veteran shouted loudly to encourage a recruit at his side. Imperceptibly, the marching pace quickened as the files and columns, with a rumbling in their throats, plunged forward in a shuffling run. The officers were waving their swords and screaming the order to "fire," "fire," "fire"; the little drummer in the rear of Roussillon was running fast to catch up, the deep drum pounding his shoulder as he ran. He had drawn his sword. Everyone was yelling behind the slanting glint of polished bayonets.

The British infantry, according to their custom, fought in

silence, firing and advancing on order and to the tap of th
drum. While Montcalm was forming up his regiment
Wolfe's regulars in line were lying on the ground. The
had done so on their colonel's orders. The fire from th
French skirmish line and Montbeillard's guns was telling
it was senseless to stand up boldly in noble defiance. Wit
an officer's work to do, General Wolfe walked about, heed
less of the enemy fire. On the left, Brigadier Townshenc
with the 15th and the two battalions of the 60th, was en
gaged in a sharp fire fight with Dumas's troops across th
St. Foy Road. Colonel Howe's light infantry, hastil
fetched back after having driven the enemy from th
Samos Battery, was fighting, under Townshend's com
mand, for two houses on the road. Smoke was rising fror
the thatch of one building when Wolfe, who had gone t
estimate the situation on the left, left Townshend. It was
walk of 400 or 500 yards to where Monckton held the right
Wolfe was bound for there—where he had received hi
wrist wound and where the Indians and French rangers
from cliff-side positions, annoyed the 35th Foot and th
Louisbourg Grenadiers. Wounded men, moving toward th
cliff path, walked a little way with their general. The battl
line of five regiments and the grenadiers, supported by th
35th on the right and the 48th in reserve, was rising to it
feet. All eyes were looking to their front, the east, towarc
the city where the French were. Wolfe stepped through th
opening between the 28th and the grenadiers, to see his ol
enemy, enticed out at long last and attacking. One of th
British guns was close at hand, its crew frantically loading
with canister to greet the massing enemy. The French, i
appeared to all the silent men ranked in a double line, wer
coming toward them in three groups. Behind the advancing
men in white, mounted officers rode, high as the battl
flags borne by the ensigns.

The French fire began from about 130 yards. After fir

ing, many of the French threw themselves down to reload. It was the way of the Canadians, who were filling in the regiments of Old France. The British officers noted that the custom broke the solid front of the advancing Frenchmen, as they knew it from European fields of battle. The double line of British soldiers stood stiff and still.

The French were coming on at a shuffling run. One by one, company by company, the British officers gave the order for a quarter turn to the right. The front rank dropped to one knee, and the muskets of both ranks came up. An irascible sergeant shouted for the men to mind their dressing, while he shoved at them with his halberd staff to straighten out the line. An occasional soldier dropped in the ranks or staggered out of it, wounded.

The French were but forty yards away when the order to fire by platoons was given. There is a pause—a second of eternity—between the fall of the hammer, the spark igniting the powder in the pan, and the ultimate roar of the discharge. Quickly, the British infantrymen reloaded in the long, numbered count of the exercise. They were behind a veil of smoke made by their own volley and they watched to see if the running Frenchmen would burst through its acrid gauze.

Reloaded now, the column heard the platoon officer's calm order to advance through the murk for a second volley. The files stepped off, hands tight on musket-stock and barrel, bayonets presented. On the other side of the smoke they saw that the French had recoiled. As platoon after platoon came up onto the new firing line, the new order of fire by regimental volley was passed. Silently, the British infantry stood waiting for the order which would shatter the already shaken enemy in their front.

Few, if any, of the men in the ranks saw that General Wolfe had been hit. The shock of the bullet which entered his breast staggered the tall general. He did not fall, but turned to a lieutenant of the Louisbourg Grenadiers and asked that he be supported a little toward the rear of the firing line. Wolfe had gone only a few steps before he sagged, and the lieutenant gently let him down to the ground. A regimental doctor hurried up and knelt beside the general whose eyes were heavy, as on the point of sleep. The two volleys fired by the two nearby regiments roared out—they heard them on the ships in the river, and Captain Chad's men, unloading shovels from a boat, looked up to the top of the high cliff as if expecting the din to be visible.

An irrepressible cheer burst from the British troops in line, as they saw the whole French army, except for the dead and those wounded by the volleys, break ranks and run. Behind the red backs, the British general roused himself to give an order. It was a good order, to cut off the fleeing French from their bridge to the Beauport lines. It was an exact order, for Colonel Burton to execute with his regiment. It was General Wolfe's last order, at the moment of a long-denied, long-delayed, last-minute victory. Having given the order which would win the battle, James Wolfe died in peace.

But the victory was not immediately won. Brigadier Monckton was summoned from Wolfe's side by a tearful aide, but before Monckton could take hold, a bullet struck him in the right breast and coursed around under his skin, to lodge finally and painfully in his shoulder blade. After the French ran, Murray, next in command, had put himself at the head of the Highlanders, as mad as he himself. They had gone haring off with drawn broadswords to do some close killing of the coursing French.

In the confusion, it was rumored that, like Monckton and Wolfe, Murray, too, was down, and it was Brigadier Townshend who eventually ordered the general pursuit. Neither Murray nor Townshend caught up with the main body of the French, retreating across the St. Charles River bridges.

The Marquis de Montcalm did not go with his regulars back to the Beauport lines. He could not. A ball of grape-shot from one of Colonel George Williamson's cannon had hit the mounted general in the thigh and passed up its length to lodge in his stomach. Williamson was aiming the little 6-pounder at Montcalm but did not see his target fall. The marquis held to his saddle. Seeing the blood on his thigh, the panicked men about him shouted that he was killed. The marquis tried to reassure them but the big ball in his body was fast robbing him of the strength to keep a fair counte-nance on the disaster about him.

Driving off one of his guns, Montbeillard saw his general, still on his black horse, being led into Quebec through the St. Louis gate. Three of Montcalm's white-coated regulars were supporting him. They bore him tenderly into the house of a doctor and laid him on the bed. There, in the few hours left to him to live, he attended to the duty re-maining to him as a soldier. Ramezay came to his general for advice as to how to defend the city. The dying man framed a plea to the British commander to protect the French pris-oners. The bishop came to shrive him, as the last duty of a soldier to his own mortal soul. The Marquis de Montcalm died and was buried in a grave beneath the chapel floor of the Ursuline Monastery. The men who dug the quiet tomb, so far from Candiac, had only to enlarge the crater of a bomb.

XX

The Fleets Sail Out

Louis Antoine Bougainville did not see his friend and his general again, nor did he attend the Mass for the late Marquis that was said in the bombed-out chapel. On the morning of 13 September, Holmes's flagship, which Colonel Bougainville watched as though it were a weathervane, still lay off Cap Rouge, though the admiral himself had crept away in *Lowestoft*. Not until nine o'clock in the morning did a messenger come with the incredible news that the English were on the heights. By that time Montcalm and Wolfe were ready to engage, and, though Bougainville forced the pace of his march, he did not—he could not—arrive at the field until the battle had been lost by the French. Tentatively, the grenadiers of the colonel's command probed toward the Samos Battery, but the response of the victorious British was savage. Brigadier Townshend had spent his first hour in command in regrouping his scattered forces and in bringing up the engineering stores from the beach. So Bougainville's force fell on the prickly back of a porcupine army in all-around defense.

Prudently, the colonel withdrew to make his own firm stand as a rallying point for the French troops coming from the now useless Beauport lines. The tired, beaten regiments

ime from the old trenches; they came marching the wide
ay around by Charlesbourg, Lorette, and Ancient Lorette.
ew were left to lead the battalions. Both of the newly
ised brigadiers, Sennezergue of La Sarre and Fortbonne
f Guyenne, were wounded prisoners aboard a British ship.
Inly Vaudreuil could claim the rank of higher command.
ut the elderly governor was content to accompany the
roops on their march away from the besieged capital of
Jew France. Bougainville, waiting for instructions, did
ot receive them from the Marquis de Vaudreuil; he had
o wait for the arrival of Lévis.

The chevalier reached Cap Rouge on 18 September, and
t once set an attack in motion. Bougainville and Lévis were
rithin a mile and a quarter of the city where the Marquis
e Montcalm lay buried when they realized that Quebec
ad fallen to the enemy. After suffering a bombardment of
xty-eight hours, M. de Ramezay had capitulated.

On 19 September, Brigadier General Murray marched
ito the upper town, crowning General Wolfe's bold vic-
ory on the Plains of Abraham. The general's thin body lay
mbalmed aboard an English ship-of-war, for burial in Eng-
ind. At a quay in the lower town, British sailors were land-
ig, as the soldiers' drums beat triumphantly through the
ates. Captain Hugh Palliser, of *Shrewsbury*, entered Que-
ec in acknowledgment of the Royal Navy's triumph in the
ong campaign. Aboard his flagship, Admiral Saunders
eadied the orders which would take the tall ships out of
he narrow river. The battle for Quebec was won, and the
avy was needed elsewhere in the war around the world.

The wind on Lake Champlain blew lightly out of the
outh—where the British were—all day on 11 October. At
unset the wind dropped, and Captain Doloboratz, of the
'rench Navy, rowed his three xebecs into the Quatre Vents
slands off the west shore of the lake. The three crews of

soldiers and sailors cooked and ate their dinner in the glory
of a salmon and gray sunset. Then they settled down for
the night on board their slim vessels. The wind rose again
out of the south before Doloboratz had retired for the night,
leaving orders to be called at dawn.

It was still dark when the watch roused the captain with
a warning that boats, British boats, were approaching.
Quietly, the French crews came awake and moved silently
to their battle stations. They could hear the British calling
to each other not far away. From their voices, the English
appeared to be lost. At first light, the two fleets sighted
each other at the same moment, the big xebecs and a flotilla
of troop-laden bateaux. Shouting, the Scots (they were
Highlanders) turned and pulled away to the south. Shouting, the Frenchmen cleared their cannon for action. The
fight was brief, for the small boats were quicker away
against the wind. But from the small quarter-deck of *La
Musquelonguy*, Doloboratz could call out his "Bravo!" to
the gun crew who had sunk a British bateau with twenty
men aboard.

The French captain dared not pursue. If Amherst's army
was abroad on the lake, then his big ships were cruising at
last. It troubled the sailor that he had not yet sighted *Duke
of Cumberland* and *Boscawen*. Perhaps they had passed him
in the night. In that case he could swoop south among the
light British craft, protected only by the lumbering radeau,
and scatter the water-borne army. Or perhaps Doloboratz's
duty lay in rejoining the schooner *Vigilante*, now doubtless
being chased by Commodore Loring's two ships. Captain
Doloboratz also had to consider the wind. It had veered
twice within an hour, and from what the Mediterranean
sailor had learned of these narrow waters, that meant a
shift to a wind from the north. So, while he still had the
weather gage of a fleet to the north of him, Doloboratz took
the advantage. He did not keep it for long. Before after-

oon, the French crews were straining at the sweeps to
ake slow headway against a northeast wind that flecked
white spray off the top of the angry waves.

The three French captains kept their crews at galley-
laves' work throughout the afternoon. The southward-
eaching tip of Cumberland Head came abreast of the star-
oard side. With aching arms and straining backs, the
Frenchmen watched the point drop astern. But their labors
were for nothing. Late in the afternoon, the lowering sun
icked up the glint of white sails ahead, and Doloboratz
knew that their set was British. Soon after, the lookout
potted the sails of another vessel. She was not *Vigilante*,
of which there was no trace.

With a tired crew and a downwind position, there was
ittle hope of bringing on an advantageous fight with the
British commodore. Doloboratz's only chance was to flee
outh into the gathering dusk and hide in one of the many
places he had found during his long summer of cruising the
ake. The place he chose lay in behind a small island in the
open mouth of Plattsburg Bay. There, on an evening of
owery clouds, the three xebecs dropped anchor in the lee.
As Commodore Loring, aboard *Duke of Cumberland*,
rounded Cumberland Point in the gathering gloom, he got
a glimpse of a lateen sail coming down behind the island.
Giving the signal to *Boscawen* astern, Loring sailed into the
bay and dropped his anchor. He watched with navy scepti-
cism as *Boscawen*'s captain mimicked the maneuver. The
fellow was a soldier out of a Highland regiment.

Captain Doloboratz watched the two Britishers come in
to anchor and watch him, in turn, through the night. The
French captains held council, and came to the conclusion
that their position and their plight were hopeless. In the
darkness of a dark night, they set their crews ashore, and,
with their carpenters, the captains scuttled their vessels.

The French Lake Champlain navy, which had held up

Amherst's advance through all the good campaigning day
of summer, died that night by its own hand, its job c
"being in being" done. Though the fleet was gone, the ad
vancing season was ready to take up the guard over th
water gate to Montreal. Winter marched to its post on Lak
Champlain to the cadence of a rising gale, the stamp o
waves on the southwest shore, and a plume of dark cloud
swirling overhead.

Before the northeast storm, General Amherst's water
borne army, one day north of Crown Point, fled for shelte
to the land. Under the gale-whipped trees the soldiers o
nine regiments, regulars and colonials, made a cold, we
camp in makeshift shelters and windbreaks. They had
long wait. On the fourth morning of the storm Private
Robert Webster, of Fitch's 4th Connecticut Regiment, as
signed to row the artillery boats, woke to find hard ice or
the rain puddles. The sky was clear and deep, but the lake
was a roil of whitecaps and it was very blue. The rangers
whom Amherst sent north in whaleboats to look for Commodore Loring, missing since the night of 11 October, were
turned back, drenched with spray, nearly frozen, and
beaten by the wind-whipped waves. Private Webster was
in the woods on the eternal search for dry firewood, when
the "flying news" reached him that Quebec had fallen. He
had the "certain news" on returning to the bivouac on the
shore of Lake Champlain. A whaleboat had won its way
through the narrows, where the waves were less high, to
tell Amherst of Wolfe's and Saunders's victory, and of the
death of the former.

When the wind finally shifted into the south, as it did on
18 October, an exultant general led an exuberant army out
onto the lake to continue its march. Where Doloboratz had
sunk his navy, Amherst found Loring, pleased as a drake in
a frog pond. He had chased away the French schooner,

aused the xebecs to scuttle, and had raised one of the latter, which he had already christened *Amherst*.

But the next morning the wind came up again out of the orth. No progress toward Montreal could be made that ay, nor any day that autumn. General Amherst gave the rder to turn back.

The chance of another storm was too great to risk an rmy, likely to be cut off far down the lake without sup-lies. It was probable, too, that Colonel Bourlamaque's 2000 efenders at Isle aux Noix would be reinforced by the not nconsiderable French army that had escaped from Quebec. ieneral Amherst went back to Crown Point and disas-embled his 1759 army.

As the advancing autumn season had stopped his ad-ance down Lake Champlain, so, he felt, would the force f winter weaken the French defenders of New France, ow compressed into the island city of Montreal. In the pring he could set the British armies marching again, from Crown Point, from Oswego, from Quebec, for a rendez-ous at Montreal.

Around the world, the year 1759 was a great and won-erful year for British arms. Time and again the bells of London rang out "Victory over the French!" Bonfires were ighted from the South Downs to the Yorkshire moors to cclaim the success of the British infantry who, with roses n their hats, had routed all the French king's horse at Minden-am-weser in Hanover. From Plymouth, where the lispatch boat landed, a train of celebration set all England cheering for Admiral Boscawen, who had trounced the French Mediterranean fleet in Lagos Bay. In parish churches everywhere that George was king, thanks were offered for the victories at Ticonderoga, Niagara, and, late in a mild autumn, at Quebec.

Messengers came from far and wide to give their good

news to Pitt in his office or at the entrance to the House ɑ
Commons. From Africa, from the European mainland, an
from North America, the young officers came to "th
Great Commoner" on their way to an audience with the
king. In far away India, the sword and genius of Robe
Clive, the hero of Plassey, was building a British empir
from the cities and provinces that had been French.

But, despite Britain's triumphs all over the worlɑ
throughout the year of 1759 Pitt's government and Eng
land were under a serious threat of invasion from across th
Channel. The Duc de Choiseul did not attempt to invad
the island until late in November of that year. As a neces
sary prelude to invasion, he summoned the Maréchal d
Conflans, with eighteen ships of the French navy, to act a
escort for the troop transports. Admiral Sir Edward Hawke
with the Channel fleet, had been watching Conflans all dur
ing the summer, and when the Frenchman moved the Eng
lish acted at once. Hawke drove Conflans into Quibero
Bay, and immediately behind his admiral, "Black Dick
Howe sailed into the bay and destroyed the French flee
there, making an end to France as a naval power.

With the defeat in Quiberon Bay, Choiseul's dream o
invading England abruptly came to an end. Without th
necessity of defending the homeland, Pitt could send 20,00ɑ
soldiers to reinforce the British army fighting on the con
tinent of Europe.

In the new year of 1760, from the North Sea to Bayonn
the British blockade held the remnant of Louis's ships i
harbor. The Lords of Admiralty gave to Saunders of Que
bec the Mediterranean station, with its sunny skies, anɑ
the Barbary pirates to play with. Admiral Holmes, late o
the upriver squadron in the St. Lawrence, went to the Wes
Indies. Pitt's greedy eye was on the other French island
there. Admiral the Lord Colville cruised in North Ameri
can waters in 1760.

Though cut off from the sea by the English in Quebec
City, the government of New France looked seaward for
salvation. Through all her 150 years, French Canada each
spring expected and received the fleet from home. Each
spring, the wealth of North America which the Canadians
had heaped upon the mother country came back to them
as goods, sustenance, and the pleasant fripperies of life. During her whole existence, New France had depended on Old
France for trade and bounty. Since the Baron Dieskau had
reached Quebec in 1755 with four regiments of regulars,
the colony had been defended by the king's men. Not that
the Marine did not have stalwart soldiers, or the parish
militia lacked the will and courage to defend themselves.
Rather, it was because the former were too weak and scattered, and the latter had first to sow and reap against the
winter, with their military duties spread between.

Although the French coast was blockaded and Montreal
had lost her easy access to the sea, the government of New
France confidently expected the fleet to arrive as usual in
the spring of 1760. Since the day Quebec fell, the governor
general, the intendant, even the bishop, each in his own
fashion, anticipated the arrival of the ships.

The Marquis de Vaudreuil sent his report of the last campaign by emissary to M. Berryer, the minister of Marine and
colonies, and begged instructions for the next one. Bigot,
who had conveniently escaped from Quebec, wrote both
to Berryer and to Fouquet de Belle-Ile, the minister of war.
To the former he wrote confidently of a reorganization of
his department; to the latter Bigot unctuously cited all that
he had done to give food and help to the army.

Henri de Pontbriand, bishop of Quebec since 1741, saw
in the spring fleet an argosy of mercy, with charity at the
helm and the holds filled with alms. The bishop, too, had
abandoned Quebec before the English came. He had left
its ecclesiastical buildings in such ruins that only in the

nunnery of the Ursulines could Mass be said with dignity
As wretched as the people of Quebec were, the country
folk were in even worse plight. They had acted as allies and
harborers of the French Indians, and as such, had felt the
force of Wolfe's retaliatory raids, carried out by the Amer
ican rangers under the British general who scorned the
colonials for doing his work. For these destitute people
Bishop de Pontbriand asked linen, stuff, pork, flour, brandy
wine—things which Bigot had to sell, but for a price. For
the priests, the bishop asked for silk gowns which they
could fashion into proper vestments to replace those stolen
and desecrated by the heretical New England rangers. The
practical bishop named agents in Brest, Bordeaux, and
Rochelle who would receive and ship the alms.

The Chevalier de Lévis, by succession commander in
chief of the French army in Canada, was also concerned
with the arrival of the spring fleet, for it would bring him
reinforcements and replacements. But, first, he had to provide a safe shore upon which the ships could land. As the
government of Canada was, in effect, besieged in Montreal
and in the St. Lawrence Valley, from the rivers rising in
Lake Ontario to the Jacques Cartier River above Quebec,
the chevalier had to break the British siege ring. But he had
not only to break the siege but also the naval blockade at
Quebec. To do so General de Lévis had to capture Quebec, with its docks and defenses, at the very moment when
the ice broke on the river. The French fleet of succor,
which sailed in February 1760, and which had avoided
the blockade on the French coast, would be waiting to
come up the river the very day the ice went out. If they
found the British still in Quebec, the ships would sail away
with their alms for the bishop, their trade goods for Bigot,
and their soldiers for Lévis. A British fleet, too, probably
based in Louisbourg or in Halifax, would ascend the river

: the earliest possible moment. If that fleet reached Quebec
efore Lévis recaptured the old capital, not only would
ie French convoy be seized, but Lévis's troops could not
ike the reinforced city.

There was an even more pressing consideration for the
ewly raised commander. The troops he needed for the
)uebec expedition must leave there by the time the ice left
.ake Ontario and Lake Champlain, and before the mud dried
n the portage roads over which Amherst's army would close
n the city of Montreal. Only if it moved early would the
imetable of the thaw permit the army of Canada to go to
)uebec and back.

On 10 April, the ice in the river at Montreal was dark
vith rot. On the 17th, the Chevalier de Lévis sent a staff
fficer to select a landing place near Quebec and to mark it
or a secret landing at night. On the 20th, Colonel Bourla-
naque set out from Montreal by way of the river with all
he troops, upward of 8000 men. He had the eight regi-
nents of regulars, no one of which, after the long years in
:anada, was now over 400 strong. But to them, and to the
wo regiments of the Marine, militia had been attached to
narch in pride with the old battalions. Bougainville's cav-
lry of 200 troopers were in the boats with their mounts,
nd 270 Indians paddled with the flotilla, which carried
ield guns and artillerymen to man them.

The Chevalier de Lévis followed the army a day later,
vith the blessing of the governor, with whom he was in
avor because he was ranked by Vaudreuil and, as yet, had
iot contradicted the old Canadian. Lévis soon caught up
vith his soldiers, and pulling alongside Bourlamaque's boat,
ioted with pleasure that the nearer they approached to
)uebec, the thicker were the ice floes in the water. Under
hese conditions, no fleet was likely to be in the river.

On 24 April, Lévis arrived near Pointe aux Trembles. The
flotilla was now a brave sight in the ice-filled river, having

been joined at Trois Rivières by the two French frigate
L'Atalante and *La Pomone*, which had been lying at tha
place since the English had come to Quebec in 1759. Bu
the chevalier believed that the element of surprise had bee
lost, and he gave up his intent to land at Sillery, close t
the Plains of Abraham, for a landing at St. Augustin, twelv
miles from Quebec.

The troops began coming ashore behind a screen of Mon
sieur de St. Luc's Indians. They landed on the shore ice
without mishap, until the dark of evening. Then an artiller
boat coming in to land was battered by a floating chunk o
ice. The sergeant, standing in the stern of the boat, fell int
the freezing water. In the dusk, his mates could not see hir
until he had been whisked away by the current. Later, the
heard a cry, far-off in the river. Some thought it was th
sergeant, on an ice floe. But the concensus was that it was
seal, or the cry of a gull. No man could live, wet, on tha
river on an April night.

From the day that Saunders sailed away, taking with hir
the wounded Monckton and the sardonic Townshend
Brigadier General the Honorable James Murray com
manded and governed in the city of Quebec. As command
ing general his responsibility was for the king's property
and the king's troops; as military governor he was respon
sible for all the conquered townspeople.

Quebec faced a lean winter. There was little food in th
town. Earlier in the spring Montcalm had sent the reserv
stores out of the beleagered city. The nearby farms eithe
had not been tended by their workers turned militiamen
or had been the object of reprisal raids by Wolfe's eage
American rangers. With the fall of the city, a garrison o
hungry British soldiers had moved in, and when it sailed
away, the British fleet could not leave behind supplies o
food sufficient to feed all. As bleak as were the prospects o.

unger, more ominous yet was the gaunt, blanched specter
f cold that stared hard at the city. During the summer of
erts, no one had had the time to cut and cord and stack
rewood for the city, nor indeed, had it been safe to do so,
vith rangers and Indians of both sides roaming the perime-
er of the siege. Even during the last months of 1759 it
vas not safe to do so.

From the attacks made by Canadians and Indians on
voodchopping parties, Brigadier Murray found that his
ole had subtly changed from that of the besieger of Que-
ec to that of one besieged in Quebec. Captain Dumas of
he Ohio commanded the Canadians left by Lévis on the
acques Cartier River line. The aggressive Dumas, now
enior officer of the Marine in Canada, kept his Canadians
rowling the autumn woods, harrying Murray's men and
he *habitants* who had taken the oath of allegiance to
ritain. There were many *Quebecois* who considered them-
elves well rid of the intendant Bigot and his retinue of pale
eeches. Dumas's activities kept Murray's men on the alert.
n October, 600 Britishers had to march out to punish an
lusive band of partisans. Murray's soldiers grumbled when
hey were called out in November to chase a French foray,
oo near the town. The men of the British regiments were
ired of the long-continuing campaign. The alarms con-
inued through December and into January, when the St.
Lawrence froze over with ice thick enough for pleasure
aleshes to take picnickers to the snow cone, piled below the
rozen falls of Montmorency.

At midnight on 30 January, the soldiers were tumbled out
f their beds to stand to in the dark, cold streets. They shiv-
red as they stood in their makeshift blanket coats, and they
lipped and fell as they were marched down the steep, icy
treets to the lower town. The wind on the river, blowing
p Lieutenant Malcolm Fraser's philabeg, stung the bed-
varm flesh of his thighs. Across the river, under the black

rise of the Point Lévis shore, stabs of flame flecked the dark
ness, and the crack of musket fire sounded sharply acros
the ice.

In the morning there were cherry-colored spots of froze
blood on the ice, counted by the British as French casualties
They had brought back their own dead, and the woundec
lay in the hospital in the care of the nuns. A whole detachment of light infantry was missing, presumably taken prisoner. Dumas, with officers sent down from Quebec, took
the British post at Point Lévis that night, and had attemptec
a raid on the lower town. The French held Point Lévis for
two weeks, when Murray drove them off. Eight hundrec
French attacked again on 24 February, and Murray callec
out three regiments to drive them away.

It was so cold, and the men were so weak on short rations
that the guards at night were relieved every half-hour. The
hospitals were filled with the shivering sick. Once each
week, Brigadier General Murray led his officers in a day o
fast, and the rations they saved went to the starving *habitants*. The soldiers loved their mad general for his consideration of them that winter, and the common people of Quebec
came to appreciate the qualities of sympathy and understanding in their conquerers' governor.

Less sympathetic to Murray was the redoubtable Reverend Mother de Sainte Hélène, Superior of the Hospitalers,
who entirely reciprocated the Scotsman's feeling for her.
Being a Ramezay, she was a Frenchwoman and a Canadian,
as well as a nun to whom all Britons were Godless foreigners. Though she could weep at the bedside of Captain
Ouchterlony, she could also plot for the overthrow of the
invaders. Vaudreuil had given free pardon to the French
soldiers, men of many nationalities, who had gone over to
English Service during the confusion following the death of
Montcalm. The Reverend Mother was his agent in this and
other secular duties akin to that of spying. In all her activi-

cies, Mlle. Ramezay exasperated the quick-tempered Scottish general. In a fiery interview, Murray once ordered the nun to confine herself to her religious duties or he would enlist her for a grenadier. She towered more than six feet toward the rafters, a noble figure of a woman.

The religious orders of Quebec had reason to complain of their treatment at the hands of Murray. Though he permitted them their belief, their teaching, and their ceremonies, he made use of their property in a most irreverent manner. The sanctity of church buildings meant nothing to the governor, if they had a roof intact, to shelter British soldiers. At St. Foy and at Ancient Lorette, on the roads west of the town, Brigadier Murray had made strongholds of the churches. In these two towns and at Cap Rouge, outposts watched Dumas, and there was little doubt that the French would try to regain the city from that quarter when the spring came again.

On 23 April, the ice broke up in the river at Quebec. Spring was coming at long last. Six hundred and eighty-two British soldiers—a battalion, as battalions run after a hard campaign—had died that winter. Of the 5600 remaining, 2300 were on the doctors' sick-lists for regiments.

His Majesty's frigate *Race Horse*, under command of Captain Macartney, had wintered in Quebec. The sailors had kept the ice cut away from the hull at her moorings in the basin at the mouth of the Charles River. By the night of 26 April, Captain Macartney had moved his vessel out beyond the old boom, to a position where he could watch the main channel of the river, yet stay safe from the ice floes. Behind the ice, the French frigates might be riding in a dash for the sea. A sloop-of-war rode at anchor close by. As the sun set on that day, the tide was beginning to ebb, and the big ice floes off Cape Diamond had begun their inexorable movement. Night had fallen, the watch had changed, and four bells had been rung on *Race Horse*. The watch on the sloop had heard the brisk chimes. He also heard a faint call for help from out in the river, where the ice floes were moving with the tide toward the bluff of Point Lévis. The lookout called the watch. They, too, heard the sound, almost imperceptible in the distance. A boat was lowered and a party went off, hallo-ing, with a lantern held high by a man in the bows. Somehow, among the ice islands they found the French sergeant who had fallen from the artillery boat. The man was taken to *Race Horse*, where he was warmed, fed, and given clothing. With good navy rum in him, he began to talk. He told of the coming of Lévis and of the landing that was still going on up the river at St. Augustin.

At three o'clock the next morning, the rescued Frenchman, warmed with rum and wrapped in a blanket, stood before Murray in his dressing-gown and repeated his story. Before he had finished, an aide had gone to the guardroom to awaken the duty drummer. Soon all Quebec City was aroused to another attack.

XXI

The Plains of Abraham—Again

The second battle of the Plains of Abraham was not fought on the day that Murray, rousted out of his bed by the arrival of the lucky French sergeant, called out the troops before dawn. That day, 27 April 1760, was used by the British commander to reconnoiter, plan, prepare, and maneuver. Murray drew in his outposts from Ancient Lorette, St. Foy, and Cap Rouge, blowing up the churches of the first two places as he left.

Lévis used that day before the battle to bring up his troops from St. Augustin. If he had not expected to maintain complete surprise, Lévis could reasonably have believed that the presence of his whole army at Quebec was unknown to Murray. Rebuilding bridges and crossing a marsh, the French troops advanced behind a screen of St. Luc de la Corne's Indians. Bourlamaque led the advance with ten companies of grenadiers. They marched to the pyre of the St. Foy church and on to the house and windmill of a M. Dumont, where they ran into the rear guard of British light infantry. The French van stopped.

Lévis's men were grateful for the halt. The rain of the day before had lasted throughout the night, and soaking showers had punctuated the day with misery. The men were

tired. They had worked hard at unloading the boats and
rebuilding the bridges, and the road was either mud, wet
slush, snow, or in low places it was flooded. Lévis had gaged
the fatigue of his army, and had also marked its high temper
of confidence and basic cheer. He had planned to give the
fighting troops a rest on the 28th. The weather was clearing,
and the men could rest in bivouac. On that day the French
vessels would arrive at Anse-au-Foulon, on the French right,
and guns and stores and provisions and baggage would be
brought up the road that Wolfe had used the previous autumn. On the evening of the 27th, a messenger from the
grenadiers found the Chevalier de Lévis camped on a site
of higher ground in the center of the French line. On the
right and left, from the palisades to the St. Foy road, the
flames of cookfires winked where nearly 8000 Frenchmen
and Canadians lay under arms. The message brought to the
general was that the English had retired from Dumont's
house, and that patrols had fixed the enemy picquets on the
ground where Montcalm had formed his regiments for his
last charge.

Again, reveille was early for the British troops on 28
April. By eight o'clock in the morning they had fallen in,
been counted, had been issued picks and shovels, fallen in
again, been counted, brought to attention, and marched out
in a preordained sequence to a prearranged place outside the
walls of Quebec. As each regiment marched out of its gate,
a guide led it to its place in the battle line, forming where
the French had formed eight months before. With each
regiment had gone two field guns, dragged along by their
gunners and a detail from the ranks. In a long, thin line, the
guns formed up in the wide gap between their own battalion
and the next one to the right. The whole British line supported the guns, and was itself supported by some 150 cannon on the city walls at their back. General Murray was de-

pending heavily on his guns to balance the odds of more than two-to-one against him.

As the line of infantry dressed and took up its spacing, the gunners laid out their tools and ammunition. Other British soldiers hurried eagerly from the town, like schoolboys released to form a bucket brigade. Quickly, they slipped into the rear ranks of the regiments or busied themselves about a gun, with a glance for the officers and sergeants, a look of innocence on their faces. The late-comers were the convalescents of the army, some 500 feverish, gaunt, pale, wasted men who, despite orders, would not be left behind.

No Englishman in Quebec that morning wanted to stay in the miserable city that had been a winter prison. They sought their chance on the open Plains of Abraham, where, once before, they had gloriously succeeded. From the general to the smallest drummer boy, they were "in the habit of beating the enemy," as Murray wrote to William Pitt.

Seen from Brigadier Murray's vantage point, the French line, at the edge of an open wood that jutted out toward the British, was undecided and out of order. Murray ordered the whole British line to advance, by the right, for 100 paces. In the new position, the guns went into action all up and down the line. At that range, the cannoneers were loading with round shot. When aimed low, the balls skipped and bounced over the wet ground and through or over the white-coated ranks formed in the open plain. When the quoin was pulled back and the muzzle raised, the balls caromed and ricocheted in crazy flight among the trees. French soldiers running up to find their places were struck by falling branches or had to duck away from the screaming thing flying past their heads.

It was during this cannonade that the unlucky Bourlamaque was wounded. A cannon ball cut and bruised the calf of his leg so that he fell, crippled and useless, to be carried to the rear. When he was hit, the colonel was supervis-

ing the withdrawal of the grenadiers from the Dumont
house. Lévis had been caught with his battalions still forming when Murray advanced to bring his guns into play. To
give the regimental officers time to make their array, the
chevalier sent orders to those troops already in line to give
ground. When all were ready, Lévis would launch his
charge on the thin British line.

The chevalier's orders, shouted by an excited aide as he
galloped by, were misunderstood by the French. The retro-
grade movement by the French grenadiers, who had received the order correctly, was misinterpreted by Murray as
retreat. Seizing the opportunity, Brigadier Murray sent the
British light infantry pelting down the St. Foy road toward
the outstretched arms of Dumont's welcoming mill. With a
wave of his hat, the British general led forward the whole
long line of infantry and guns. For the gunners and their
assistants, dragging the heavy pieces and carrying up the
heavy boxes of shells and kegs of powder, the way was not
hard. Enthusiasm and a gentle down-slope aided them at
their arduous task. They cursed and laughed at once, as they
slipped in the icy mud and heaved the iron-shod wheels
through the slushy snow that lay deep and gray in the hollows. Beside the gunners the double line of infantry kept
pace, advancing and halting at the orders of the officers. On
the right of the British line, the ranks were firing a volley at
each halt of their paced advance.

Misunderstanding Lévis's order, Lt. Colonel Falquier,
commanding the brigade La Sarre-Béarn, on the French
left, pressed forward instead of back. In meeting Bourlamaque's grenadiers in retreat, Falquier saw an open door to
glory, if he could retake Dumont's house. With 1100 men
as eager as he, Falquier charged up the St. Foy road. The
colonel fell with a bullet in his side, but the regulars of La
Sarre and Béarn, and the Canadian militia attached to them,
swept by the fallen officer in a tumultuous wave of white.

They met the British light infantrymen in the farmyard, and they fought them in the cow barn, in the hay mow, and in the rooms of the house where the family had slept and had eaten the miller's flour. The French fought with their long, heavy knives; for the British, it was bayonet and gun-butt and sharp camp axe.

At the far other end of the battle line, at the top of the cliff looking down on the drifting ice in the river, Captain Donald McDonald and most of his hundred men lay, twisted dead, as the French Indians scalped them. During the boring days of winter, the captain had sought out and found, along the soldiers of the Quebec army, a hundred other blithe souls of an adventurous and reckless nature. With them as rangers in the colonial model set by Robert Rogers, McDonald had scourged the countryside in a successful "little war" against Dumas. The raid on St. Augustin in mid-March had been particularly rewarding. On the morning of 28 April, when he set out to make contact and infiltrate the French right, McDonald had in his pocket the gold watch that he had taken from the bedside table of Captain Hebin, the French commander at St. Augustin. The noise of battle was on his right as he walked through the brush at the cliff top. The left of the British line (the 28th Foot, Townshend's, late Bragg's) was out on the plain, slowly advancing. Once, McDonald stopped to view the French regiment, the Royal Roussillon, by their blue facings and white plumes, lined up on the right. They had three field guns in their front. As he passed by, Captain McDonald had paused to look down the steep slope he had climbed with Billy Howe in the darkness of a September morning. The British rangers were walking cautiously now. They had passed the redoubts built on the Anse-au-Foulon road, and were on a path through thick evergreen brush. The sound of French cannon fire was on the right. The ambush was complete, as Dumas's Canadians rose up to fire into the British flank at

pointblank range, and St. Luc de la Corne's Indians rushed
in to kill. McDonald died at once, and most of his hundred
with him. Only the rear of the column escaped. There,
Lieutenant Moses Hazen, the colonial ranger, and his few
men wisely turned and ran for their lives.

Between the end of the firing line of the 28th Foot and
the edge of the cliff there was a vacuum. Into it the Canadians and Indians moved, followed closely by Lieutenant
Colonel de Poulhariès and the soldiers of Roussillon. White-
clad soldiers lay on the ground where the Royal regiments
had stood. Red-coated figures marked the furthest advance
of the 28th, who were falling back, fighting at each step.
Next to the 28th, the Highlanders, their flank exposed,
turned smartly and marched back to rejoin their left, with
the 28th. Opposite, the regiment Guyenne cheered and ran
forward, stopping to fire as they came. The British 47th
Foot, whose fire ahead was masked by rising ground, was
taken in flank by the advancing right of Lévis's line. Over
by Dumont's house, the British light infantry were retiring,
too. The whole French line was beginning to move. Before
the two battalions of the regiment of Berry topped the rise
in front of the 47th, that regiment, on the general's orders,
had begun to move back. Brigadier Murray had seen the
flanks crumbling, and had given the order to leave the field.

The British guns, which for two hours had fired long and
hard at the enemy, one by one were falling silent. Gun captains were calling for more ammunition, ammunition which
did not come. The loaded tumbrils coming from the town
had bogged down in the heavy slush and mud. The invalids,
who had attempted to make a carry line of powder and
shell, were down, exhausted by their exertion. Spirit alone
could not bear the weight of iron. As the infantry fell back,
the gunners tried to bring off their precious guns. But now
the way was uphill, and the slushy snow in the hollows

eemed deeper than before. Cursing fate, the gun captains took the spikes from their pockets, and with the mallets drove them home into the powder-stained touchholes of their pieces. Some of the gun numbers found muskets and attached themselves to the slowly retiring lines of infantry.

So Murray's army, in a fighting retreat, marched back under the protecting fire of the guns on the walls of Quebec, and in good order entered the town. The attack had cost Murray 1000 men killed, wounded, and taken prisoner, in addition to the twenty guns.

As for Lévis, he had suffered heavily at the hands of the British guns and muskets. In the bloodiest battle of the whole long war, the chevalier could count over 100 of his officers killed or wounded, and nearly 1000 men, regulars and Canadians. Stung by the red hornets, the French general followed Murray cautiously up to the range of the wall guns. Then he ordered the halt, and let his men take the rest that he had planned for them on that 28th day of April.

That night the French soldiers of La Reine and Languedoc, who had not been engaged in the battle, opened the siege lines 600 yards from the walls of Quebec. It was not until 10 May that Lévis completed the building of his first siege battery. By that time it was too late.

The frigate *Lowestoft* had arrived in the Quebec roads on 9 May. The English officers and men, working side by side on the defenses of the wall, rushed to the heights of Cape Diamond to see the familiar vessel come around the bulk of Point Lévis. They cheered until they were hoarse, and the gunners loaded and fired their cannon in a frenzy of joy.

For another six days, the Chevalier de Lévis kept up the siege, though with the few heavy guns that he had it was more of a blockade than a siege. He still hoped that a French fleet would come up the river, and with it, the siege train of guns that he expected from Bordeaux. In St. Foy, the

French regulars made scaling ladders measured to the height of the walls of Quebec.

The fleet of twenty-one store ships and an escort frigate for which Lévis waited was in the Gulf of St. Lawrence. The convoy commodore had made his way through the British blockading squadrons guarding the French coast. He had missed, or been missed by, the British squadron that cruised out of Louisbourg and, early in May, lay in Chaleur Bay, under the Gaspé Peninsula, preparing to run up the St. Lawrence. For Captain John Byron ("Foul Weather Jack," whose son would sire a poet), Chaleur Bay was a port of call for his Louisbourg squadron searching for the spring fleet. When the tall British ships sailed into the deep bay, all the French vessels lay there at anchor. The commodore, on the flush deck of his single frigate, was trapped under the tiered guns of Captain Byron's ships of the line. Wisely, the Frenchman chose to strike his colors, and the twenty-one chunky merchantmen followed suit.

In any case, the fleet which was Byron's prize in Chaleur Bay could not have reached Lévis to succor him. The French had already lost the race to the St. Lawrence. When the French commodore struck, Commodore Swanton's squadron of Admiral Colville's fleet was sailing up the river.

Commodore Swanton arrived off Quebec aboard *Vanguard*, late on 15 May. Sailing in his wake, returning to the city, came Captain Schomberg, on the quarter-deck of the repaired frigate *Diana*. He tarried only long enough to pay his compliments to Brigadier Murray, and to gather up Captain Deane of *Lowestoft*. With the early-morning tide, he took his squadron up the river. But the two French frigates, short-handed and without guns, made off, only to run aground. In the hard current of the river, and in the gusty wind off the cliffs that day, *Lowestoft*, too, struck an underwater rock and stove in her bottom. She was abandoned, and the British soldiers on the walls of the citadel watched "their" frigate founder and break up.

After dark on the night that Swanton came up the river, the French troops abandoned the siege of Quebec. In the night of a rising wind, they silently left the trenches under the walls for the line of the Cap Rouge River. For four days, Lévis tarried while the northwest wind blew itself out. Then he left the vicinity of Quebec, and with the general went his army. In Montreal the spring flowers would be blooming, and there would be fleurs-de-lis in the garden where the old governor general took his daily walks.

Murray did not follow his retiring adversary; he could not. The casualties of the battle on the plain, compounded with the exertion of the siege, had further reduced the stamina of the garrison. But the spirits of the soldiers soared. Men who had thought of themselves as "Wolfe's terriers" now boasted that they were "Murray's pack of wolves."

When he finally got his orders, the Honorable James Murray accepted them cautiously and with suspicion, to be sniffed at all around, as an old dog accepts a proferred bone. Four tattered strangers were brought to him one morning at the very end of June, with a tale of an overturned raft and written orders from General Amherst which had been lost over the falls of the river. One at a time, Murray had the messengers (the spies?) admitted to the high, mirrored room where he sat. Surrounded by his own reflected image, the ragged implausibility of each man stood out in contrast to the immaculate figure of the keen-eyed general. Each of the four was dressed in shreds of torn buckskin, modestly covered with dirty but rich brocade, and conveniently pieced with misfit garments that a *habitant* farmer might have worn for work. Only two of the men had brought weapons, which, though inconclusive as evidence, were English army issue.

Yet each one told the same story, and though he kept the glass filled with brandy, Murray could not trip them up. Shute, Beavely, Goodwin, and Eastman were rangers in Robert Rogers's corps. They had been put ashore from a sloop, in daylight, at the far northern end of Lake Champlain. That was 150 miles away, through swamps, across rivers, in deserted and hostile lands. At the crossing of the St. Francis River, the raft had overturned, leaving two of the four men naked and without arms. It was there that Amherst's orders to Murray and a packet of officers' mail had been lost. After traveling several days through an interminable swamp, they came to a village on a Sunday morning. While the *habitants* were at Mass, the rangers entered a house and stole clothing and food. At a log house in the woods, they found a chest containing women's clothing of the finest quality, from which they made breech-cloths of brocade in the Indian fashion. They also killed and butchered a calf, which they cooked and ate while they made moccasins to replace those rotted off their feet by the long days in the bogs.

Each of the four rangers had memorized a set of verbal instructions from General Amherst to Murray: Brigadier Murray's Quebec army would march on Montreal from the east. Brigadier Haviland would arrive with his army from Lake Champlain on the south side of the city. Amherst himself would bring the main British army down the St. Lawrence from the west. The general would meet his brigadiers outside Montreal in the first week of September.

The four rangers had delivered their message, which the old, siege-worn general sitting in the mirrored room finally had accepted as the truth. Now Rogers's men wanted to return the way they had come. Major Rogers needed them, and besides, they had to collect the £50 "danger pay" that had been offered them to make the dangerous journey. But Murray, elated at the prospect of the new campaign, prom-

sed them a speedy rendezvous with Rogers, and their £50
t Montreal. To prove his optimism, Murray gave each of
he men £4 from his own purse to spend in the last French
:ity of New France.

Sergeant Beavely knew the city of Montreal. He had
ived in the house of the Marquis de Vaudreuil as recently
s late April of that same year. Taken prisoner in February
ɔy French Indians between Ticonderoga and Crown Point,
he sergeant had been ransomed by the governor. As he
vorked off his debt in the pantry and in the halls of Vau-
lreuil's "court," Beavely had overheard the loose, boasting
alk of the governor's coterie. Piece by piece, the quiet serv-
ɪnt learned the details of Lévis's plan to retake Quebec.
That information was needed by Rogers and by General
Amherst. Other captured rangers, too, were serving and
ɔiding their time in Montreal. Among them, it was agreed
hat Sergeant Beavely would escape first, with his news of
Lévis's attack on Quebec and all the other bits of military,
:conomic, and political intelligence that, together, they had
ɪmassed. Later, when the news warranted it, the other rang-
ɛrs in Montreal would likewise break their parole and their
bond.

Since 1755, the role of Rogers's rangers in the army had
been that of scouting, making careful observation, and ren-
dering true intelligence. While prisoners of war, Sergeant
Beavely and the others continued to perform the ranger's
duty. In the five years of its existence, Rogers's company of
rangers had grown into a corps, and the captain had become
a major, with all the responsibilities of big command. In
addition, on Rogers's shoulders had been laid the heavy ac-
colade of an idol to the army, a home-grown hero to the
British colonies, and a legendary figure to the English. The
years of war brought additional duties to the rangers. In
October and November of 1759, General Amherst had sent
the corps on a deep, penetrating raid of retaliation. The

rangers had struck at dawn, 150 miles behind the French
lines. When they left about noon, the Indian town of St
Francis was a flaming ruin. English scalps, 600 of them
taken on many raids, were found hanging on poles outside
the lodges. They were redeemed in kind and in destruction.

When Sergeant Beavely escaped, bringing the news of
Lévis's march with the whole French army (sparing only
the fort guards), Amherst called on Rogers to create a diversion, intended to relieve the pressure on Murray, who
was besieged in Quebec. It was not until June that the expedition got under way. Rogers sailed north with the British
fleet, riding comfortably in the captain's cabin with his
friend Grant, the Scottish sailor. For three weeks, the rangers and the fleet operated at the northern end of Lake Champlain, stirring up the French in their fort at Ile aux Noix and
spreading alarm all down the Richelieu River from the foot
of the lake to the St. Lawrence.

Robert Rogers's diversion was the first probing finger of
Amherst's campaign against Montreal. It tapped lightly but
firmly on the shoulder of Colonel Bougainville, the French
commander at Ile aux Noix. General de Lévis of the army
and Governor General de Vaudreuil of New France had
given Montcalm's former aide 1450 soldiers and men of the
Marine to guard the southern way to Montreal. Bougainville
had a fort built on Ile aux Noix in the Richelieu River drain-
ing Lake Champlain. The remnant of the French lake navy
guarded the swift waters of the channel. The Chevalier de
Lévis had ordered Bougainville, for the honor of the French
army, to hold his position to the last man. The colonel and
his men waited through all the warm month of July. It was
past the middle of August when scouts returned with the
news that Britain's Lake Champlain army was moving down
the lake.

Colonel William Haviland of the 27th Foot, acting

as brigadier general, commanded the British force going against Bougainville. He had 3400 men in his army, together with the four ships of the navy and an artillery train. Colonel Timothy Ruggles of Massachusetts was Haviland's second-in-command. Though only a colonial by birth and rank, Ruggles bore witness, by his position, to the long years and hard service of the New England men on this frontier. There were only two regiments of regulars on the lake: Haviland's 27th, and the 17th, that Forbes had commanded. The whole flotilla was led by Rogers and his rangers in their whaleboats, rowing with a swing to the long oars, flashing wet in the sunlight.

Brigadier General James Murray headed for the rendezvous at Montreal fully a month before Haviland departed from Crown Point. He left the sick and convalescent in Quebec as its garrison, took 2400 men with him, and sailed upriver in forty vessels, including British warships, so tall of mast in the channels of the river. Murray's way was slow, for his road was through the heartland of Canada, where villages and towns strung the thread of the river like a rosary of New France. At every parish the conqueror pilgrim stopped to tell that bead. In one hand, Murray held a burning brand, in the other, the cargo from the transports of the river. At those houses where the men were away with the militia, the torch was given. Few Canadians were away from home that summer, and those that were away hurried back before General Murray came. At most of the towns the *habitants* delivered up their arms to the red-coated soldiery, and took the oath of neutrality. Down at the shore, British work-parties unloaded gifts of grain and stores, things that had once come out from France, things that had once been bought from Bigot, the intendant, but in the year 1760, things that could not be bought with the valueless scrip of a ruined economy.

At Trois Rivières, the third city in New France, Dumas of the Marine, with a force meant to delay the Quebec army, awaited Murray's coming. But the British general passed by in his ships and sailed out into Lac St. Pierre. Dumas followed meekly along the shore. He met Lévis, riding out from Montreal, and together the two old soldiers watched the big fleet sail into the nest of islands at Lac St. Pierre's eastern end, where the River Richelieu flowed into the St. Lawrence at Sorel. Murray burned that town, because all the men had gone to join Bourlamaque, set by Lévis to intercept the Quebec army. Murray did his duty with a reluctant hand and a heavy heart, but the hard example of the burning town sufficed for his purpose. When he moved a step nearer to Montreal, Colonel Bourlamaque's army had disappeared.

General Murray's Quebec army was first to the rendezvous, a week ahead of Haviland. The Champlain army had laid siege to Ile aux Noix. Robert Rogers, with the grenadiers and light infantry of the regulars, had worked his way around Bougainville's fort and had attacked the French fleet in the river. In a whooping, shooting avalanche, the rangers and regulars boarded the fleet and made it their own. Bougainville, with new orders from the governor countermanding those of Lévis to "stand and fight," gave up the fort. Quietly, he slipped away in the darkness of a late August night. Haviland followed slowly after his rangers, who were rollicking in pursuit of the French rear guard, backing down the long road across the prairie to Montreal.

Early in September, Haviland and Murray made lateral contact by patrols. Brigadier Haviland was marching on Longueuil, on the south bank of the St. Lawrence opposite the city. Brigadier Murray was approaching the island of Ste. Thérèse, just below Montreal.

Major General Jeffrey Amherst was still somewhere up-river.

XXII

The Lilies Fade

From Albany on Hudson's River to Oswego on Lake Ontario, and thence by the chute of the St. Lawrence to Montreal, it is 420 miles or more. It was that route that Amherst took to keep his rendezvous with Murray and with Haviland. He made of his progress a summer-long parade.

The Indians counted the regiments as they passed by. On the shore of the Mohawk River, a greased Iroquois girl watched the loaded bateaux working their way up stream. The baby at her breast moved his head from time to time to suck on a finger of army pork, given to him by a passing soldier. At the shipyard at Oswego, stately chiefs of the Onondaga Nation broke a bottle over the bows of the new *Onondaga* as she took the water. Later they went aboard Britain's newest warship, where the greatest chief among them hoisted a new flag to the masthead: on it was painted an Onondaga warrior. Then Commodore Loring and *Onondaga*'s Captain Thornton ladled punch for their guests from the big bowl set out on a table covered with a white linen cloth.

There were few Indian Nations anywhere in North America that summer that did not know the British king's men were parading in their might. Sir William Johnson saw to it that the western Nations knew of Amherst's army. He told the "praying Indians" of the St. Lawrence, who then forgot to answer the priest's call to Mass. Even the Abenakis, in the east, buried the hatchets given them by the French king while they followed the redcoats' progress on the march to Montreal.

Indians, when attached to a well-ordered army, were apt to be an irksome liability to the general who employed them. Amherst's orderly-room seemed constantly to be plagued by incidents of disorder caused by the warriors and their ever-present women, none of them subject to regulations, discipline, or punishment. For a general with a perpetually inadequate war chest, the demand for presents seemed incessant. The custom of paying a bounty for scalps was as questionable as it was repugnant to the old campaigner. Furthermore, the Indians were not the scouts and woods fighters that their past success seemed to proclaim. James Braddock's defeat in 1755, and Major Grant's defeat at the same place three years later, had been due in great part to successful French leadership of the Indians, an ability that the British neither possessed nor made any attempt to develop. King George's generals had relied on their rangers to scout the enemy, and His Majesty's army had developed the light infantry. The generalship of Jeffrey Amherst had used Rogers's colonial rangers to their fullest capacity, though for his march through the wilderness Amherst was relying largely upon the regular light infantry. These troops, with the men of the bateau service, pioneered by John Bradstreet, were now doing the work that had been done by the native Indian during the early and less successful years of Britain's war for French North America. The Indians had never become a part of British army discipline and order, and the Indian customs and morality were abhorrent to an English gentleman and officer. The Oswegatchi chief whom Johnson brought to Amherst as a valuable turncoat was said to have killed thirty people, men, women, and children, all of them British. The colonial wing of Amherst's army, many of whom numbered those thirty as relatives, shared their general's suspicious mistrust of the Indian as an ally.

Major General Jeffrey Amherst, adjudicating the case of an Indian who had cut up a sutler's horse, found little satisfaction in the 700 Iroquois warriors brought by Sir William Johnson to the well-run camp on the shores of Lake Ontario. He gave a cool welcome to "the Baronet of the Mohawk," who, on a recent visit to Johnson's manor, had forced the general's recognition of "the brown Lady Johnson" as his hostess. Too, the knighted colonial had rather usurped the command over British troops, following the untimely death of Prideaux at Fort Niagara. The friction between homespun rank and court-tailored commission—a friction that had driven young George Washington out of the army—still raised the nap after six years of rubbing shoulders. Amherst had refused to acknowledge as military Johnson's title of "Colonel," nor would he grant Johnson's request for the same rank, and £600, in the army. Sir William's work with the savages was political and could remain so, as far as the commander in chief was concerned. As Indian agent in the north, it was the task of Sir William to placate the Indian Nations and to maneuver and manipulate their shifting loyalties, as it was John Stuart's job to keep at peace the Nations in the south.

The latter Indian agent already had cost the supreme British military commander one regiment of regulars. For all the long years of the war, Stuart, whose appointment as Indian agent in the south bore the same date as did Johnson's commission, had kept the great Cherokee Nation actively allied to the British. For many campaigns, the pale-skinned Cherokee warriors had traveled north into Virginia and Pennsylvania to fight the French, but more particularly to make their own war on the enemy Indians of the Ohio, allied to the French. With their fine, straight eyes, the Cherokee men watched the French power wane in the north and saw their implacable foes go over to the English, who accepted them as brothers. John Stuart, the Cherokees' friend, was hard put to explain away the covetous greed of the coastal colonists, as they gazed at the land beyond the Appalachian Mountains, which France no longer "owned." The wise men viewed with alarm the drunken militiamen, who garrisoned the posts on the headwaters of the Tennessee and the Savannah Rivers, which were in Cherokee land.

The Cherokee war started with a roistering carousal at Fort Prince George, on the Keeowee River, and progressed across that stream to the Cherokee town where the women were alone. Lieutenant Richard Coytmore, the fort's commander of militia, led the revelers in the orgy of rape. A year later, in February of 1760, he received his reward when he was killed in ambush by Oconostota, the war chief. By the time Coytmore died, the war had grown from isolated incidents of angry reprisal into a struggle for existence by one Indian Nation against the restless westward advance of the English colonists. Thus it was, that when the Carolinian commander of Fort Loudoun, deep in Cherokee country, lay staked out for torture, the Cherokee women began the ritual by cramming the coveted earth into the Englishman's mouth.

In March, the lieutenant governor of South Carolina appealed for troops to relieve Fort Loudoun and to put down the Cherokee rising. Amherst had sent him six companies of Highlanders from his own army, and as many companies of the 1st Foot from Haviland. Colonel Archibald Montgomery was put in command, and with him went that Major James Grant who had jeopardized his chance of promotion on the Monongahela. In early June, when Amherst was

eady to leave his Albany base for the Oswego starting
ine, Lieutenant Governor William Bull wrote that Mont-
omery's expedition had started for Fort Prince George and
he wild country that lay beyond. General Amherst had not
et reached Oswego when the chastened Montgomery and
Grant turned back in a hasty withdrawal out of the terrible
ind well-defended mountain fastness of the Cherokees. Un-
elieved, Fort Loudoun fell to Oconostota's warriors. Be-
ore Amherst left Oswego, Captain Paul Demere was eating
earth on the torture ground.

Jeffrey Amherst was a tall, straight man with red hair and
ed eyebrows. But his normally florid complexion had
urned pale, almost ashen, when he was helped into bed
n the guest quarters at Fort Schuyler. On the way from Al-
any, the forty-three-year-old general had been taken with
a pain in the chest. His hurt kept him close to his quarters
or several days. Then, in spite of the admonitions of the
doctors, he pushed on after the twelve horses of his stable.
As a soldier, Amherst spared neither himself, nor his men,
nor his animals, though he was meticulous in the care of all.
The general rested, while his army flowed westward around
the red rock of his ailing body. The bateaumen hushed their
singing as they passed by the house where their general lay,
and the drovers cursed their teams in muted voices. In calm,
undoubting confidence, General Amherst relaxed away the
pain. At every point of the march, in every department of
the army, Amherst's own staff officers functioned like the
grease in the smooth-turning axle of his army.

For a month after Amherst's arrival at Oswego on 9 July,
the staff worked at bringing the troops and supplies from
Albany. Step by systematic step, the barrels and the bundles came forward with the men. As July gave way to August, the staging depots along the Mohawk River were shut
down, and the bateaux went forward over the portage to

form the invasion fleet. Then the teams of horses and the spans of oxen turned back, their carts empty, to an all-but-deserted Albany.

Through six years of campaigns, the inland city had transshipped the stuff of war. The burghers of Albany had prospered on the armies that had gone north and west through their town at the crossroads. The merchants and business men had dealt in goods and foodstuffs and credit. The entrepreneurs and the craftsmen had hired out the wheels and built the bateaux to send the regiments on their way. Innkeepers and opportunists had catered to the needs and wants of the transient soldiers. Housewives cashed billeting chits for the young subalterns from England, going to "join up," and made a bit for their compassion for the sick or wounded gentlemen convalescing in their rearranged downstairs parlors. With the campaign of 1760, the war boom in Albany was over—unless Amherst's carefully contrived campaign stumbled to failure. The prospect for Albany residents was bright, however, in the new sun of peace, shining at the edge of the passing war clouds. The prosperous time of armies was passing by the pivotal city, set midway between the Atlantic and the St. Lawrence, but a new horizon of wealth was showing clear, over and beyond the five great inland lakes. The peace that could be glimpsed on the Hudson in 1760 had already come to the Ohio, where Virginians and Pennsylvanians were trading along the army roads over the Appalachian Mountains. But Forbes's road and the road that George Washington had pioneered to the new Fort Pitt would not interfere too much with the prospects of the Albany burghers, who sat, secure, at the branch of the time-old water-level route to the north and the beckoning west. The last man of General Amherst's army went up the Mohawk River in July 1760.

That last man was a sergeant of New England troops, shepherding the reluctant recruits for an incomplete regi-

ment already at Oswego. The colonels of the four Connecticut regiments detailed to Amherst's army had a sluggish
response to their recruiting drive that year. All over New
England, the colonists were settling down to peace. Farmers on the back lots were anxious to open the northern pas-
ture for a crop. No more would the priest-led Abenakis
come down out of Canada. There was a better day's work
for the fisherman on the banks, for a sailor on the West
Indies-England-home triangle, or for a shipwright in the
yards on Long Island Sound than there was in pulling the
oar of a bateau over the freshwater lakes. All of New
France was compressed into the city of Montreal, where
were the remnants of Montcalm's regiments of regulars.
Twenty-one battalions of British regular infantry con-
verged on Montreal that summer. There was no need for a
New Englander to "go for a soldier" when there was a ship
to be rigged or a new field to be cleared of cobble.

Yet the New Englanders finally came to the armies gathering at Albany. The Massachusetts men, with the Rhode
Islanders and the New Hampshire Regiment, had gone
north to join Haviland. The Connecticut men came to Amherst 2000 strong. With the New York regiments and
Schuyler's tenacious Jersey "Blues," Amherst's provincials
were equal in numbers to his regulars.

On 7 August, the first contingent moved from Oswego to
secure the mouth of the St. Lawrence River. A day or so
later, the whole army set out in 800 boats, coasting the
shores of Lake Ontario with a naval escort to seaward. One
French warship was still at large on the lake. For a month,
Commodore Loring had swept the big lake without finding
Outwas. It fell to George Williamson, Amherst's heavy-
jowled commander of artillery, to start the French vessel
from behind an island in the St. Lawrence. With a view
halloo and a taunt to the absent commodore, the gunner
colonel rowed down on *Outwas* with five gunboats in full

cry and took her with a rush. He renamed his prize *Williamson*, and left her in the river for Loring to repair, as the guns had used her hard. Two days' march down the shore the French Fort Lévis stood on its island in the middle of the river.

The Chevalier de Lévis had seen and approved the island site of the fort that carried his name. Like a Mallard duck, the island sat in the middle of the stream, bresting a fast current that squeezed between opposite points of land, each within a good cannon shot of Fort Lévis. The island had been chosen because it was in a defile, and because it was above the first of the St. Lawrence rapids, which Amherst would have to assay with caution. For generations, the Canadians had shot those rapids to bring home the canoe brigades, laden with furs from the west. The *voyageurs'* skill and daring in the white water was inherited. They knew the hidden rocks and the crossovers as they knew the grunting paddle-song which was taking them home to Montreal, a hundred miles away. But the Englishmen and the "*Bostonais*" would need pilots for the river below Fort Lévis.

The fort had been built by Captain Pouchot, of Béarn, he who had lost Fort Niagara to Prideaux's sappers and Johnson's Indian horde. Fort Lévis was not a strong fort. Digging the ditches, the men soon struck the bedrock of the island, and the low earth walls they threw up were pieced out with logs, to hide rather than to shield, the soldiers behind them. The abatis on the shore was sparce and weak, being made of the puny brush which could be cut on the island. The Frenchmen and Canadians that Pouchot had as defenders were still building the fort when General Amherst came with the might of his army.

Captain Pouchot stood in the great angle of battery, watching through his glass the approach of the British gunboats, and behind them, the whaleboats of the van. All round him, the gun numbers were laying the guns to the sharp orders of the gun captains. The guns began to fire as he boats came abreast of the point on the north. Pouchot leaned into the earth of the rampart, his eye to the long tube of the spyglass. White flowers of spume broke into life around the gunboats. Quite suddenly, the inshore British boat reared up in the water like a young horse on a frosty morning. Pouchot saw the crew of the gun in the bow of he stricken boat tumble over, some of them falling into the water, some into the piece. Then the rowers dove over the side, and the Frenchman saw the boat's commander, standing in the stern as he carefully removed his blue-and-red artillery coat. Swinging his glass away from the sinking gunboat, Pouchot picked up, one by one, the other gunboats of Williamson's flotilla, and the whaleboats crowded with light infantry. All were backing water, the gunboats clumsily in their unwieldy weight and size, the whaleboats easily swinging round between the splashes of the French artillery balls. In one of the whaleboats, there was confusion in the bows, where a shattered gunwale showed clearly in the round eye of Pouchot's glass.

It was not until that night, 18 August, that General Amherst succeeded in bringing his gunboats and a part of his force past the guard at Fort Lévis. By then, he had troops ashore on both the north and south points. When, on the morning of the following day, Commodore Loring came down with two of his vessels and anchored, the French fort was sealed off and siege operations began. General Amherst had no intention of by-passing Captain Pouchot and his 300 men. He expected Lévis to attack him on the river, perhaps at the rapids lower down, where Amherst knew that St. Luc de la Corne was waiting with a militia force. It was not in Jeffrey Amherst's training to leave behind him a willful, determined Pouchot, with well-served cannon. Nor did the British commander in chief have the spur of fleeting time to

force him into the character, so alien to his nature, of a bold
dashing, but distraught James Wolfe. Amherst had thre
weeks at his disposal before keeping the rendezvous with
Murray and Haviland, because he and his staff had planne
it that way. So the British army from out of the west began
its siege by building batteries. One of these was on the south
point, and two others bore on Fort Lévis from islands 50
yards distant, under the north shore.

At eight o'clock on the morning of 23 August, the island
batteries of 12-pound and big 24-pound guns began the op
erations against Fort Lévis. Two heavy mortars, crouching
on their beds, joined in to arch their shells high over the wa
ter, to fall and burst among the people and buildings behind
the walls. At eleven o'clock, after three hours of continuou
bombardment, Amherst was ready to begin the second stage
of the attack. The general planned to bring down two of
Loring's ships to anchor close to the French island. While
they fired their broadsides into the breached walls, marks
men in the rigging would give plunging small-arms fire onto
the French gun crews. At that moment, Lieutenant Colone
Eyre Massey's men would assault ashore from their boats
The grenadiers had stripped off their heavy coats and al
their equipment, to be free for hand-to-hand fighting with
the swords, axes, and tomahawks which were their only
weapons. They had pulled out from shore and were ready
and waiting when the first ship, *Mohawk*, made her run
down. The shore batteries fell silent as the sloop masked
their target. Upstream, *Williamson* was shaking out her sail
like a dowager about to make her entry into a drawing-
room. But she came in slowly, like a very old dowager
Without a wind to fill her sails or to give her steerage way
she was completely at the mercy of the current.

The French in Fort Lévis had run out a gun and in spite
of the marksmen in the rigging, were firing almost muzzle

o muzzle with the sailors of *Mohawk*. The French fire was accurate. Loring was hit on the quarter-deck, and the vessel was hulled between wind and water. With the deck settling under him, the wounded captain gave the order to cut cable. *Mohawk* drifted down out of the fight and was taken in tow by the gunboats. Following her consort, *Williamson* was helpless in the swift-running stream, which took her wide of the French fort to an ignominious beaching on the Ile de l'Abbé Picquot, more than a mile downriver. The grenadiers in their boats were called back to shore.

There was yet one vessel of the British navy unengaged and upstream from Fort Lévis. She was *Onondaga*, with a Mr. Thornton her captain under the Indian flag. Stirred by the scene of his commodore's failure, Mr. Thornton gave his orders to heave in the anchor and make sail. *Onondaga* was a proud sight as she came round the north point, and the grenadiers cheered her and turned their boats about. On shore, Amherst cursed the fool that commanded her. The general had given no orders for *Onondaga* to engage, and he had already called off the assault, the wind not being subject to his staff planning. *Onondaga* passed close to Fort Lévis, so close that musket fire was exchanged. Just south of Pouchot's island, while the small arms were still rattling between the ship and the shore, *Onondaga* ran aground.

Lying there, helpless, Mr. Thornton quickly struck his colors—too quickly, in Amherst's opinion—as he ordered the island battery to fire on the ship's company in the boats, "deserting" to the French island. Colonel Massey, too, was raging in indignation at the conduct of the sailors. At the water's edge, he found Lieutenant Pennington, still in his assault boat with his forty grenadiers. The colonel commanded him to raise the British Jack on *Onondaga*, and to "keep the deck for England's honor." Through all the long hours of the afternoon on which he died, Pennington, hud-

dled in the canted scuppers under the Jack that he ha
raised and under the strange device of the Indian flag
obeyed his colonel's orders.

Before dark, those remaining of Pennington's grenadier
came away from the stranded hulk. After nightfall, Am
herst sent boats to bring off the artillery stores that wer
Onondaga's cargo. These stores were needed at the battery
sites, as the bombardment, after the failure of the attack
would be protracted. But through all the night Pouchot and
his soldiers kept the English from their work.

With the coming of dawn, both sides set a watch over the
stranded vessel. British Grenadiers rowed in the river, out o
gunshot range, while Frenchmen stood ready to launch
their boats, should the enemy try again for the valuable
stores. The British gunners meanwhile kept up the cannonading of Fort Lévis, but with an eye, now, on the dwindling
pile of shot in the magazines.

Sunday night, Amherst sent out twenty-five of the light
infantrymen that his brother William commanded to guard
Onondaga. On the empty deck, the night was still. The
crash of the big guns was pillowed by the darkness. The
light infantrymen, straining their ears for nearer sounds
heard only the lapping of the waves against the hull.

Next morning, the British guns further slackened their
fire to save their ammunition. On all the shores around stood
idle British soldiers, watching the beleaguered French island. The cooks called the men to their meal, which they
ate hurriedly, to return expectantly to their watch. At four
o'clock in the afternoon, their patience and the gunners' efforts were rewarded: a white flag was raised over the walls
of Fort Lévis. Suddenly the bombardment stopped, as a
boat came over with Pouchot's terms of surrender. By eight
o'clock, all was arranged, and Colonel Massey, with three
companies of grenadiers, marched into Fort Lévis, its desolation illuminated by the flickering torch-light.

For another week, General Amherst remained at Fort
Lévis. There was much to be done. The staff was busy, and
he clerks swarmed over the fort, counting and recounting
tems for their interminable lists. Everything that had be-
onged to the French king was now Crown property,
narked with George II's broad arrow. All the cargo from
he Lake Ontario fleet, which remained above the rapids,
had to be off-loaded, listed, and repacked in the bateaux and
he whaleboats. In this task the commissary, Colonel Rob-
rtson, was assisted by Major Moneypenny, who, since
Abercromby's expedition, had been preparing loading sched-
ules. The provost guard strutted importantly as they paraded Mr. Thornton, sometime captain of His Majesty's
loop *Onondaga,* between his place of confinement and the
board sitting in unfavorable judgment upon him. The work
of the chaplains was soon over, as they laid away in their
graves twenty-one British soldiers. Out on the island, the
British Grenadiers helped the French prisoners bury again
their thirteen dead, disinterred by the Iroquois. Forbidden
to massacre the French prisoners, Johnson's warriors had
raided the graves for scalps before returning sullenly to
their homes. But other Indians came in from the French
ands to do homage to General Amherst. They claimed to
know the secrets of the rapids, and joined the band of
French pilots who had been employed after a canvass of the
Canadians among the prisoners of war.

With the skillful help of these steersmen, Amherst's army
coursed the first series of rapids without mishap. By 2 Sep-
ember, the British army was on that wide stretch of the St.
Lawrence known as Lake St. Francis. To the south and east,
the soldiers could see the mountains beyond which lay the
coastal colonies. From the shore, a priest and a few blank-
faced Canadians watched the bateaux go by. The whaleboats and the heavily laden artillery boats pushed off from
the shore, the men's hands white with the tight grip on their

setting poles and steering oars. Not far from land they fel
the grip of the current seizing them, and soon, before the
were quite ready, the sliding mass of water held them and
hurled them like darts down the chute of the river. A black
rock, plumed with a white mane of water, grabbed, missed
and scraped the length of a bateau's side. In the bow of
whaleboat, a sweating soldier stabbed with a green pine oa
at the face of a boulder, leering up at him from just below
the surface. The oar broke, and the boulder crashed up
through the frail bottom of the whaleboat, overturning it
Bobbing and plunging in the water, another boat raced by
only a few feet away, its crew powerless to help the strug
gling, gasping, drowning men. Further down, a big artillery
boat lay overturned, capping a rock, while a mound o
black water pressed on its upstream side. A bateau slid by
its steersman intent on an ominous ripple 200 yards beyond
He steered wide, and suddenly and unexpectedly the bateau
was itself again, free and floating in the deeper water of
Lake St. Louis. The pilot leaned on his steering oar. Al
ready, the four rowers had their oars out and the bowman
exhausted, was leaning on the long shaft of his setting pole

A staff officer checked the boats ashore below the rapids
A later tally showed that thirty of the boats had been
wrecked and eighty men lost to the river. On shore, Gen
eral Amherst watched the first of the boats come in, until he
was called away to hear the intelligence reports. These con
firmed the rumor that St. Luc de la Corne and his Canadians
had gone from Ile Perrot, just across from the landing place.
In the afternoon of 4 September, Amherst crossed to the is
land and made camp. There Lieutenant Eliot found the gen
eral and reported that Brigadier Haviland's force was in
position, awaiting orders, on the south shore of the St. Law
rence opposite Montreal. Brigadier Murray, with the fleet,
was below the town. Montreal lay between the jaws and the
paws of the British Lion.

Early in the morning of 6 September, Jeffrey Amherst crossed over from Ile Perrot to the island on which was the city of Montreal. The army landed before noon, a little below the church at Lachine. The landing place was a good one—the place from which the fur brigades set out, up the St. Lawrence to the west, or up the Ottawa River by the old, old way to the upper lakes. Light infantrymen landed on the ramp where, seven years before, Chaussegros de Léry had launched the canoes of the third brigade, bound for the Beautiful River, before the long war had begun. There had been skim ice on the slats that April of 1754; there was slippery scum on the boards now, in September of 1760. A battalion soldier, carrying his pack, blanket, and musket, slipped and fell. Quickly, he scrambled to his feet and went, grumbling, after the laughing men of his company. Together, they marched off after the light infantry and the grenadiers, stepping down the last stretch of the road to Montreal.

The afternoon sun was still high when the British troops deployed outside the walls of Montreal. They were drawn up in two ranks, with the grenadiers on the right and the light infantry on the left, all in correct parade order. For a long while, as soldiers count the time in ranks, General Amherst's army stared at the blank picket wall of Montreal, and the steeples and towers of the churches behind the wall. For a long while, as doomed men watch the minutes pass, the government of New France looked out on the serried ranks of Britain with the red sun setting behind them. Before darkness fell, Jeffrey Amherst marched his regiments a little to their rear and made camp. In Montreal, the Marquis de Vaudreuil called all the chief men to his palace on the parade, to begin the final and complete surrender of New France. The Seven Years' War for all North America had come to an end.

Afterword

The French were reluctant to depart from New France. The Chevalier de Lévis resisted the inclusion of the French army in Vaudreuil's terms of capitulation and refused to be a party to the polite formalities when the governor general surrendered the army. At one point Lévis, hopeless but determined to uphold the honor of the king's regiments under his command, asked permission to take the eight proud battalions and escape to Louisiana. When General Amherst was closing in on Montreal, the redoubtable chevalier sought the governor's consent to his taking the regulars to the Ile Ste. Hélène, to make a desperate last stand. After the final surrender Lévis refused to meet with the conquerors of Montreal. It fell to the grievously wounded Bourlamaque and the tactful linguist, Bougainville, to coordinate the withdrawal of French troops from Canada, but even they could not locate the regimental colors when the time came to turn them over to the English. There was reason, however, in the French commander's reluctance to lay down his arms, for Amherst, holding the French regulars accountable for many of the Indian atrocities and massacres, demanded harsh terms from them, without according them the customary honors.

On his return to France, Lévis prospered in his career and eventually was made a duke and a marshal of France. Less fortunate was the fate of the Marquis de Vaudreuil. He was put on trial for the malpractices of his government of New France; but justice prevailed, and he was exonerated from the culpable blame that rightly stripped the intendant Bigot and his man Cadet of all the wealth they had amassed. Vaudreuil loved Canada, and left the land of his birth with deep regret. On 18 September General Amherst called to take his leave of Monsieur and Madame de Vaudreuil. The following day Vaudreuil, with exquisite courtesy, returned the visit and bade farewell to the British general. On 23 September the vessel carrying the marquis to France ran aground in the St. Lawrence thirty miles above Montreal. It was as though Canada would hold back her son and her first French governor.

Fate intervened in the departure for France of one other Canadian. He was the Indian leader and the scourge of the English, the Chevalier St. Luc de la Corne. The ship taking him to France was wrecked in a storm, and St. Luc de la Corne was miraculously thrown back on the Canadian coast. He remained in Canada, assisting (on both the civil and the military side) the first two British governors of Canada: Brigadier General Murray and Murray's successor, Wolfe's onetime Lieutenant Colonel of Grenadiers, Guy Carleton.

When the French government had left Canada, General Amherst had much to do to consolidate the vast new empire that his army had won. Of all the elements of French rule, only the Catholic Church remained, an instrument of British policy in the management of the *habitants*. In immediate recognition of the Church's help to him, Amherst sent a gift of two dozen bottles of madeira to the Sisters, who had cared for the sick soldiers so tenderly. With tolerance for the Catholic Church came religious recognition, too, for other faiths. One of the British army quartermasters was a Jew, who settled in Montreal and founded the Jewish community of that city.

Away from the St. Lawrence, from Montreal to Quebec, enormous tasks confronted the new rulers of Canada. Robert Rogers, the ranger, was sent to take the surrender of Detroit and all the other western forts and posts of the Great Lakes water system. At Louisbourg that summer, Governor Whitmore was demolishing that mighty fortress. The base of the British navy was now to be concentrated in Halifax.

When the convoy taking the regulars and the troops of the Marine had sailed for France, no French soldiers remained in Canada. The militiamen gratefully and peaceably took their amnesty and went back to work. Amherst was left with a large army of regulars and colonials, to be disbanded or re-employed.

The colonials went home. Like the *habitants* they had work to do — much work. The war they had just fought had opened new and wide horizons for their future. The threat from the French and France's Indians had gone from their back lots. Opportunities for trade and commerce along the Atlantic seaboard seemed unlimited, and for the young, the adventurous, and the restless there were the western lands. The colonials took home with them from the army a new feeling of self-confidence and self-reliance, gained at the charge on the French entrenchments at Ticonderoga, at the ambushes on the road to the Ohio, and in countless skirmishes. The vaunted British regulars were no better than they, and the proud contempt of the British officers for the colonials merely underlined the equality, or the superiority, of the American fighting man. The colonials who went home from Montreal in the autumn of 1760, and all the others who had fought in the war, returned to civil life as Americans.

General Amherst's regulars went into winter quarters. For them, the war was not over. The commander in chief in North America still had to settle the Cherokee war, a vicious "little war" that foreshadowed the rising discontent among all the Indians in the old French lands. Then, too, Amherst had to consider the French colony of Louisiana, a newer part of the old Canadian colony of New France. With an eye to New Orleans, above the delta of the Mississippi, General Amherst conferred with Admiral Colville. The soldier asked the sailor to make available a fleet in the Gulf of Mexico, in case the army should go that way.

But Louisiana was not in William Pitt's war plans. From a conquered Canada, the builder of a British empire turned his attention to the West Indies. Louisiana could and did wait for its disposition at the conference table where, in 1763, the Seven Years' War finally ended, and the transfer of North America to British domination took place.

About four months after General Amherst took Montreal, the King of England died in his private chamber, alone with his valet. On 17 January 1761 George III was proclaimed king. He was heir to an empire, to have and, if possible, to hold.

Chronology

of events during the battle for the North American continent

1754

28 May   British attack the French in The Glade (Ohio Front)

3–4 July   French attack and capture Fort Necessity (Ohio Front)

1755

10 June   British Navy takes French ships *Alcide* and *Lys* off the Newfoundland Banks

16 June   British siege and capture of Forts Beauséjour and Gaspereau (Maritime Front)

9 July   French victory over British Army on the Monongahela River (Ohio Front)

8 September   British turn back French attack in battles at Lake George (Northern Front)

October   French Indians raid into eastern Pennsylvania

Autumn   Expulsion of French Acadians from Nova Scotia

353

1756

27 March   French raid destroys Fort Bull (Oswego Front)

March   British raid to Shawnee towns is unsuccessful (Ohio Front)

18 May   War declared between France and England

27 July   Naval action off Louisbourg (Maritime Front)

2 August   French and Indians burn Fort Granville (Ohio Front)

14 August   French Army captures and razes forts at Oswego

8 September   British raid Indian town of Kittanning (Ohio Front)

1757

March   French attack over the ice on Fort William Henry fails (Northern Front)

9 August   French besiege and capture Fort William Henry (Northern Front)

27 September   British blockading fleet off Louisbourg scattered and wrecked in hurricane

November   French raid Palatine towns along the Mohawk River (Oswego Front)

1758

13 March   French and British rangers fight on snowshoes near Ticonderoga (Northern Front)

4 April   French fleet with supplies and reinforcements for Canada destroyed by the British channel fleet

28 April   French fleet bound for Louisbourg defeated and turned back by the British Navy in the Mediterranean

Spring   French Indians raid into Augusta County, Pennsylvania

8 July   French victory over British Army attacking Fort Carillon (Northern Front)

26 July   British Army and Navy besiege and capture Louisbourg (Maritime Front)

27 August   British take Fort Frontenac (Lake Ontario)

September   British expedition up St. John's River (Maritime Front)

July–November   British campaign to Fort Duquesne on the Ohio River

14 September   British reconnaissance in force toward Fort Duquesne is driven back

12 October   French attack on British camp at Fort Ligonier fails

25 November   British Army occupies an evacuated Fort Duquesne

1759

June–September   British Army and Navy lay siege to Quebec

31 July   British fail in attack on Beauport lines

5–25 August   British combined operations against towns up-river from Quebec

11 September   British defeat French Army on the Plains of Abraham

17 September   Quebec capitulates to British

25 July   British and Indians turn back relief column at Fort Niagara and the fort surrenders (Lake Ontario)

26 July   British Army occupies Fort Carillon after a short siege; Fort St. Frédéric also falls to the British (Northern Front)

1–2 August   French mount unsuccessful attack on Oswego

12 October   French fleet on Lake Champlain scuttles itself (Northern Front)

November | Punitive expedition of British rangers destroys French Indian town of St. Francis (St. Lawrence River)

20 November | By its victory in Quiberon Bay on the coast of France, British Navy cuts off Canada from aid from France

1760

24 February | French launch minor but unsuccessful attack on Quebec across the frozen St. Lawrence River

26 April–16 May | French lay siege to Quebec

28 April | French defeat British Army on the Plains of Abraham

9 May | First of the British fleet arrives at Quebec

16 May | French raise the siege of Quebec

8 August | Cherokee Indians take British Fort Loudoun on the Tennessee River (Southern Front)

19–25 August | Siege and surrender of Fort Lévis to the British Army on the upper St. Lawrence River

May | British squadron captures a small French provision fleet in the Baie de Chaleur (Maritime Front)

25–26 August | French evacuate and British Army occupies Ile aux Noix at the north end of Lake Champlain

8 September | Montreal capitulates to three British armies converging on the city

1763

10 February | Treaty of Paris is signed, ending the Seven Years' War and ratifying the British conquest of French colonies in North America

British Government and Army

Persons in authority in the governments in England and in North America during the war

His Majesty George II	1727–60
His Majesty George III	17 January 1761—

First Commissioners of the Treasury:

Duke of Newcastle	1754–56
Duke of Devonshire	1756–57
Earl of Waldegrave	1757
Duke of Newcastle	1757–62

N.B. William Pitt, as Secretary of State, Southern Department, was in power as virtual Prime Minister from 4 December 1756 until 6 April 1757 and again from 18 June 1757 until 9 October 1761.

First Lord of Admiralty:

Lord Anson	1751–56
Earl Temple	1756–57
Earl of Nottingham and Winchilsea (April–July)	1757
Lord Anson	1757–62

Secretary of War:

Henry Fox	1746–55
Lord Barrington	1755–61

Governors, Lieutenant Governors, and Deputy Governors in North America:

Nova Scotia	Charles Lawrence	1753–55
	Robert Monckton	1755
New Hampshire	Benning Wentworth	1741—
Massachusetts	William Shirley	1741–56
	Thomas Pownall	1757–60
	Francis Bernard	1760—
Rhode Island	William Greene	1748–55
	Stephen Hopkins	1755–57
	William Greene	1757–58
	Stephen Hopkins	1758
Connecticut	Robert Wolcott	1751–54
	Thomas Fitch	1754–60
New York	James DeLancey	1753–55
	Charles Hardy	1755–57
	James DeLancey	1757–60
New Jersey	Jonathan Belcher	1748–58
	Francis Bernard	1758–60
	Thomas Boone	1760
	Josiah Hardy	1760
Pennsylvania	Robert Hunter Morris	1754–56
	William Denny	1756–60
	James Hamilton	1760
Maryland	Horatio Sharpe	1755
Delaware	(*See* Pennsylvania)	
Virginia	Robert Dinwiddie	1752–58
	Lord Loudoun	1758
	(appointed governor but never took office)	
	Francis Fauquier	1758
North Carolina	Arthur Dobbs	1754
South Carolina	James Glenn	1743–56
	William Lyttelton	1756–60
	William Bull	1760
Georgia	James Reynolds	1754–57
	Henry Ellis	1757–60
	James Wright	1760

Regiments of the British Army serving in North America during the war, with date of arrival or recruitment in North America

Regimental Number	Arrival in North America
1st	1757
15th	1758
17th	1757
22nd	1756 (December)
27th	1757
28th	1757
35th	1756
40th	In garrison in Nova Scotia before 1754
42nd Highlanders	
1st Btn.	1756
2nd Btn.	1760
43rd	1757
44th	1755
45th	In garrison in Nova Scotia before 1754
46th	1757
47th	In garrison in Nova Scotia before 1754
48th	1755
50th	Raised in North America 1755, disbanded 1756
51st	Raised in North America 1755, disbanded 1756
55th	1757
58th	1758
60th Royal Americans	
1st Btn.	Raised in North America 1755–56
2nd Btn.	" " " " 1755–56
3rd Btn.	" " " " 1755–56
4th Btn.	" " " " 1755–56
77th Highlanders	1757
78th Highlanders	1757
80th Light Infantry	Raised in North America 1757
90th	1760
95th Light Infantry	

1st Btn.	1760
2nd Btn.	1760
Royal Artillery	1755

Notes on Special Units

The 60th (Royal American Regiment) was raised as the 62nd (Royal American Regiment). When the 50th and 51st were disbanded after their capture at Oswego, their numbers were vacant on the army list and in order to close ranks the 62nd moved down two digits, becoming the 60th.

In 1757 two regiments of Highlanders were raised and numbered the 62nd and 63rd. Their seniority numbers were soon changed to the 77th and 78th, respectively.

A third "62nd Regiment" appears in North America briefly in 1758. A detachment of the latest 62nd apparently served as marines on the British fleet at Louisbourg in 1758 and again, with a detachment of the 69th Regiment, with Saunders's fleet at Quebec in 1759. Neither of these regiments, serving only aboard ship, is included in the list of British regiments serving in North America.

It should be noted that the grenadiers and light infantry were not distinct regiments on the establishment of the British army. It was customary, but optional, for a commander in the field to detach the grenadier companies from all the regiments in his force, put them under command of a trusted officer, and use them together as a shock unit. When in North America the use of rangers proved so valuable, "light infantry" companies were formed of the youngest and most agile soldiers, to serve as skirmishers. Following the example of the grenadiers, the light infantry of regiments were united as a separate unit for an action or for a campaign.

The "new" idea of light infantry was so fashionable in America that permission was granted to raise a regiment of light infantry; it was given the number 80 on the army list. It appears that the idea of having a whole and separate regiment of light infantry was given up in favor of a light infantry company in each regiment of the line. This system made of each regiment a force unto itself, consisting of the battalion companies, a company of light infantry, and a company of grenadiers.

The Louisbourg Grenadiers were the grenadiers of three regiments, the 22nd, 40th, and 45th. They appear to have been assembled together in 1757 to go with the army to Louisbourg. The battalion companies of the three-parent regiment of the Louisbourg Grenadiers were destined for garrison duty in Nova Scotia. In 1758 at Louisbourg and in 1759 at Quebec, the Louisbourg Grenadiers were the only soldiers of their regiments who were present. They were used as a small attack force to supplement the grenadiers of regiments.

The Independent Companies were on the establishment of the British army. In 1754 there were four Independent Companies in New York Colony and three in South Carolina. The other colonies, except for Nova Scotia, which was in effect under a military rather than a civil government, do not seem to have had Independent Companies stationed within their borders in that year.

Later, Captain Robert Rogers's Company of Rangers, which came to the war as the Ranger Company of the New Hampshire Regiment, was taken on the establishment of the British army as an Independent Company of rangers. They later expanded into a corps.

Independent Companies of rangers were on the establishment in Nova Scotia as early as 1750. These seem to have been Gorham's Rangers, named for John Gorham, who raised them first as part of the Massachusetts forces for the campaign to Annapolis Royal in 1743. During the war of 1754–60 the "Gorham of the Rangers" referred to John's brother Joseph. Gorham's Rangers, like Rogers's Rangers, expanded, and at Quebec in 1759 they appear to be a corps under command of a Major Scott, presumably a British officer. Joseph Gorham received a king's commission as major in 1761.

Bradstreet's Bateaumen was an administrative unit organized by Colonel John Bradstreet for the special duty of manning the water transport service. However, the bateaumen appear in a body ashore at the northern end of Lake George during the Abercromby campaign of 1758. It seems strange that these watermen specialists were used in that instance for fighting, as their services surely would be needed to supply the army across the thirty-six miles of Lake George.

Cavalry, or mounted troops, usually are a neglected consideration when the armies of the war of 1754–60 are mentioned. Captain Walter Stewart's Virginia Light Horse served with distinction during Braddock's expedition of 1755 and in other campaigns. There is mention of troops of cavalry in New York Colony during the period 1754–60. The Albany troopers are known to have worn blue coats, with hats laced with silver. Mention is made in the text of French cavalry at the battle for Quebec in 1759.

French Government and Army

Persons in authority in the governments in France and in Canada (New France) during the war

His Most Christian Majesty Louis XV   1715–74
(La Marquise de Pompadour)

Ministers of Foreign Affairs:

Barberie	1751–54 24 July
Rovillé	28 July 1754–57
Pierre	25 June 1757–58
Choiseul	1 November 1758–61

Ministers of Marine and Colonies:

Rovillé	1749–54 28 July
Machault	28 July 1754–57 1 February
Peirenne de Moras	1 February 1757–58 1 June
Massiac Lenormand de Mezy }	1 June 1758–58 1 November
Berryer	1 November 1758–61

Ministers of War:

Voyer d'Argenson	1743–57 1 February
Paulmy	1 February 1757–58 25 February
Fouquet de Belle-Ile	3 March 1758–61

Governors General of New France:

Duquesne	1752–55
Vaudreuil	1755–60

Regiments of the French Army serving in North America during the war, with date of arrival in New France

Name of Regiment	Arrival in New France	
La Reine	1755	
Béarn	1755	
Languedoc	1755	
Guyenne	1755	
Artois	1755	At Louisbourg
Bourgogne	1755	At Louisbourg
Royal Roussillon	1756	
La Sarre	1756	
1st Btn. Berry	1757	
2nd Btn. Berry	1757	
Cambise	1758	At Louisbourg
Les Volontaires Etrangers	1758	At Louisbourg

Notes on the Marine and on Army Organization

The troops of the Marine were on the regular French establishment but were under the direction of the Minister of Marine (Navy) and Colonies. They were recruited both in France and in the colony where the companies served. Thirty companies were serving in Canada in 1754. Each was a separate and independent command, taking direction from the governor general, who reported to the Minister of Marine and Colonies.

During the war of 1754–60 some of the companies of the Marine were brought together to form a larger unit of regiment or brigade. They served beside the other regular units of General Montcalm's army.

The ideal table of organization of a French battalion (the regiments listed above were, in fact, a battalion of the regiment, unless noted, as in the case of Berry) was as follows:

> 1 colonel
> 1 aide major
> 2 ensigns

> 1 company of grenadiers
> 12 companies of fusiliers

The grenadier company called for 3 officers and 45 soldiers; a fusilier company had 2 to 4 officers and 40 soldiers.

A company of the Marine consisted of 65 soldiers.

A Note on Source Material

The basic research for this book was done from a study of contemporary writings in the form of journals, diaries, orderly books, and letters, of which there is a plenitude surviving and readily available in reprints. Most of these are listed in an invaluable volume published in 1945 by the University of California Press: *American Diaries* by William Mathews.

Further aid to the researcher has been rendered by those students and editors who have gathered together the contemporary accounts relating to a single campaign or place. The six large volumes, the *Siege of Quebec*, by A. G. Doughty and G. W. Parmelee, 1901, is a monumental work. The Fort Ticonderoga Bulletin has published eye witness accounts, letters, and notes on battles, campaigns, and life in that key fort. Other material, as yet unpublished, is in the extensive library at the fort. In his book *Louisbourg from Its Foundation to Its Fall, 1713–1758*, J. S. McLennan catalogs the pertinent documents on this subject and lists ships, military units, ordnance, and supplies. E. B. O'Callaghan approached the compilation of source material from the larger consideration of geography. His *Documentary History of the State of New York*, in fifteen volumes, includes in one volume (Vol. X, 1858) papers relating to New France. Biographers and compilers have documented the lives of the leaders in the French and Indian War, or, as it is referred to in France, *La Guerre de Sept Ans aux Colonies*. Men like Washington, Bougainville, and Bouquet, who made their fame in later times, in another conflict, or in other fields, have had their days in the old war memorialized in print.

There are as many secondary sources as there are primary ones. No one can write today of the seven-year battle for the North American continent without mention of Francis Parkman and his *Montcalm and Wolfe*, published in 1884. During most of the eighty years since its publication, this work has constituted the definitive study of the period. In recent years, however, working from material unavailable to Parkman, historians have tended to doubt some of the conclusions of the great Bostonian, especially in his dismissal of the Indians and in the field of biography. John Shy of Princeton University, himself a trained soldier, has done much work on the logistics of the mid-eighteenth century, and has given James Abercromby credit and stature as a commander in chief, if not as a battle leader. In his book, *Robert Rogers of the Rangers*, 1959, John Cuneo has retrieved the reputation of his subject character and has given him the stature as a soldier that Kenneth Roberts, the historian-novelist, first recognized in *Northwest Passage*, 1937. Charles P. Stacey, sometime historian for the Canadian Army, in his *Quebec, 1759: the Siege and the Battle*, has newly evaluated that campaign. Now, the Royal Navy under Admiral Saunders is given its just credit in the conduct of the summer-long siege, and Wolfe, while maintaining his position as an undoubted hero, has been downgraded, to a certain measure, as a general.

In writing this book, I have consciously avoided the study or re-reading of *Montcalm and Wolfe*.

Index

369

Northeastern North Ameri
1754 ~ 1760

Showing:

The St Lawrence River as the key to
the Great Lakes and the Northwest

The Ohio River way to the Mississippi
River and Louisiana

The Hudson-Champlain-Mohawk
waterway through the
Appalachian Mountain chain

Nova Scotia - Cape Breton Island
dominating the sea lanes to Europe

LAKE SUPERIOR
(LAC DE TRACY)

Trois

Mont

WINNEBAGO

Ottawa R.

FOX

ALGONQUIN

Cham

LAKE
MICHIGAN
(LAC ILLINOIS)

LAKE
HURON
(LA MER
DOUCE)

F

S

Famine B.

HURON

G

LAKE ONTARIO
(LAC DE FRONTENAC)

Mohawk

POTTAWATOMI

H

Alba

Detroit

St. Joseph R.

T

IROQUOIS

LAKE ERIE
(LAC DE CONTY)

I

Maumee R.

J

MIAMI

K

ILLINOIS

Wabash River

MINGO

PENNSYLVANIA COLONY

FORT's LINE

Susquehanna R.

Delaware R.

Phil

River

DELAWARE

6

N

SHAWNEE

Ohio River

Monongahela R.

4

Carlisle

5

Potomac R.

Alexandria

CHOCTAW

James River

Williamsburg

0   100   200   300

scale of miles